Getting Skills Right

Enhancing Training Opportunities in SMEs in Korea

OECD

BETTER POLICIES FOR BETTER LIVES

Please cite this publication as:
OECD (2020), *Enhancing Training Opportunities in SMEs in Korea*, Getting Skills Right, OECD Publishing, Paris, *https://doi.org/10.1787/7aa1c1db-en*.

ISBN 978-92-64-37351-8 (print)
ISBN 978-92-64-68729-5 (pdf)

Getting Skills Right
ISSN 2520-6117 (print)
ISSN 2520-6125 (online)

Photo credits: Cover Cell phone: © Creative Commons/Alfredo Hernandez, clock: © Creative Commons/Hakan Yalcin, cloud upload: Creative Commons/Warslab, join: © Creative Commons/Tom Ingebretsen, doctor: © Creative Commons/Joseph Wilson, chef: © Creative Commons/Alfonso Melolontha

Corrigenda to publications may be found on line at: *www.oecd.org/about/publishing/corrigenda.htm*.

Foreword

The world of work is changing. Digitalisation, globalisation, and population ageing are having a profound impact on the type and quality of jobs that are available and the skills required to perform them. The extent to which individuals, firms and economies can reap the benefits of these changes will depend critically on the readiness of adult learning systems to help people develop and maintain relevant skills over their working careers.

To explore this issue, the OECD Directorate for Employment, Labour and Social Affairs has undertaken an ambitious programme of work on the functioning, effectiveness and resilience of adult learning systems across countries. This includes the creation of the Priorities for Adult Learning (PAL) dashboard for comparing the readiness of each country's adult learning system to address future skills challenges, as well as a cross-country report, "Getting Skills Right: Future-Ready Adult Learning Systems," which showcases relevant policy examples from OECD and emerging countries.

The Directorate is also carrying out a series of in-depth country reviews of adult learning systems to offer a comprehensive analysis of the key areas where policy action is required. This report 'Getting Skills Right: Enhancing Training Opportunities in SMEs in Korea' assesses whether training for SME workers in Korea is adequate, relevant, and aligned to skills needs. It analyses policy options to expand access to training for SMEs, remove the barriers to training participation/provision, and ensure that training provided by SMEs is relevant to skills needs, particularly in the context of the 4th industrial revolution. Based on this analysis, this report provides actionable policy recommendations as well as good practice examples from OECD countries.

The report is structured as follows. Chapter 1 paints a picture of the place that SMEs occupy in the economy and assesses current skills imbalances in the Korean labour market. The chapter also looks at how the mega-trends that are changing the skills needed in the labour market may be particularly disrupting for SMEs. Chapter 2 assesses the extent to which SMEs support the acquisition of skills, highlights training participation patterns among SME workers, and explores the key obstacles that SMEs are facing in providing training to their employees. Chapter 3 highlights the key training obstacles that SME workers face. Chapter 4 analyses whether training is useful, of high quality, and aligned with labour market needs. Chapter 5 provides an overview of the architecture of the Korean adult learning system, looking at governance and financing.

This report was prepared by Alessia Forti from the Directorate for Employment, Labour and Social Affairs, under the supervision of Glenda Quintini (Skills team manager) and Mark Keese (Head of the Skills and Employability Division). Taehoon Lee provided research analysis support and helped co-ordinate the work of the OECD Secretariat with its counterparts in Korea. Useful comments were provided by colleagues in the OECD Directorate for Employment, Labour and Social Affairs, the Centre for Skills, and the Economics Department. The OECD Secretariat would like to thank the Korea Research Institute for Vocational Education and Training (KRIVET), and the Ministry of Employment and Labor (MoEL) for their support in carrying out this project, as well as for organising an initial fact-finding mission in June 2019 and a workshop in December 2019. The OECD Secretariat is particularly grateful to Chul-Hee Kim for the technical assistance and statistical support provided throughout the project. Jai-Joon Hur and Sun-Jung

Oh also deserve special thanks for providing technical assistance with the construction of the OECD Skills for Jobs indicators for Korea.

This report is published under the responsibility of the Secretary General of the OECD, with the financial assistance of the Korean Ministry of Employment and Labor and KRIVET. The views expressed in this report should not be taken to reflect the official position of OECD member countries.

Table of contents

FIGURES

TABLES

Executive summary

Enhancing training opportunities in SMEs should be a policy priority for Korea. SMEs are the backbone of the Korean economy, representing 99.9% of firms and providing 80% of business sector jobs. Yet, they lag behind large companies when it comes to productivity and working conditions.

While investing in adult learning in SMEs is already urgent, this will be accentuated further by several mega-trends such as digitalisation, population ageing and globalisation. OECD estimates show that 44.3% of SME jobs in Korea could be partially/completely automated should new cutting-edge technologies be introduced (against 36.5% of jobs in larger firms) highlighting the need for SME workers' continuous reskilling. Population ageing, which is taking place very rapidly in Korea, will also increase the need for adult learning over longer working careers. Given that most older workers in Korea work for or run an SME, closing the skills gaps between youth and older generations will be crucial.

Despite the urgency of skills investments, Korean SMEs lag considerably behind large firms when it comes to training:

- Korea has the second largest variation in training participation across firm sizes in the OECD. Only 30% of workers in micro-firms (10 employees or less) participate in job-related training in a given year, a share that gradually increases to about 70% in large firms (over 250 employees).
- Korean SMEs provide far less training opportunities to their workers than large firms. In 2015, only 43% of small firms provided training (other than mandatory) to their workers, against 53% of medium-sized firms and 64% of large firms.
- There are several reasons behind low skills investments in SMEs. The attitudes of business owners and SME managers are not always supportive of training. Moreover, lack of staff, fear of poaching, absence of a dedicated HR department, and training costs, also contribute to poor skills investments by SMEs. Adult learning policy measures should be put in place to tackle these barriers and encourage SMEs to offer training to their employees.
- On top of receiving less training opportunities from their employers, SME workers also face additional obstacles to training. Lack of time is a key barrier, cited by 63% of SME workers who would have liked to participate in (more) training but did not, above any other OECD country. Lack of information and financial constraints are also important obstacles to training for SME workers. Korea needs to ensure that SME workers are able to find the time to train in more flexible ways, are supported in their training decisions (e.g. through career guidance), and are able to benefit from the plethora of financial incentives available.
- Training quality is another key issue in Korea. According to PIAAC, only 32.7% of SME workers in Korea found their job-related training activity very useful for the job – lower than any OECD country except for Japan. Considerable efforts have been put in place to improve and monitor training quality. However, more could be done. There is a need to ensure that adult learning teachers are sufficiently prepared, that training quality is adequately measured, and that adult learning programmes are updated continuously in line with changing labour market needs.

- The governance and financing of the adult learning system could be improved. Like in other OECD countries, in Korea a variety of ministries, the local government, and different stakeholders have some degree of responsibility over adult learning. Going forward, the policy priorities for Korea revolve around streamlining the governance and financing of the adult learning system and better involving social partners.
- There is only so much that adult learning policy can do to increase training opportunities in SMEs. Contextual factors – such as labour market duality, the tradition of seniority wages that potentially creates a wedge between workers' wages and productivity, and the dependency of Korean SMEs on large conglomerates – significantly contribute to low training patterns in SMEs. This suggests that complementary policies that go beyond the scope of adult learning (e.g. labour market and industrial policies) also need to be put in place to promote skills investments in SMEs.

Post-script: While this report was being finalised, Korea and the rest of the world were responding to a global health pandemic, COVID-19. The policy measures taken to contain the virus will have long-lasting impacts on the economy and labour markets. While the labour market context has changed significantly, the need for SMEs to adapt, and for SME workers to learn quickly, has never been greater. The analysis and recommendations offered in this report are intended to support these efforts. The policy recommendations for enhancing the provision of distance learning and the digital skills of SME workers to take up these opportunities as well as strengthening career guidance are particularly relevant.

Assessment and recommendations

Why adult learning is important for Korean SMEs

The Korean social and economic context makes adult learning investments particularly important for small and medium-sized enterprises (SMEs) – i.e. firms which employ less than 250 employees. SMEs are the backbone of the Korean economy: they account for nearly all firms (99.9%) and provide 80% of all business sector employment, the second highest share in the OECD after Greece.

Yet, Korean SMEs lag behind large companies when it comes to productivity and working conditions. The productivity gap between large firms and SMEs is the largest in the OECD. SMEs also offer lower wages, less job stability, and fewer career progression opportunities compared to large firms.

Adult learning – i.e. job-related adult education and training that is expected to enhance performance and productivity at work – is a key policy tool that Korea can use to close these gaps. Adult learning can help SMEs to close the productivity gap with large firms. It can help SMEs improve their productivity, while ensuring that SME workers can update their skills and improve their employment opportunities. It can strengthen position of SMEs in global value chains (GVCs) by helping them to specialise in high value-added activities (e.g. technologically advanced industries, complex business services). Adult learning is also valuable for SMEs going through changes due to company transitions, such as growth, restructuring, introduction of new technologies, or exporting for the first time.

While investing in adult learning in SMEs is already urgent today, it is likely that mega-trends such as digitalisation, population ageing, and globalisation, will make adult learning even more important in the future.

The adoption of new technologies, for example, may further increase the need for adult learning. OECD estimates show that some 44.3% of SME jobs in Korea could be partially/completely automated should new cutting-edge technologies be introduced, against 36.5% of jobs in larger firms. This suggests that many SME workers may need to retrain to adapt to these changes.

Population ageing may also increase the need for adult learning in SMEs. In Korea, the skills gaps between youth and older generations is among the highest in the OECD. Given that about 85% of older employees (ages 50-65) in Korea work for SMEs and many people start and run a small businesses upon retirement, closing the skills gaps with younger generations will be key for the competitiveness of SMEs.

Adult learning is also key to address ongoing skills imbalances. The OECD Skills for Jobs data shows that high-level cognitive skills (e.g. reasoning and verbal abilities; complex problem solving skills) are in shortage in the Korean labour market, a trend that is similar to that experienced in most other OECD countries. On the contrary, the demand for physical and manual skills (e.g. physical strengths) is found to be in line with supply, unlike what can be observed in the OECD area where the supply of these skills exceeds what is required in the labour market.

Enhancing SMEs' training efforts

Despite the benefits of skills investments, relatively few SMEs in Korea support the acquisition of skills. In 2015, only 43% of micro (1-10 employees) and small firms (11-50 employees) provided training to their workers, against 53% of medium-sized firms (51-250 employees) and 64% of large firms (over 250 employees). The remainder of firms provided either only legally mandatory training or no training at all.

There are several reasons as to why so many SMEs in Korea do not offer training opportunities to their workers. Lack of staff resources (i.e. lack of time of employees, shortages of labour) is the most important reason for not implementing or supporting training, cited as the key training barrier by 30% of SMEs in Korea.

Fear of poaching – i.e. the fear that the worker would leave the company shortly after training – is another key barrier to training provision. This is not surprising in a context where Korean SMEs typically offer less attractive working conditions, job turnover is high, and workers are often looking for better employment opportunities elsewhere.

Financial constraints are another reason for not providing training. Many SMEs are not able to use the plethora of financial incentives available to cover training costs, either because they are not aware of these schemes, or because they do not meet eligibility criteria (e.g. enrolment in Employment Insurance; minimum training hours).

Another key issue is that managers and business owners are not always supportive of training. Low demand for high-level skills, poor perception of training quality, lack of awareness of the benefits of training, as well as poor entrepreneurship skills among managers/business owners may all contribute to a poor learning culture in SMEs.

Finally, in Korea like in other OECD countries, SMEs typically lack dedicated HR departments/staff and training facilities – which put them at a disadvantage *vis-à-vis* large companies when it comes to training provision. The National HRD Consortium programme (i.e. CHAMP) is partly addressing these challenges but could be further improved.

Policy recommendations to enhance SME's training efforts

Tackle lack of personnel

- *Increase the take-up of job rotation schemes.* To do that, Korea should assist SMEs to secure and train replacement workers. This could be done by operating job rotation schemes in coordination with the PES and/or existing adult learning programmes (e.g. CHAMP). Ensuring that replacement workers receive adequate training before taking up the position is also important so that they can be productive as soon as they start the job.
- *Further invest in on-the-job training.* Korea should evaluate the pilot "SME structured on-the-job training programme" and scale it up if considered successful.

Reduce training costs for SMEs

- *Continue ongoing efforts to increase the coverage of Employment Insurance across SMEs.* This would allow more SMEs to be eligible to receive government-supported subsidies for training.
- *Reduce or eliminate the minimum training hours for eligibility for financial incentives.* Because short-duration training is harder to monitor, when minima are dropped, complementary action should be taken to strengthen the monitoring of potential fraud.
- *Raise awareness of existing financial incentives available*, for example through public campaigns and/or online guides. This is crucial to ensure that SMEs can take informed decisions on how to finance the training of their workers.

Ensure that managers and business owners in SMEs are supportive of workers' training

- *Make the business case for training.* For example, building and sharing the evidence on the links between skills and firms' performance could change managers and business owners' mind-sets towards learning and can ultimately be expected to raise training levels.
- *Enhance the skills of entrepreneurs and ensure that they are adequately trained* to start and run a business that nurtures its talents. This could be done by expanding initial education programmes on entrepreneurship as well as by providing more adult learning programmes targeted to managers/business owners.
- *Develop a knowledge-sharing platform* where business owners and managers can exchange on how they implement training.

Tackle the lack of dedicated HR departments/staff and training facilities

- *Improve the National HRD Consortium* programme by: encouraging training in new fields (4th industrial revolution); conducting rigorous performance evaluations of each joint training centre; and sanctioning centres with underperforming or overlapping functions. This will reduce the administrative burden involved for SMEs to take advantage of adult learning programmes and financial incentives.

Encouraging workers in SMEs to train

Korean SME workers train much less than workers in large firms, and this gap is mainly driven by low training participation among workers in micro-firms. Indeed, Korea has the second highest training gap between workers in micro and large firms in the OECD (after Chile). Only 30% of workers in micro-firms participate to job-related formal or non-formal adult learning in a given year, compared to 52% in small firms, 63% in medium-sized firms, and 70% in large firms. Training duration also tends to be shorter for SME workers. The median hours spent on (non-formal) job-related training is 32 hours per year for SME workers, compared to 48 hours for workers in larger firms.

Many Korean SME workers who miss out on training are not able to compensate with more opportunities for informal learning at work. Only 41.5% of workers in micro-firms participate to informal learning (i.e. learning by doing, learning from colleagues, or learning new things) at least once per week – a rate that progressively increases to 51.8% in large companies. These rates place Korea at the very bottom of the OECD ranking.

There are several reasons as to why SME workers do not train. On top of receiving less training opportunities from their employers, SME workers also face additional barriers to training. Lack of time (for work or family responsibilities) is the number one training barrier in Korea. Among SME workers who wanted to participate (more) in training but did not, 63% cited lack of time as a barrier – by far the highest share in the OECD.

Another key challenge for training participation is lack of money – which is more often an issue for SME workers who generally earn lower wages than workers in larger companies. Indeed, in Korea, some 15% of SME workers who wanted to participate (more) in training did not because training was too expensive for them, compared with only 6% of workers in larger firms. Cost barriers to training persist in Korea despite the plethora of financial incentives available to SME workers – suggesting that more could be done to encourage take-up of existing programmes.

Lack of information may be another key reason for not training. Indeed, often SME workers cannot rely on the support of their employers for career advice and information on training options. Moreover, public career guidance in Korea is mainly focussed on young students, older people, and the unemployed, while services for incumbent workers are piecemeal and generally less developed. Online career guidance options exist but are scattered across different websites and sources.

Policy recommendations to encourage workers in SMEs to train

Reduce time-related barriers to training

- *Increase the take-up of the education and training leave*, by: raising awareness on the existence of education and training leave options among SMEs and SME workers; and making paid educational and training leave a legal right for workers or at least re-open the debate on this issue while seeking buy-in from the social partners.
- *Further expand access for SME workers to distance learning* by encouraging SMEs to provide more e-learning opportunities and improving the basic digital skills of vulnerable groups to improve their take up of these opportunities, especially for older workers and the low-skilled who are over-represented in SMEs.
- *Expand modular learning options in formal education and strengthen the Recognition of Prior Learning system*. These modular options permit learners to combine more easily work with training outside of work.

Improving career guidance to (SME) workers

- *Expand public career guidance services beyond traditional target groups* (jobseekers; the unemployed) and towards incumbent workers. This includes better preparing the PES to provide career guidance to workers, as well as putting in place public career guidance services dedicated to all workers.
- *Encourage company career guidance provision*, particularly in smaller firms. Firms could advise workers on career progression opportunities within the firm, and guide them through available training options that would help them seize such opportunities. Public authorities together with employer representative bodies should collaborate in providing information to SMEs and their workers on the availability of career guidance services.
- *Create a one-stop-shop online career guidance platform*. Existing Skills Assessment and Anticipation (SAA) information should be put together in one place. This would avoid duplication, minimise overlaps, and help users navigate learning options in an easy way.

Tackle SME workers' financial barriers to training

- *Continue expanding the coverage of Employment Insurance to all SME workers*. This would allow all SME workers to benefit from the financial incentives to train that are available conditional on EI coverage.
- *Facilitate take-up of the National Learning Card System and closely monitor its implementation.* To ensure high up-take, Korea should: i) provide high-quality career guidance to help individuals make informed training decisions; (ii) strengthen quality assurance of training providers; (iii) foster the support of employers and a learning culture; (iv) provide financial support that is generous enough to encourage training participation; and (v) keep governance and processes simple (e.g. through well-designed and well-functioning web apps). The results of this programme should be also closely monitored.

Ensuring that training is of high quality and aligned to skills needs

In order for training to be effective, it needs to be of high quality and aligned to skills needs. Increasing participation alone is unlikely to have the desired impact on productivity and competitiveness if training is of low quality.

Considerable efforts have been put in place in Korea to improve and monitor training quality. The Korean Skills Quality Authority (KSQA) – established in 2015 as the national body dedicated to quality assurance in adult learning – is in charge of providing accreditation to training providers, assessing their effectiveness and quality, and detecting fraudulent practices. KSQA's assessments and evaluations are used in many ways, notably to establish eligibility for, and level of, government financial support, provide excellence labels for best performing training providers, and inform individuals/firms about the quality of each training provider.

Despite these efforts, evidence on the quality of training provision is mixed in Korea. On the one hand, studies based on PIAAC data estimate positive returns to formal and non-formal training, amounting to 8% and 10%, respectively.[1] On the other hand, workers' perceptions of the usefulness of their training at work are disappointing: only a third of SME workers in Korea find their formal or non-formal job-related training activity very useful for their job – well below the OECD average of 53% and lower than any OECD country except for Japan.

The alignment of training content with emerging skill needs is an essential aspect of training quality. In this context, the key challenge is that Korean SMEs often lack the capacity to assess their skill needs. Indeed, about 28% of small firms, 25% of medium-sized firms, and 17% of large firms do not review the skills and competences required by employees based on the business environment and company strategy.

The recent development of *National Competency Standards* (NCSs) – a framework that defines the set of competencies required to perform a job or task in each industry – is an important step in helping employers and providers plan training content based on job requirements. However, there are implementation challenges. For example, there is a mismatch between NCSs and industry needs. Another key challenge is that, with technological change, the NCS framework needs frequent updates. Implementation among training providers is also difficult, as teachers and lecturers lack expertise in how to adopt NCSs; while firms and workers have little incentives to use the framework.

In Korea like in other OECD countries, digital skills are becoming increasingly important in the context of the 4th industrial revolution. Yet, in Korea, some 72% of workers in micro-firms have low digital problem-solving skills, a rate that declines to 50% in large firms. Despite this challenge, IT-related training is the least frequently provided training in SMEs, and publicly financed training programmes related to the 4th industrial revolution remain scant compared to demand.

Adult learning teachers also need to keep pace with new emerging skill needs and the introduction of new technologies. Most adult learning teachers feel the need to participate in refresher training, but few of them actually update their skills continuously. Recent measure to address this issue are steps in the right direction and should be continued.

Policy recommendations to ensure that training is of high quality and aligned to skills needs

Build the capacity of employers to train for a changing world of work

- *Encourage SMEs to conduct an analysis of their training needs on a regular basis*. For this to happen, Korea should increase the take-up of programmes that aim to help SMEs to better understand their training needs and offer training accordingly. Korea could task Regional and Industry Skills Councils with administering these programmes or informing firms about the existence of these programmes.

Enhance the adoption of National Competency Standards (NCSs) by firms and training providers

- *Improve the process of developing/updating NCSs*, by ensuring that users' views are fully reflected in the process. In particular, it will be crucial to expand the roles of industry and labour representatives in updating current NCSs and developing new ones. This will ensure that NCSs are aligned with industry needs.
- *Monitor the implementation of NCSs through dedicated assessments*. These assessments should monitor whether NCSs are being used by firms and training providers, and what challenges they are facing. The results should be used to review NCS-related processes accordingly.
- *Apply NCSs to training institutes in a more flexible way*. For example, minimum NCS adoption standards for training should be eased. Training providers should be given greater autonomy in the provision of short-term (less than 40 hours) NCS-based training.

Provide the skills for the 4th industrial revolution

- *Continue providing free or subsidised basic ICT training programmes*, particularly to at-risk population groups. Basic ICT courses could be targeted to SME workers, or to vulnerable groups who are over-represented in SMEs (e.g. older workers; low-qualified).
- *Continue channelling financial incentives to innovative training options*. For example, Korea should continue providing more generous financial incentives for training programmes in emerging industries/sectors.
- *Expand the training offer of Industry 4.0 training programmes* by, for example, making these programmes more widely available and reducing waiting lists.
- *Develop new National Competency Standards (NCSs) to cover emerging sectors*. Ensure that all relevant stakeholders are involved in the process in a timely manner. The process for adding new NCSs could be made shorter so NCSs are more responsive to changing needs.

Better prepare adult learning teachers

- *Make refresher training mandatory for adult learning teachers,* as is currently being discussed by the government.
- *Enhance working conditions and wages of adult learning teachers* as a way to make the profession more attractive and increase teachers' willingness to train and upskill.

Improving the governance and financing of the Korean adult learning system

In Korea, like in other OECD countries, the governance and financing of the adult learning system involve several actors. A variety of ministries, local governments and other stakeholders have responsibility over adult learning.

While the Ministry of Employment and Labor (MoEL) is the primary actor and funder of adult learning in SMEs, other ministries also play a role – including the Ministry of SMEs and Start-ups, and the Ministry of Education. With a view to promote horizontal coordination, Korea has recently updated the legal framework to prevent different ministries from implementing similar and overlapping adult learning programmes.

Recognising the important role that local actors could play in adult learning, MoEL has steadily increased the funding for local governments to implement adult learning programmes. The central government is also empowering local governance bodies (e.g. quadripartite councils) to deal with human resource development at the local level.

In recent years, the government has also been taking steps to better involve social partners in adult learning. One important initiative was the establishment of regional skills councils (RSCs) and industry skills councils (ISCs). These bodies are composed of social partners and other stakeholders and have the objective to promote training in line with industry and regional needs.

However, much remains to be done to ensure that RSCs and ISCs can successfully fulfil their roles. Some of the challenges they face revolve around the lack of experience of the personnel; the weak cooperation between RSCs and ISCs; the imbalance of responsibilities between employers' organisations and trade unions; and the fact that RSCs and ISCs are financially dependent upon the government.

Social dialogue at firm level could also be improved further in Korea. Labour-Management Councils (LMCs) – i.e. consultative bodies that promote dialogue between a firm and its employees – could represent a valid tool for workers and firms to jointly identify training needs, regularly discuss the quality of training programmes undertaken, and explore best learning options. Despite their potential, the influence of LMCs on adult learning issues remains weak, especially in SMEs.

How the adult learning system is financed has also implications for training participation patterns in SMEs. In Korea, training programmes for employees are mainly financed through a levy-grant system paid by employers that feeds into the Employment Insurance (EI) Fund. All employers have to contribute to the EI fund, and are entitled to rebates to recover the training costs for their workers.

The Korean EI system was designed to be more favourable towards SMEs. Indeed, premium rates vary from 0.25% to 0.85% of the total taxable wage bill, with lowest rates applying to smallest firms. Moreover, when they provide training, SMEs are able to recover a higher share of the levies paid compared to large firms.

Despite the preferential support given to smaller firms, SMEs still do not use the EI system as much as large firms do. In 2018, about 30% of insured SME workers took part in employees training, compared to 55% of workers in large firms – pointing to the fact that SMEs and SME workers face additional barriers to training other than financial. Another issue is that EI coverage is still far from universal, and is particularly low among SMEs – which means that many workers and firms are still not entitled to benefit from training programmes financed through EI.

Another key challenge is that social partners have very limited responsibilities in the management of adult learning funds. This is very different from what can be observed in many OECD countries with a training levy in place – where social partners manage part of the funding through training funds (e.g. Italy) or skills councils (e.g. Sweden).

Policy recommendations to improve the governance and financing of the Korean adult learning system

Ensure that Regional and Industry Skills Councils can successfully fulfil their roles and effectively promote social dialogue on adult learning

- *Invest in capacity building of Regional and Industry Skills Councils* and provide adequate training to their personnel.
- *Allow Regional and Industry Skills Councils to autonomously manage a training budget*. This would give them greater autonomy and recognition as a social partners' body rather than as a government body.
- *Ensure better cooperation between Regional and Industry Skills Councils*. This would ensure better coordination and fewer overlaps in roles and responsibilities.
- *Balance the power between employers' organisations and trade unions*. Ensure that trade unions are more equally represented in Regional and Industry Skills Councils.

Make quality assurance a joint responsibility with social partners

- *Ensure that social partners have* representation on national agencies responsible for the quality assurance of adult learning (e.g. the Korean Skills Quality Authority).
- *Allow social partners to participate in the accreditation of training providers*.
- *Encourage social partners to actively collect information on training quality*, for example through surveys among workers and firms.

Ensure that trade unions are more actively engaged in adult learning

- *Build expertise on adult learning among trade union members*. For example, Korean trade unions could appoint dedicated 'training' specialists, whose objectives are to encourage the take-up of learning in the workplace and/or to develop an understanding of the workers' skills needs. Efforts should be made to ensure that trade unions undertake sufficient training themselves, notably on adult learning issues.

Strengthen dialogue within firms between employers and workers on adult learning issues

- This could be done by continuing to enhance the role that Labour-Management Councils play in establishing training priorities within firms. Recent government efforts go in the right direction and should be continued.

Set up complementary policies to develop a learning-friendly environment

There is only so much that adult learning can do to enhance training opportunities in SMEs. On top of improving how adult learning programmes operate and function, complementary policies need to be implemented by the government to reduce differences in working conditions between SMEs and large firms, and raise SMEs' demand for high-level skills. While these policies fall outside the realm of adult learning, they are fundamental to ensure that SMEs are able to train their staff and SME workers have adequate access to skills development opportunities. For example, reducing differences in working conditions between SMEs and large firms can make it easier for SMEs to attract and retain talent, which in turns may reduce job turnover, decrease fear of poaching, and ultimately encourage SMEs to invest in workers' long-term skills development. To give another example, raising SMEs' demand for high-level skills

– e.g. by encouraging technology adoption – may likely increase firms' needs to train their workers. Korea also needs to carefully evaluate the impact that new (e.g. labour market, industrial) policies may have on training.

Policy recommendations to develop a learning-friendly environment

- *Reduce the gap in working conditions across firms of different sizes.* This should be a long-term goal that will require a number of structural policies (e.g. industrial and labour market policies) that go beyond the scope of adult learning policies.
- *Raise the demand for high-level skills in SMEs.* Encourage larger firms to engage in greater transfer of technological and organisational know-how with smaller companies in their supply chains. This will of course require action in a number areas beyond adult learning measures.

Note

[1] The results are statistically significant only for non-formal training.

1 Why adult learning is important for Korean SMEs?

The Korean social and economic context makes adult learning investments particularly important for SMEs. This chapter paints a picture of the place that SMEs occupy in the economy. It looks at the key mega-trends that are changing the skills needed in the labour market, and how these changes may be particularly disrupting for SMEs. Finally, the chapter also looks at current skills shortages, surpluses, and mismatches in the Korean labour market, focussing particularly on skills imbalances in SMEs.

In Brief

Enhancing training opportunities in SMEs is key for Korea

This chapter paints a picture of the place that SMEs occupy in the economy and highlights the reasons why adult learning is important for them. The key findings of the chapter can be summarised as follows:

- SMEs are the backbone of the Korean economy: they account for nearly all firms (99.9%) and provide 80% of all business sector employment, the second highest share in the OECD after Greece. Yet, SMEs lag behind large firms when it comes to productivity and working conditions. The productivity gap between large firms and SMEs is the largest in the OECD. SMEs also offer lower wages, more unstable contracts, and fewer career progression opportunities compared to large companies. Adult learning can help to close these gaps by increasing the productivity of SMEs and upskilling its workers.
- New technologies may increase the need for adult learning in SMEs. If new cutting edge technologies were introduced, some 44.3% of jobs in Korean SMEs could be partially or completely automated – against 36.5% of jobs in larger firms. This suggests that many SME workers may need to retrain to adapt to these changes.
- Population ageing may also increase the need for adult learning. In Korea, the skills gaps between youth and older generations is among the highest in the OECD. Closing these skills gaps will be key considered that older workers are over-represented in SMEs and many of them start and run small businesses in their old age.
- Despite the fact that the Korean adult population is highly educated, Korean SMEs face significant labour shortages and struggle to attract and retain talents. About 80.5% of SMEs are experiencing difficulty finding employees.
- Skills imbalances are already emerging in Korea. Like in other OECD countries – in Korea certain high-level cognitive skills are in shortage (reasoning and verbal abilities; complex problem solving skills). Physical and manual skills (e.g. physical strengths) seem to be at an equilibrium level – unlike what can be observed in the OECD area where these skills are in surplus.

Introduction

The Korean social and economic context makes adult learning[1] investments particularly important for SMEs. In Korea, SMEs account for a significant proportion of employment. Yet, they contribute little to value added compared to larger companies, suggesting that more could be done to increase the productivity of SMEs and their employees. Moreover, key mega-trends (population ageing, digitalisation, and globalisation) are putting pressures on the Korean adult learning system, making skills investments in SMEs very urgent to tackle chronic labour shortages and skills imbalances. This chapter is structured as follows. Section 1.1 paints a picture of the place that SMEs occupy in the Korean labour market. Section 1.2 highlights the extent to which the megatrends make training investment in Korean SMEs particularly urgent. Section 1.3 looks at skills imbalances in the Korean labour market, focussing particularly on SMEs. Section 1.4 highlights the contextual (labour market, industrial) conditions needed to favour adult learning in SMEs.

1.1. The place of SMEs in the Korean labour market

Korean SMEs account for a significant proportion of employment, and dominate certain economic sectors such as services, construction, and manufacturing. However, there are large gaps between SMEs and larger companies, in terms of productivity and working conditions offered to workers. This section paints a picture of SMEs in the Korean labour market, looking at the place that they occupy in the economy, their productivity, and the working conditions that they are able offer. It also offers a snapshot of the skill levels of workers in SMEs and larger companies, placing Korea in the international context.

1.1.1. Virtually all firms in Korea are SMEs and they provide 80% of business sector jobs

In Korea, similarly to other OECD countries, SMEs – defined as firms with less than 250 employees unless otherwise specified [2] – account for nearly all firms (99.9%), with micro-firms[3] accounting by themselves for 93% of all companies. SMEs in Korea provide 80% of all business sector employment, the second highest share in the OECD after Greece, well above countries such as Great Britain (53.08%), Japan (52.8%), the United States (42.41%), and Canada (58%). In terms of value-added, Korean SMEs generate over 60% of all business sector GDP (Figure 1.1).

Korean SMEs are particularly present in certain economic sectors. For example, they account for around 90% of total employment in the service sector, 85% of employment in construction, while in manufacturing they account for around 80% of employment. These rates are much higher than what can commonly be found in other OECD countries with comparable data (Figure 1.2). Sectors where Korean SMEs are least present include business facilities management and business support services (64.2% of employment), electricity, gas, steam and water supply (71.2% of employment), and professional, scientific and technical activities (72.2% of employment), according to the Census on Establishments in 2014.

Figure 1.1. SMEs and their contribution to the business economy

Percentage 2016, or latest available year

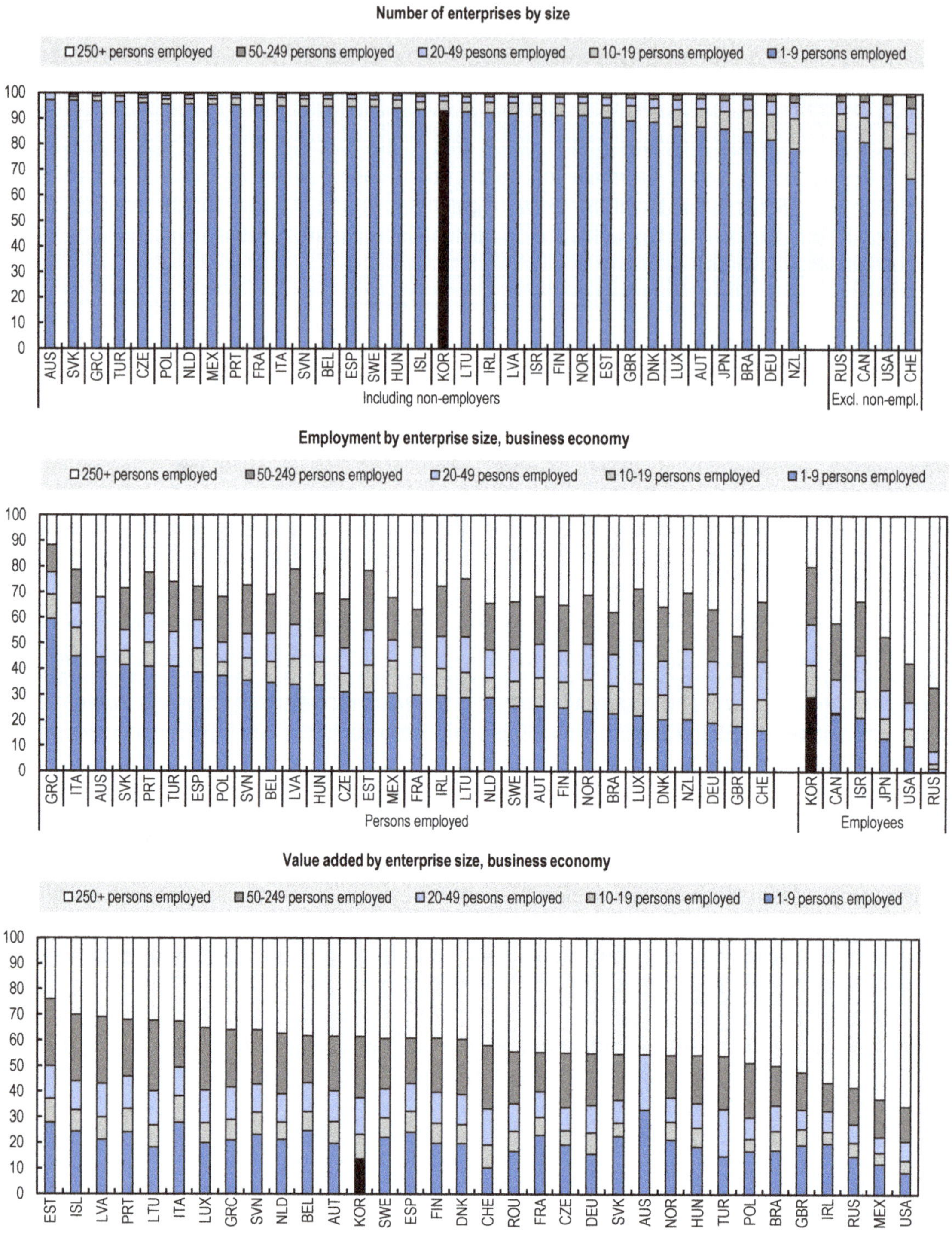

Source: OECD (2019[1]), OECD SMEs and Entrepreneurship Outlook 2019, OECD Publishing, Paris, https://doi.org/10.1787/34907e9c-en.

Figure 1.2. Employment by enterprise size, main sectors

Percentage of total employment in sector, 2014, or latest available year

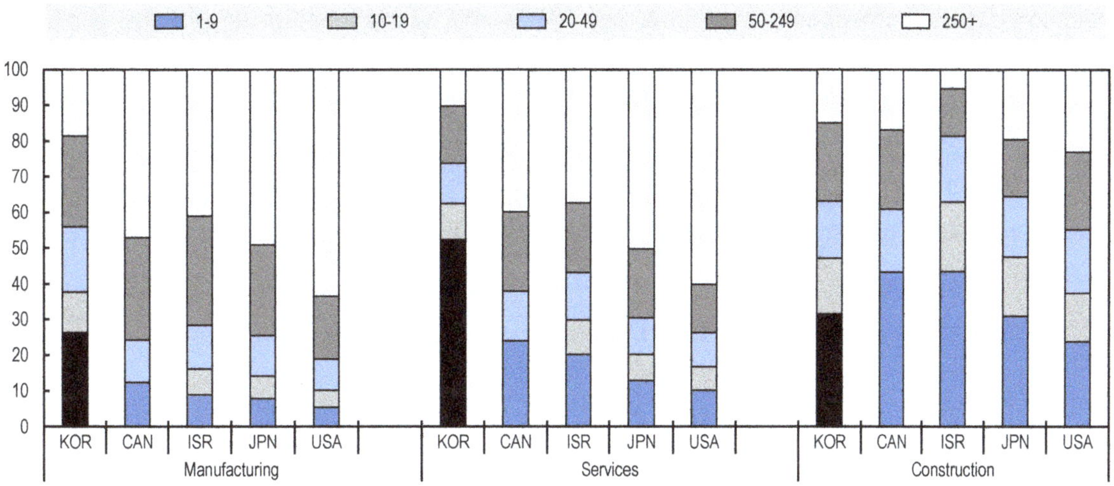

Note: Data are based on number of employees; data for KOR are based on establishments; for CAN, 1-9 refers to 1-19; for CAN, JPN, KOR: size class 50-249 refers to 50-299; 250+ refers to 300+; reference year: CAN, ISR: 2015; data for JPN were compiled in Japanese Industrial Classification and include overseas employment.
Source: OECD (2017[2]), *Entrepreneurship at a Glance*, OECD Publishing, Paris, https://doi.org/10.1787/entrepreneur_aag-2017-en.

Since the 1990s, SMEs – and micro- and small firms in particular – occupy an increasingly important role in the Korean economy. The share of employment among companies with 1-9 and 10-19 employees increased from 37.3% and 8.4% in 1993, respectively, to 40.9% and 10.9% by 2017 – while the overall share of employment among medium-sized companies has remained almost the same. Conversely, in 1993 establishments with 300 or more employees accounted for 22.6% of total employment in Korea[4], a share that declined to 14.6% by 2017 (Figure 1.3, Panel A). As shown in Figure 1.3, Panel B, increases in the number of companies over the past decades were observed primarily among micro- and small firms.

Figure 1.3. Employment by SMEs rapidly increased in Korea during the 1990s

Employees by firm size (percentages) and number of establishments by firm size (in thousands), 1993-2017

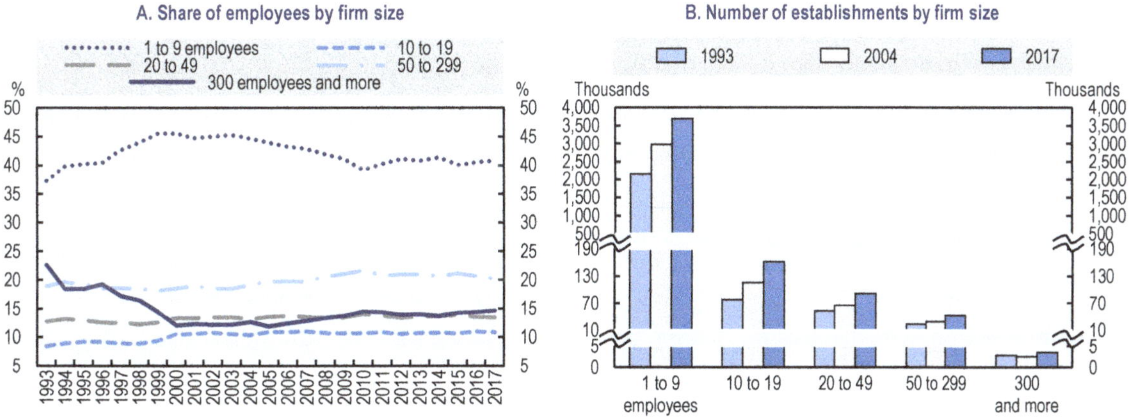

Source: Statistics Korea, Census on Establishments, 2018.

1.1.2. There are large productivity gaps between SMEs and larger firms

As is well known, Korea's rapid economic growth has been driven by export and manufacturing by large business groups, making Korea the sixth-largest exporter in the world. However, this traditional model has also led to polarisation between large firms and SMEs and has resulted in large gaps in productivity between them. Labour productivity in Korea is 46% lower than in the top half of OECD countries (OECD, 2018[3]) and the productivity gap between large firms and SMEs is the largest in the OECD (Figure 1.4).

Figure 1.4. Productivity gaps between large firms and SMEs

% difference in labour productivity between large enterprises and SMEs in the business economy, 2017 or latest year

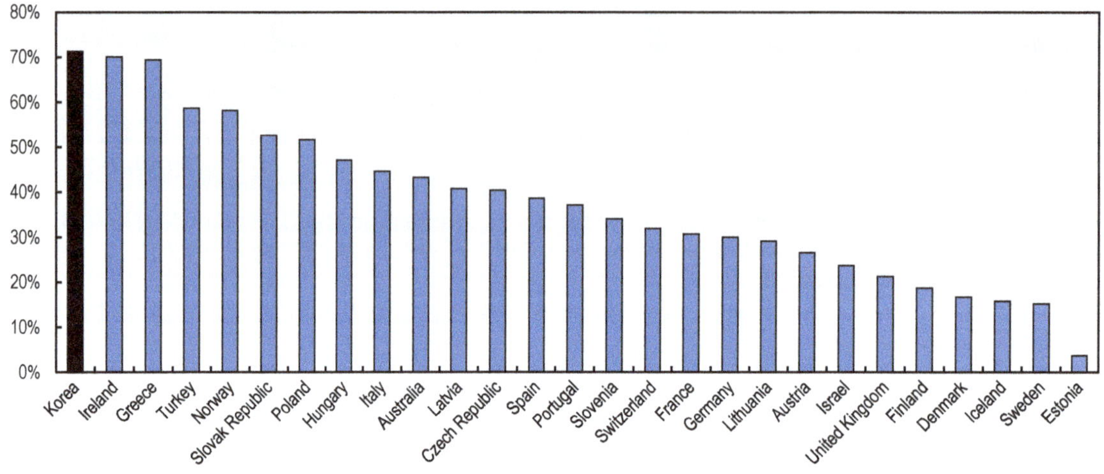

Note: Data excludes financial and insurance activities. Labour productivity is measured as value added per person employed. Data for Korea refers to 2015. SMEs refer to firms with 1-249 persons employed. Large firms refer to firms with 250+ persons employed.
Source: SDBS Structural Business Statistics (ISIC Rev. 4).

There are several reasons behind the gap in productivity between SMEs and large firms. Low technology adoption in SMEs – discussed in Section 1.2.1 – could partly explain the productivity gaps with larger companies.

Unbalanced economic growth driven by large firms, and centred on exports and manufacturing, is also a key reason for productivity gaps across firms of different sizes. For example, in the manufacture sector, labour productivity in SMEs declined from 53.8% of that in large firms in 1988 to 32.5% in 2014 (OECD, 2018[3]).

Another key reason is that SMEs are concentrated in low-productive sectors. For example, as discussed in Section 1.1.1, Korea's SMEs are concentrated in the service sector, where productivity is less than half of that in manufacturing.

Korea's widespread subcontracting culture has been pointed out as one of the main causes for the productivity gaps between large firms and SMEs (Kim, 2015[4]). Large companies in Korea, especially in manufacturing sector, had a larger share of total employment before the 1990s. Since the early 1990s, however, Korea began to face much higher competitive pressures from emerging economies such as China, along with rising wages at home.

In this context, large companies began to outsource their various production processes to SMEs in order to reduce labour costs and to achieve greater flexibility, and medium-sized enterprises also turned some of their production process over to smaller firms. After the 1997 Asian Economic Crisis, such subcontracting process was widespread in manufacturing and eventually became common also in the service sector (OECD, 2018[5]).

Raising productivity of SMEs is key for economic growth. According to recent OECD estimates, raising SMEs' productivity from its current level of about a third of that of large firms to half (which corresponds to the OECD average) would lift GDP per capita by more than 40% in 2060, amounting to an increase in the 2020-60 annual growth rate from 1.2% to 2.1% (OECD, forthcoming[6]).

1.1.3. SMEs typically offer poorer working conditions than larger companies

In Korea, SMEs offer poorer working conditions than large companies, including less job stability, lower wages, longer working hours, and less career advancement opportunities. If this is a challenge that Korea shares with other OECD countries, gaps in working conditions are particularly marked in Korea by OECD standards.

First, SMEs are more likely to offer non-regular, unstable, job contracts. In Korea, non-regular workers are largely concentrated in SMEs and particularly in micro- and small firms. As shown in Table 1.1, around 94.4% of non-regular workers are employed in SMEs, of whom 47.6% work in micro firms.[5]

Table 1.1. Regular and non-regular workers in Korea by firm size, 2018 (%)

By firm size	Regular workers	Non-regular workers	Total (all salaried workers)
Micro (1-9 employees)	29.3	47.6	35.3
Small (10-29 employees)	21.8	25.0	22.9
Medium-sized (30-299 employees)	32.8	21.7	29.2
Large (300+ employees)	16.1	5.6	12.6

Source: Statistics Korea (2018[7]), Supplementary Results of the Economically Active Population Survey by Employment Type in August 2018.

SMEs are also more likely to offer lower wages. Regular and non-regular workers in SMEs earn less than both regular and non-regular workers in large firms (Figure 1.5). As shown in Table 1.2, in 2018 the (hourly) average wage of non-regular workers in SMEs was only 41.8% of that of regular workers in large firms, while regular workers in SMEs on average earned 56.8% of the salary of regular workers in large firms.

Figure 1.5. Average gross earnings in Korea by employment type and firm size, 2018 (thousand KRW)

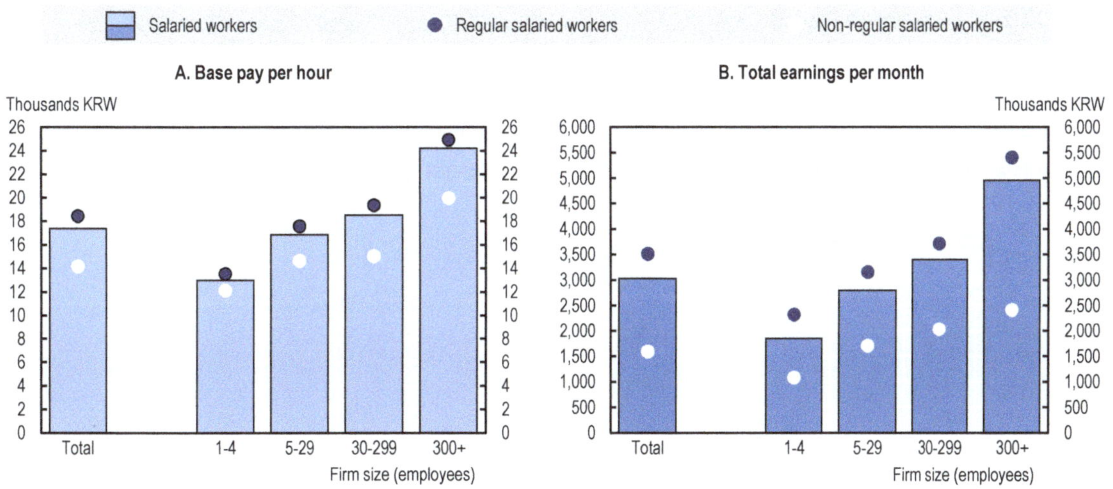

Source: OECD estimates using MOEL (2019), Survey Report on Labor Conditions by Employment Type.

Table 1.2. Wage gap between regular and non-regular workers by firm size, 2013-18

Total hourly wages by employment type and firm size (Index "Regular worker in large firm (300+)" = 100)

		2013	2014	2015	2016	2017	2018
300+	Regular workers	100.0	100.0	100.0	100.0	100.0	100.0
	Non-regular workers	65.6	64.2	65.0	62.7	65.1	63.2
1-299	Regular workers	53.8	52.3	49.7	52.7	54.3	56.8
	Non-regular workers	36.7	34.6	35.0	37.4	40.3	41.8

Note: Data refer to total hourly wage level relative to regular workers in large firms.
Source: OECD Secretariat calculations based on the Survey Report on Labor Conditions by Employment Type.

Korea has a high incidence of low-paid work. With 22.3% of full-time employees earning less than 2/3rd of median (hourly) earnings of all full-time employees, Korea has the fifth highest incidence of low-pay in the OECD area after Israel, Ireland, Latvia and the United States (Figure 1.6).

Figure 1.6. Incidence of low-pay by country, 2018 or latest year

Percentage of full-time employees earning less than 2/3rd of median (hourly) earnings of all full-time employees

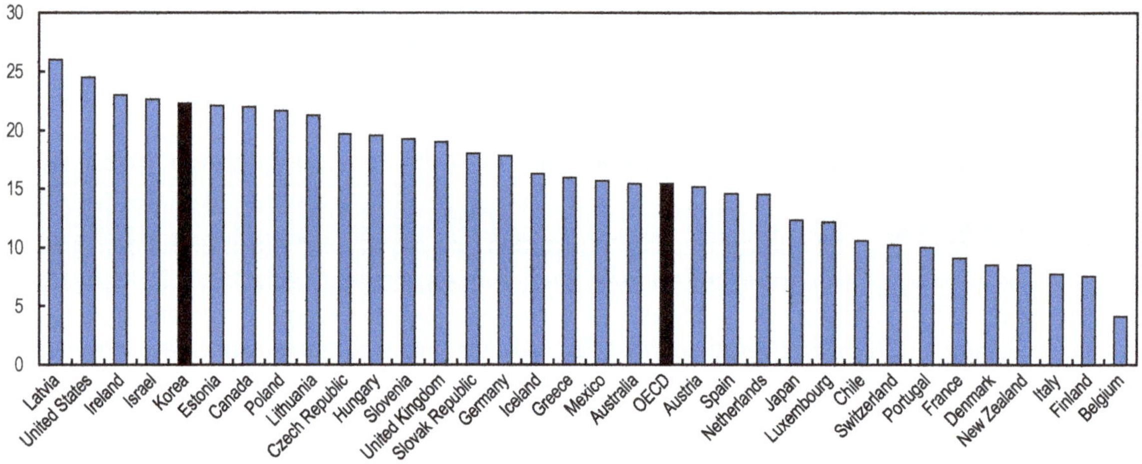

Note: data for Korea refers to 2017.
Source: OECD Earnings Distribution Database, www.oecd.org/employment/emp/employmentdatabase-earningsandwages.htm.

Unsurprisingly, the incidence of low-pay in Korea is higher in SMEs and this is largely driven by low pay in the smallest firms. As shown in Figure 1.7, although the incidence of low pay has decreased in recent years, it remains much higher in small firms (16%) than in larger companies (4.5%).

Figure 1.7. Incidence of low-pay, by firm size and year, Korea

Percentage of full-time employees earning less than 2/3rd of median (hourly) earnings of all full-time employees

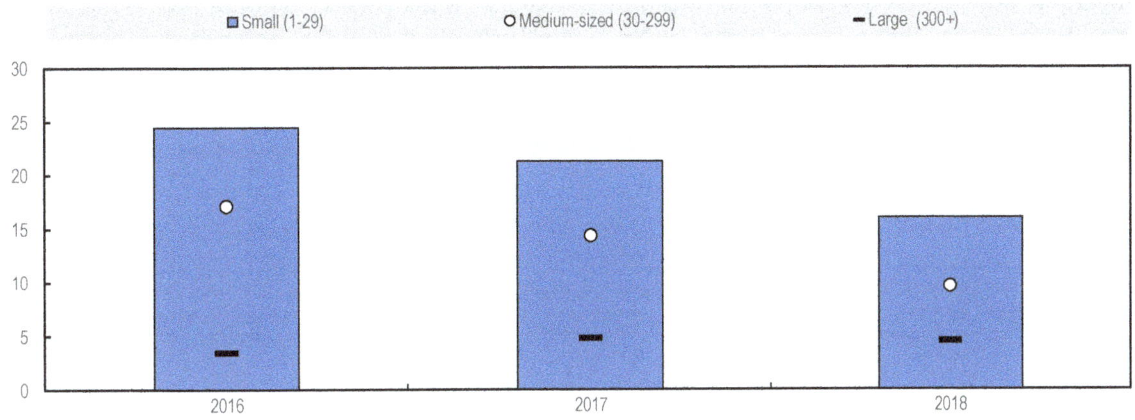

Source: KRIVET elaborations of the Survey on Labor Conditions by Type of Employment (SLCTE).

Wage gaps have increased constantly over the past decades. In the 1980s, average wages between large and small firms were relatively similar, with workers in small firms (10-29 employees) earning 90% of what workers in large firms were paid. Since the 1990s, however, the gap has been widening. As of 2016, the average hourly base pay in large firms are around twice as high as that of SMEs with less than 300 employees (Figure 1.8).

Figure 1.8. Average hourly base pay in Korea by establishment size, 1993-2016

KRW in constant 2015 prices

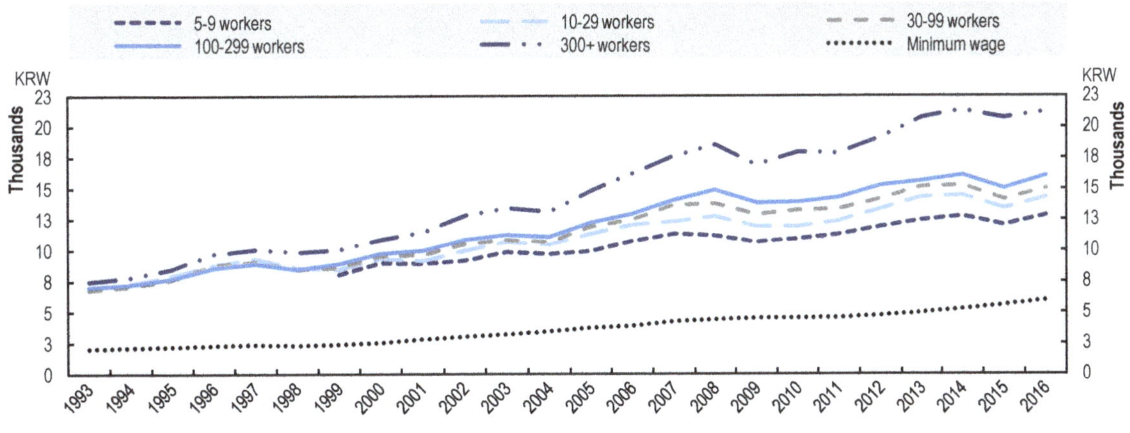

Note: Data refer to real average base pay per regular hour worked in 2015 prices. Data have been deflated using the KOSIS consumer price index (2015 = 100).

Source: OECD estimates using MOEL (2017[8]), *Survey Report on Labor Conditions by Employment Type*, http://laborstat.molab.go.kr/newOut/renewal/menu05/menu05_search_popup.jsp, Table "Age, Days, Hours, Payments, Workers by Size, Education, Age".

Working hours are another important aspect of working conditions. Although working time has been decreasing in recent years in Korea, in 2018 it still was the third longest in the OECD, at 1967 hours per year (roughly 164 hours per month). If working hours are long across the board, they are particularly long in SMEs – and this is particularly true for small and medium-sized firms.[6] In particular, in 2018, employees of small and medium-sized enterprises worked around 170 hours per month on average, about 7 hours more than workers in large firms (Figure 1.9).

In July 2018, the Korean government reduced the maximum weekly working hours from 68 to 52 hours (roughly from 272 to 208 hours per month) in large firms with more than 300 employees. This regulation was extended to firms with 50-299 employees in January 2020 and will be expanded to firms with 5-49 employees in July 2021. The extension of the new 52-hour workweek to SMEs may serve as an opportunity to reduce the gap in working hours between small and larger companies.

Figure 1.9. Working hours in Korea

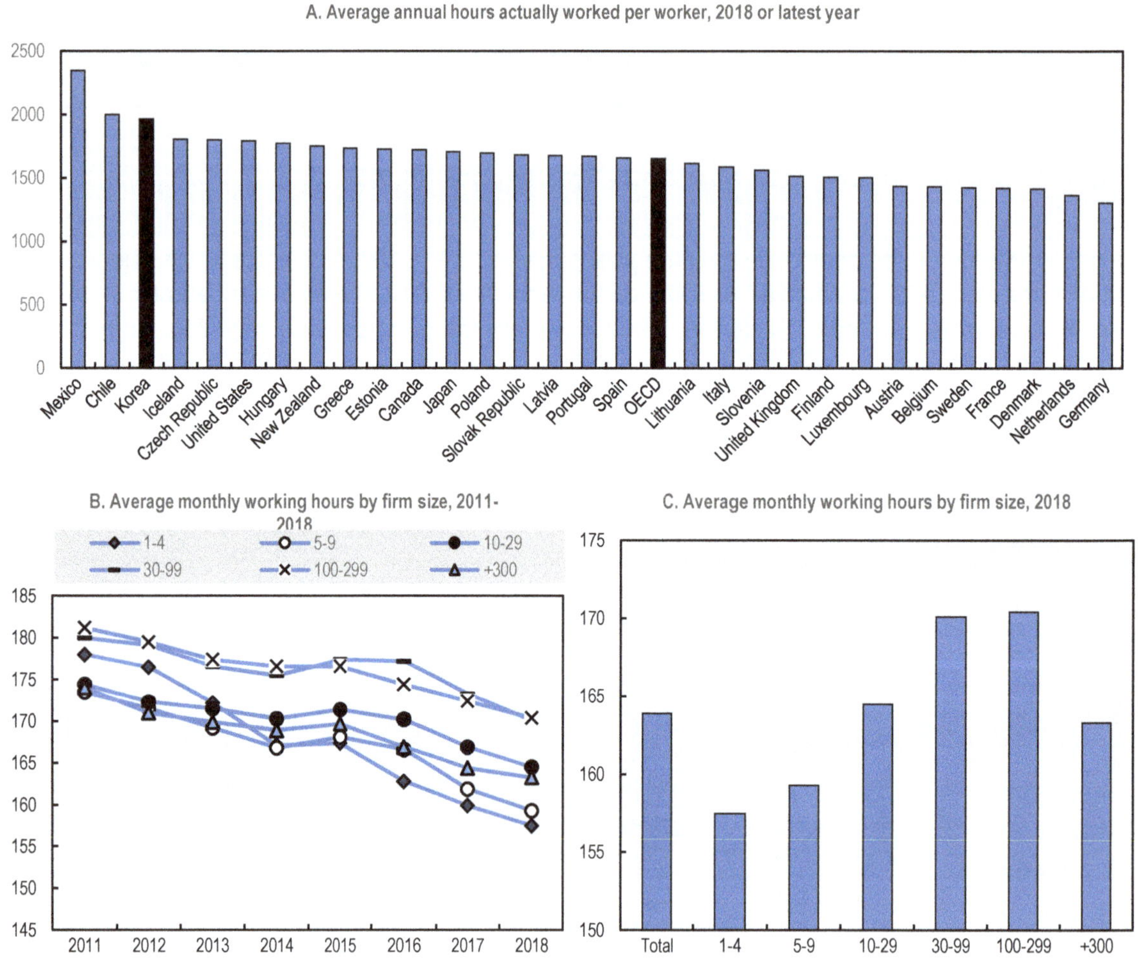

Note: For Korea data disaggregated by firm size, data refers to average monthly working hours of all employees (permanent, temporary and daily employees).

Source: Panel A: OECD Labour Force Statistics Database; Panel B and C: Ministry of Employment and Labor, Labor Force Survey at Establishments.

Career progression opportunities are another important element of working conditions. Workers may feel motivated to know that they can progress in their career and that working conditions may improve in the future. However, many SME workers feel stuck in poor jobs, and do not feel that they can grow and advance in their current career. Elaborations of the 5th Korean Working Conditions Survey show that only 32.5% of workers in micro-firms feel that their job offers good prospects for career advancement. This rate increases evenly with the size of the firm, reaching 53.1% of workers in large companies (Figure 1.10).

Figure 1.10. Career advancement opportunities in Korean SMEs, 2017

Percentage of workers who agree or strongly agree that their job offers good prospects for career advancement, by firm size

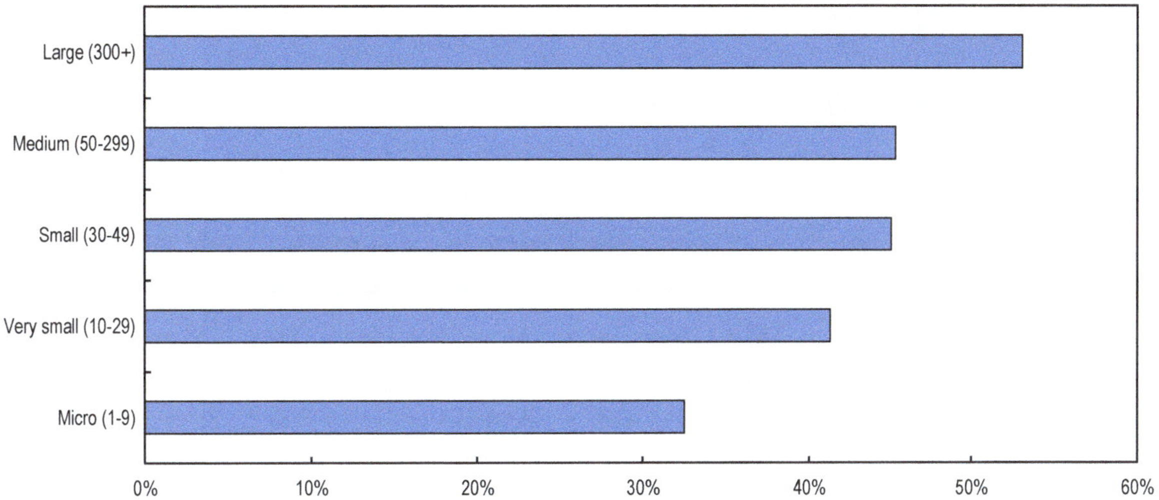

Note: data refer to 2017.
Source: KOSHA elaborations based on the 5th Korean Working Conditions Survey (KWCS).

In this context, it is not surprising that workers in SMEs appear to be much less satisfied with their job than workers in larger companies. As shown in Figure 1.11, less than 27% of workers in micro-firms are satisfied or very satisfied with their job in Korea, against around 60% of workers in large firms.

Figure 1.11. Job satisfaction in Korea, by firm size

Percentage of workers who are satisfied or very satisfied with their job, by firm size

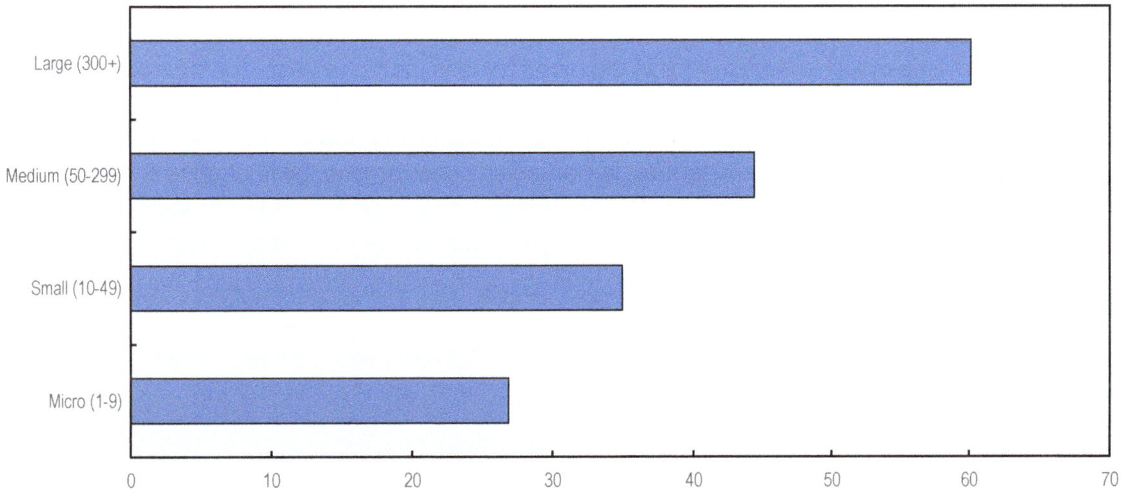

Source: OECD elaborations of the Korean Labor & Income Panel Study (19th wave, 2016).

The key reasons for job dissatisfaction among Korean workers are varied. Data from the Korean Labor & Income Panel Study shows that Korean workers are mainly dissatisfied with wages, followed by personal development opportunities, job stability, and work hours. This is true for workers in firms of all sizes, but workers in SMEs seem to be unhappy with work conditions much more frequently than workers in large firms. For example, 28% of workers in micro-firms are dissatisfied or strongly dissatisfied with wages, compared to only 12% of workers in large firms (Figure 1.12). Some 14% of workers in micro-firms are (strongly) dissatisfied with the possibility of personal development that the job can offer, which is almost three times as many as in large companies.

Figure 1.12. Reasons for job dissatisfaction

Percentage of workers who are dissatisfied or strongly dissatisfied with the following work conditions

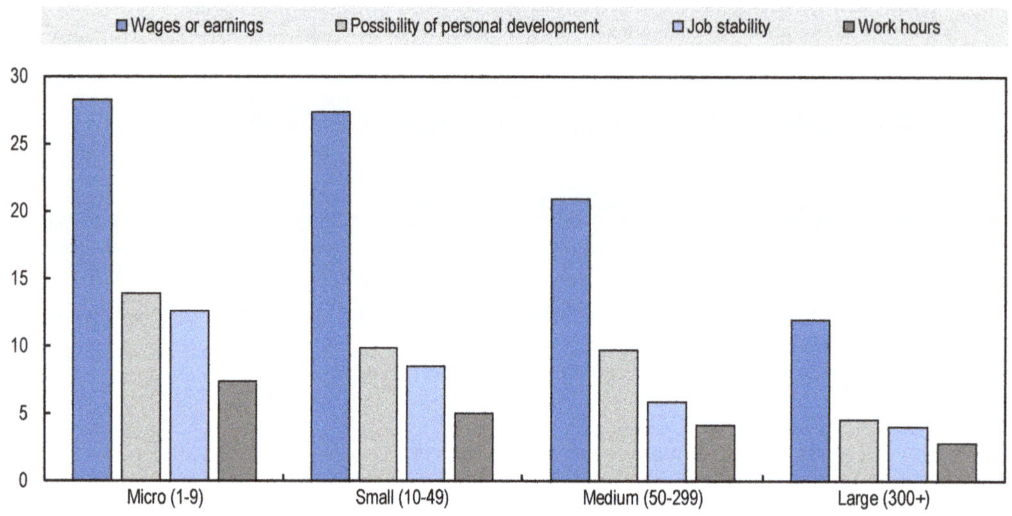

Source: OECD elaborations of the Korean Labor & Income Panel Study (19th wave, 2016).

In a context of poor working conditions, limited career progression opportunities, as well as overall low job satisfaction, it is not surprising that many SME workers look for better job prospects elsewhere, notably in a larger company or in the public sector. This translates into high turnover and low job tenure, particularly in SMEs.

In 2018, 30.4% of employees in Korea were in their jobs for less than one year – compared with an OECD average of 19.4% (Figure 1.13, Panel A). The average job tenure of workers in Korea in 2018 was a little over six years, the lowest of any OECD country and considerably lower than the OECD average of 9.4 years (Figure 1.13, Panel A). Job tenure is particularly low among SME workers, notably among workers in smallest firms. Figure 1.13, Panel C, shows that average job tenure in firms with 5-9 employees is 4.7 years as of 2018, less than half of that of large firms with 500 or more employees.

Figure 1.13. Average job tenure (years) and incidence of job tenure of less than one year (percentages)

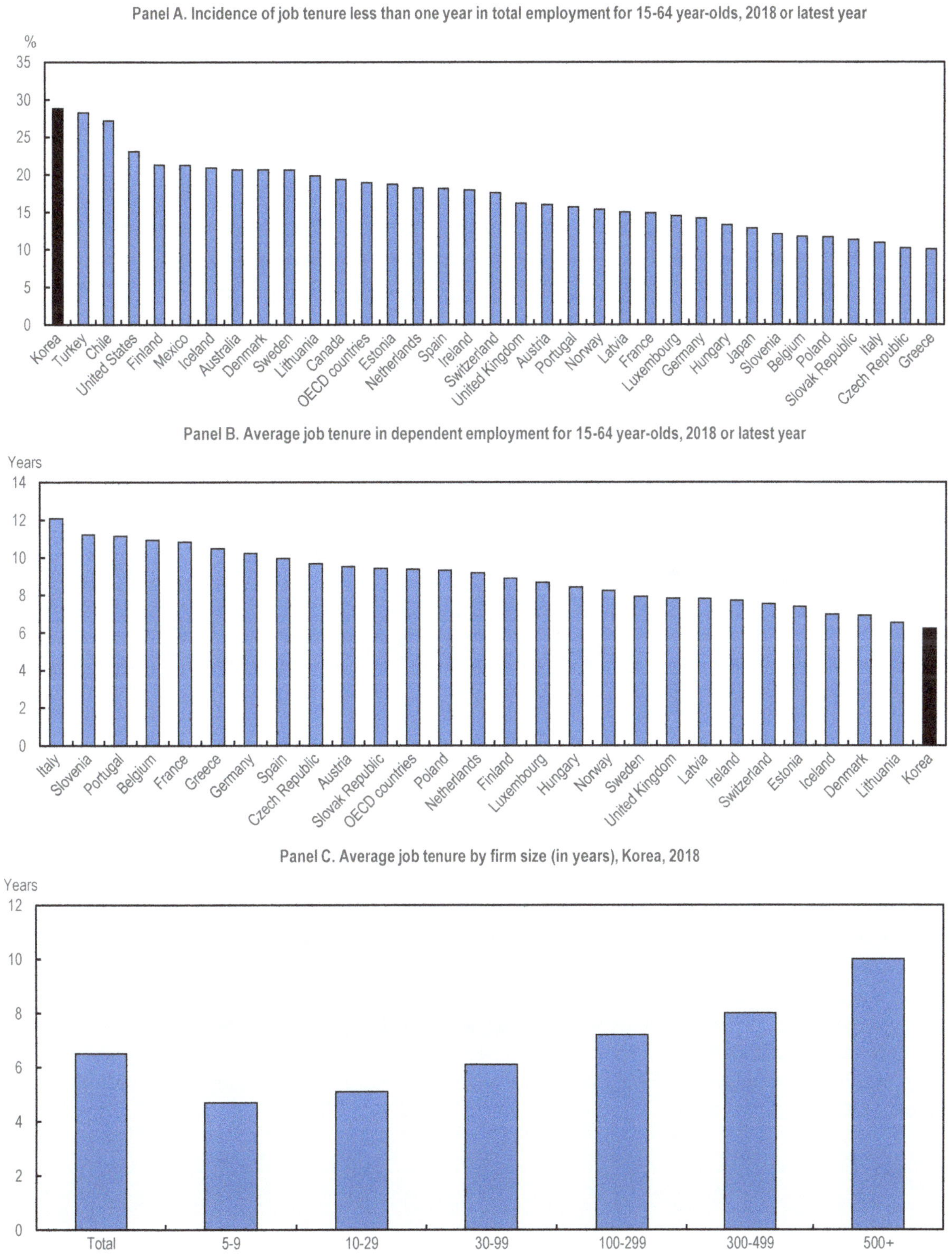

Note: For Panel C, the Size of establishments is classified on the basis of permanent employees.
Source: Panel A and B: OECD Job Tenure Dataset, a subset of the OECD Employment Database, www.oecd.org/employment/database; Panel C: Ministry of Employment and Labor, Survey Report on Labor Conditions by Employment Type.

1.1.4. SME workers have lower levels of skills

In Korea, employees in SMEs have lower levels of skills than employees in large firms. This may be due to various reasons. To some extent, SMEs may be unable to attract high-skilled workers, notably because they cannot offer attractive working conditions (see section 1.3). It may also be that, because SMEs are concentrated in low value-added sectors (see section 1.1.1), they do not require high-skilled workers. Another potential reason is that SMEs provide little opportunities for skills development and skills use at work, which in the long-term leads to workers' skills deterioration and obsolescence. Low levels of skills among SME workers may also reflect that vulnerable groups who typically have lower qualifications (e.g. older people, see section 1.2.3), are overrepresented in SMEs.

Elaborations of the Survey on Adult Skills (PIAAC) show that in Korea workers in SMEs have on average lower levels of literacy and numeracy skills, compared to workers in larger firms: the mean literacy score for a worker in a micro-firm is 267 (257 mean numeracy score) compared to 289 for a worker in a large firm (282 mean numeracy score). A similar pattern can be observed in the OECD countries on average (Figure 1.14).

Figure 1.14. Mean literacy and numeracy scores, by firm size

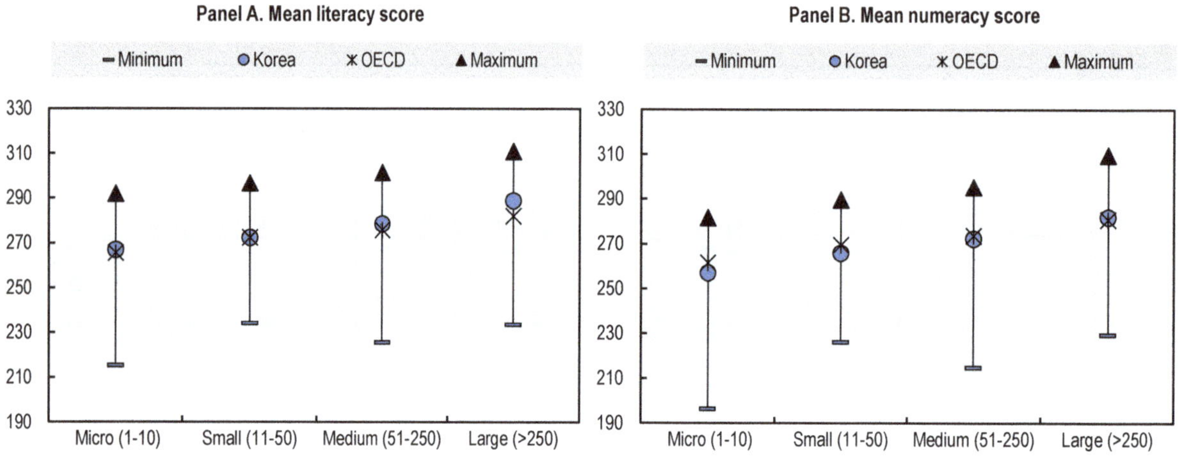

Source: OECD elaborations based on the Survey of Adult Skills (PIAAC) 2012; 2015.

As in other OECD countries, in Korea low-skilled workers are over-represented in the smallest firms. About 18.5% of workers in SMEs have low literacy and/or numeracy skills in Korea[7] (compared with 17.6% in the overall Korean population), a share that decreases as firm size increases: some 20% of workers in micro-firms have low literacy and/or numeracy skills (OECD average 24%), against 17% of workers in small firms (OECD average 19%), 13% of workers in medium-sized firms (OECD average 18%), and 8% of workers in large companies (OECD average 15%) (Figure 1.15). Age probably plays a role, since older workers are more likely to be employed in SMEs and older workers in Korea have among the lowest skill levels across the OECD.

Figure 1.15. Workers with low basic numeracy and/or literacy skills

Percentage of workers with low basic numeracy and/or literacy skills

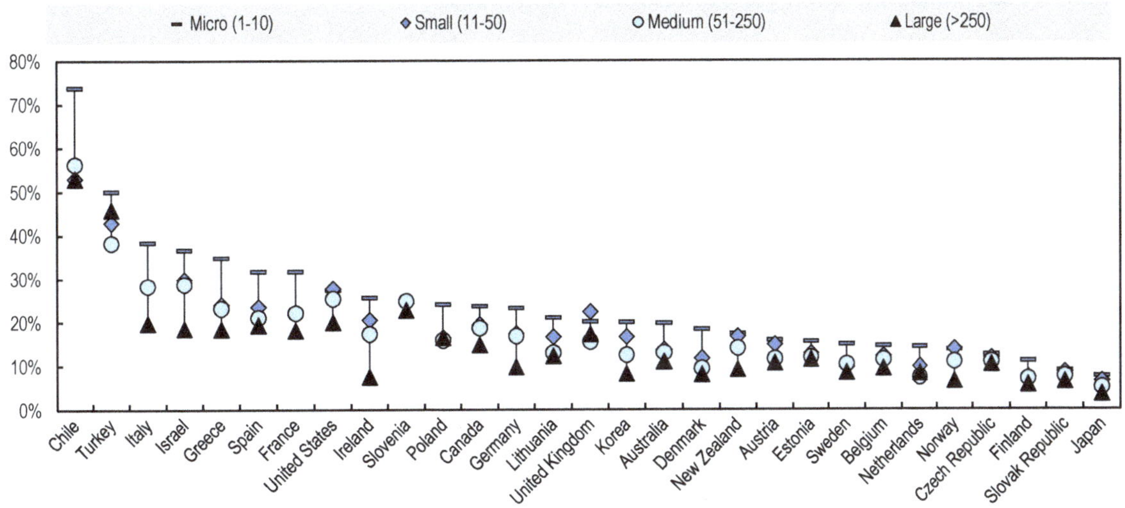

Note: The indicator refers to workers who score Level 0 or 1 in numeracy and/or literacy.
Source: OECD elaborations based on the Survey of Adult Skills (PIAAC) 2012; 2015.

In line with these patterns, Figure 1.16 shows that high-performers in numeracy and/or literacy[8] are less commonly found in Korean SMEs while they are overrepresented in larger companies: they represent around 45% of workers in micro-firms, a share that gradually increases to about 70% in large companies.

Figure 1.16. Proficiency levels in literacy and numeracy, by firm size, Korea

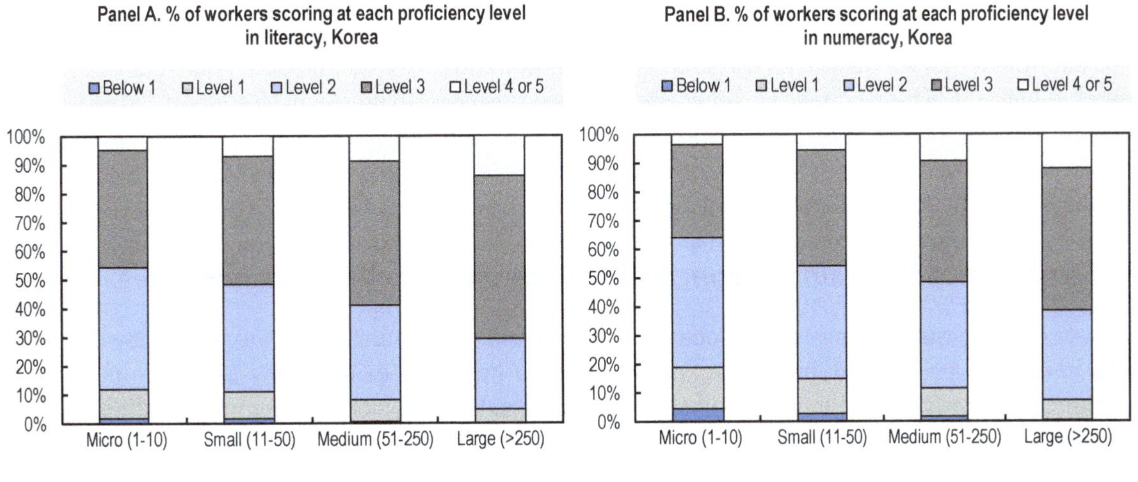

Source: OECD elaborations based on the Survey of Adult Skills (PIAAC) 2012; 2015.

As the importance of digital skills in the labour market has increased rapidly, it is striking that Korean SME workers often lack even the most basic digital problem solving skills. PIAAC data show that in Korea, 72% of workers in micro-firms have low digital problem-solving skills (OECD average 66%), a rate that declines to 50% in large firms (similar to the OECD average). This makes Korea the OECD country with one of the widest gap between micro- and large firms (22 percentage points), after Japan (30 percentage points),

Israel (26 percentage points) and Denmark (23 percentage points) (Figure 1.17). Again, these patterns may largely reflect the over-representation of older people in SMEs.

Figure 1.17. Workers with low digital problem-solving skills

Percentage of workers with low problem-solving skills in technology-rich environments, by firm size

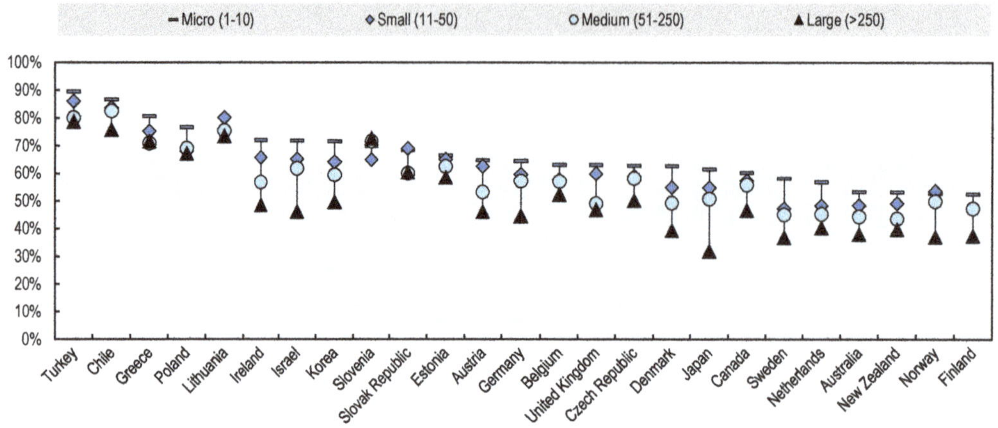

Note: The indicator refers to workers who score Level 1 or lower in problem-solving skills in technology-rich environments, or workers with no computer experience or who failed ICT core. Chile, Greece, Israel, Lithuania, New Zealand, Slovenia and Turkey: Year of reference 2015. All other countries: Year of reference 2012. Data for Belgium refer only to Flanders and data for the United Kingdom refer to England and Northern Ireland jointly.
Source: OECD elaborations based on the Survey of Adult Skills (PIAAC) 2012; 2015.

1.2. Mega-trends and implications for SMEs

Mega-trends such as technological progress, globalisation, and population ageing, are changing (or may change in the future) the quantity and quality of jobs that are available and the skills they require. If this is true for the Korean labour market as a whole, these mega-trends may be particularly disruptive for SMEs. To reap the benefits of these changes, adult learning systems need to be ready to support SMEs and SME workers in maintaining and developing the skills needed in a changing world of work. This section identifies the main drivers of change in SMEs, including structural change, automation, new technologies, globalisation, as well as population ageing.

1.2.1. Structural change, automation, and the introduction of new technologies

Structural change creates jobs in some sectors and decreases opportunities in others, thereby altering the types of skills that are needed. In the past decade, Korea has seen its economy transform more rapidly than other OECD countries. The Lilien index measures the extent to which employment in different sectors of the economy grows or shrinks at different speeds. The higher the score on the Lilien index, the more profound the transformation. Figure 1.18 shows that Korea has experienced the biggest changes in the OECD in the period 2005-15.

Figure 1.18. Structural change 2005-15

Lilien Index

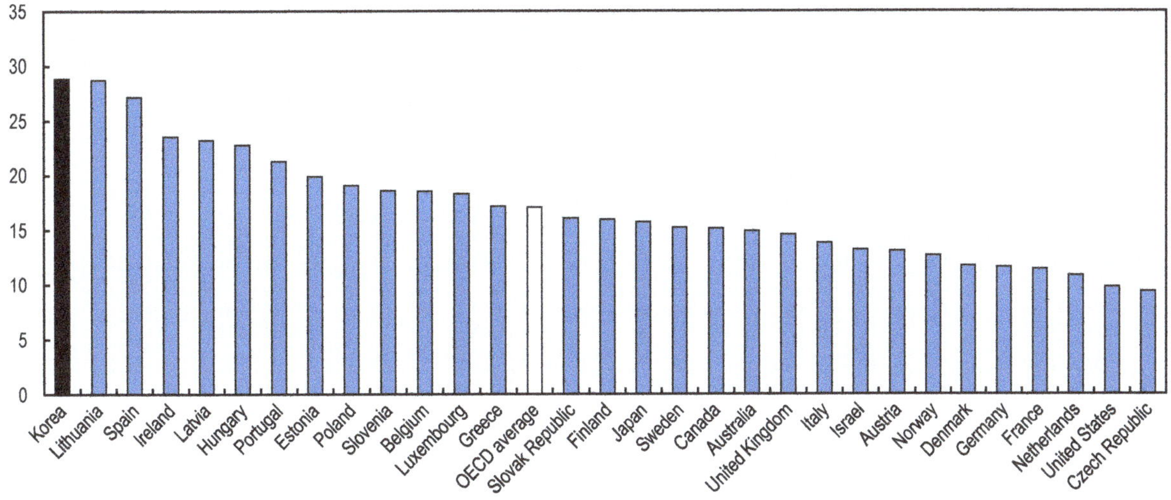

Source: OECD (2019[9]), Getting Skills Right: Future-ready adult learning systems, OECD Publishing, Paris. https://doi.org/10.1787/9789264311756-en.

But the most important changes to the Korean economic structure may lie ahead. There is a lively debate about the impact technology will have on jobs in the future. It is likely that cutting-edge technology will be able to automate more and more complex tasks at accelerating speed, fundamentally changing the skills that are required for many jobs. Other jobs may even become entirely redundant.

Recent OECD studies have estimated the share of jobs at risk of automation in OECD countries that have participated in the Survey of Adult Skills (PIAAC), including Korea (Nedelkoska and Quintini, 2019[10]; Arntz et al., 2016[11]). Using the methodology developed by Nedelkoska and Quintini (2019[10]), it is possible to estimate the share of jobs at risk of automation disaggregating the results by firm size.[9] As shown in Figure 1.19, what emerges is that:

- Some jobs may disappear altogether while others would see a significant change in the tasks they involve. Should current cutting-edge technology become widespread, 10.8% of jobs in Korean SMEs could change so dramatically as to disappear entirely and an additional 33.5% could face a significant risk of change.
- Jobs in Korean SMEs face a higher risk of automation compared to jobs in larger companies. Some 44.3% of SME jobs could be partially or completely automated as a result of the introduction of new technologies, against 36.5% of jobs in larger firms. This gap is only slightly larger than in the OECD on average, where 47.4% of SME jobs and 41.2% of jobs in large companies face a high or significant risk of automation.
- The risk of automation in Korea decreases gradually as firm size increases. In micro-firms, 48.5% of jobs are at risk of (partial or total) automation, against 42.7% in small firms, 39.4% in medium-sized firms, and 36.5% of large firms.

There may be several reasons behind the higher risk of automation being faced by Korean SMEs. First, it could be due to compositional effects relating to industry and occupation. Second, it may reflect the fact that Korean SMEs often produce low value-added goods and services, and hire low-skilled workers who need to perform only manual and routine tasks. Third, it could mirror the lower level of adoption of new technologies in SMEs, where many routine jobs that could be partially/completely automated are still performed by workers.

Figure 1.19. Jobs at risk of automation, by firm size

Share of jobs which are at a high risk of automation or a risk of significant change (%)

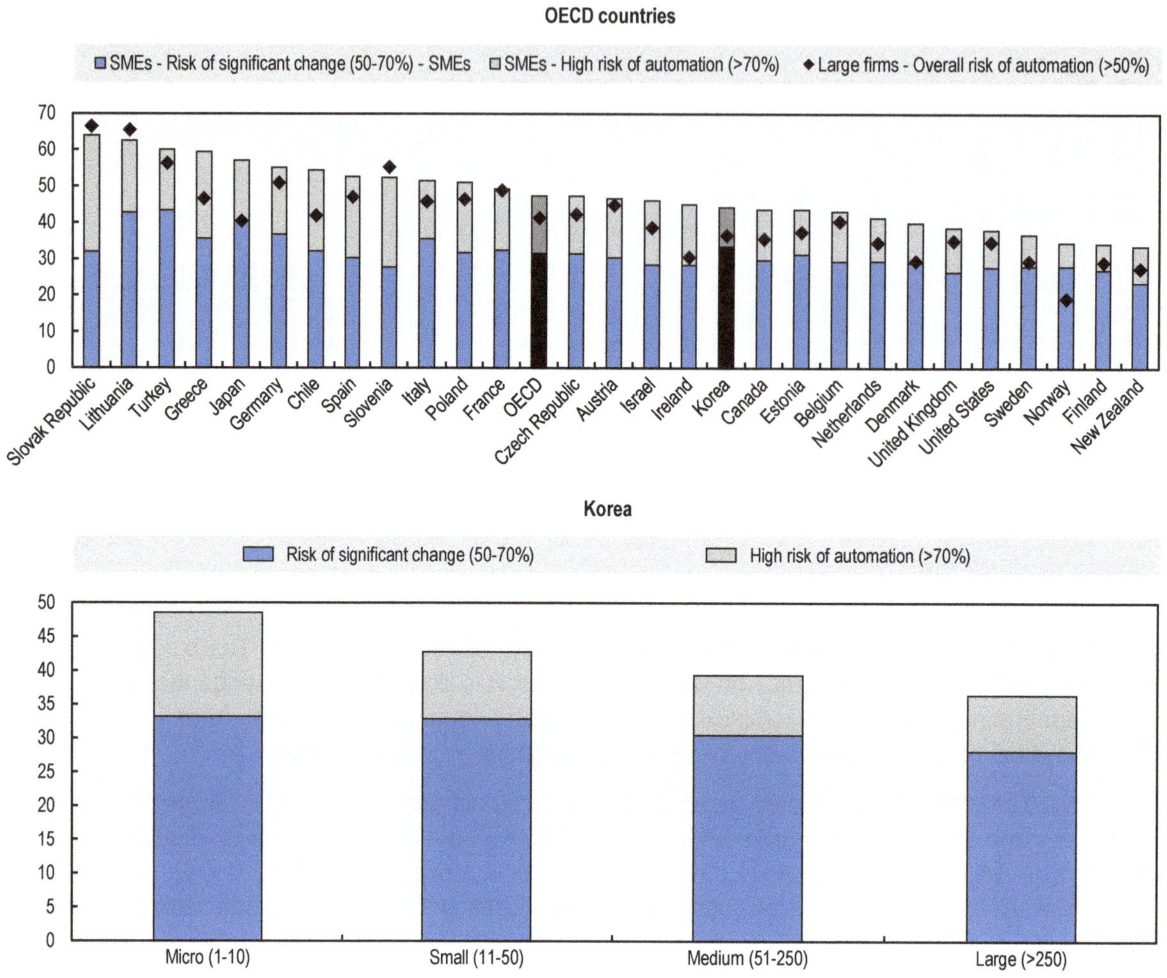

Note: Jobs are at high risk of automation if the likelihood of their job being automated is at least 70%. Jobs at risk of significant change are those with the likelihood of their job being automated estimated at between 50 and 70%. Data for Belgium correspond to Flanders and data for the United Kingdom to England and Northern Ireland.

Source: OECD calculations based on the Survey of Adult Skills (PIAAC) (2012), http://www.oecd.org/skills/piaac/; and Nedelkoska, and Quintini (2019[10]), "Automation, skills use and training", OECD Social, Employment and Migration Working Papers, No. 202, https://doi.org/10.1787/2e2f4eea-en.

Evidence shows that employment in highly automatable jobs has been increasing in Korea. For example, Seol (2019[12]) shows that employment in high-risk, highly automatable jobs, has increased from 1.6 million to 2.5 million in the period 2013-17, and in 2017 represented 28% of all SME workers.[10]

These trends are not surprising considered that in Korea the automation of processes and tasks is not yet widespread in SMEs. Chang and Lee (2017[13]) show that 62.5% of exporting SME have not yet automated their manufacturing processes. Moreover, the degree of automation that has been introduced is relatively basic, consisting of barcodes (17%) or radio-frequency identification (14%).

OECD elaborations of the Workplace Panel Survey (2015) seems to further confirm these insights. Only 25% of small firms, 32% of medium-sized firms, and 38% of large companies report a high level of work process standardisation (i.e. creating the standard of manufacturing/process).[11] Similarly, only 14% of small firms, 17% of medium-sized firms, and 22% of large companies report a high level of automation[12] (i.e. automating a process or part of work by machine, computer or electric machine) (Figure 1.19).

Figure 1.20. Standardisation and automation of the work process in Korea, by firm size

Percentage of firms reporting high standardisation or automation of the work process

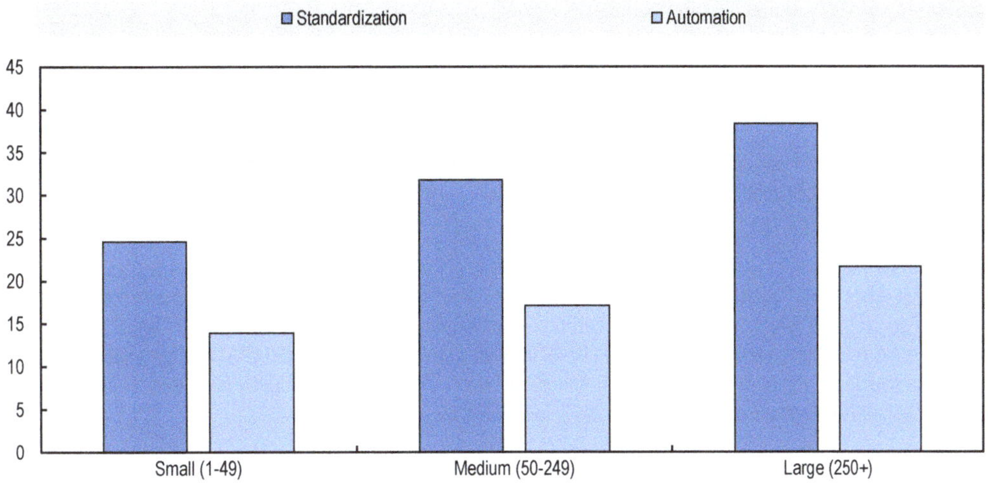

Note: 'Standardisation' refers to creating the standard of manufacturing / process, so rational activities and compatibility be improved. 'Automation' refers to automating a process or part of work by machine, computer or electric machine. Data refer to main products / delivered services. High standardisation or automation refers to the share of firms reporting a level of standardisation or automation of 80%-100%.
Source: OECD elaborations based on the Workplace Panel Survey (6th wave, 2015).

One of the reasons as to why SMEs often do not automate processes is that many of them do not feel the necessity of automation. This may suggest a lack of competition, at least in certain sectors, that would oblige SMEs to introduce automation to ensure their survival (Chang and Lee, 2017[13]).

Low automation may also be due to the inability of SMEs to adopt new technologies – as the resources that are necessary for costly investments in advanced technology may be out of reach. Indeed, Korean SMEs still lag significantly behind in their use of key digital technologies compared to larger Korean companies, and compared to SMEs in other OECD countries (OECD, forthcoming[14]; OECD, forthcoming[6]).[13]

For example, the share of SME workplaces converted to smart factories – i.e. highly digitised and connected production facilities that rely on smart manufacturing – is low at 7.4% (OECD, 2018[3]). To give another example, Korean SMEs lag far behind in their use of cloud computing technology. The share of small firms in Korea (with between 50 and 249 employees) that used cloud computing in 2016 was 10%, one-third of the OECD average (Figure 1.21). Moreover, few Korean SMEs use big data. The share of Korean SMEs using big data was only 4% in 2016, well below the 11% OECD average, and below any other OECD country with available data (Figure 1.22).

Figure 1.21. Enterprises using cloud computing services, by firm size, 2016

As a percentage of enterprises in each employment size class

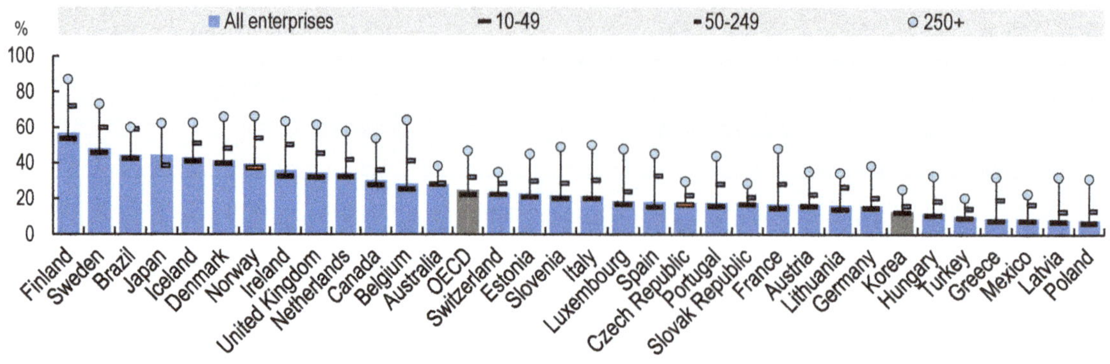

Note: Cloud computing refers to ICT services used over the Internet as a set of computing resources to access software, computing power, storage capacity and so on. Data refer to manufacturing and non-financial market services enterprises with ten or more persons employed, unless otherwise stated. Size classes are defined as: small (10-49 persons employed), medium (50-249) and large (250 and more). OECD data are based on a simple average of the available countries. For more detailed information at the country level, see endnote[14].
Source: OECD (2017[15]), OECD Digital Economy Outlook 2017, OECD Publishing, Paris.

Figure 1.22. Enterprises performing big data analysis, by firm size, 2016

As a percentage of enterprises in each employment size class

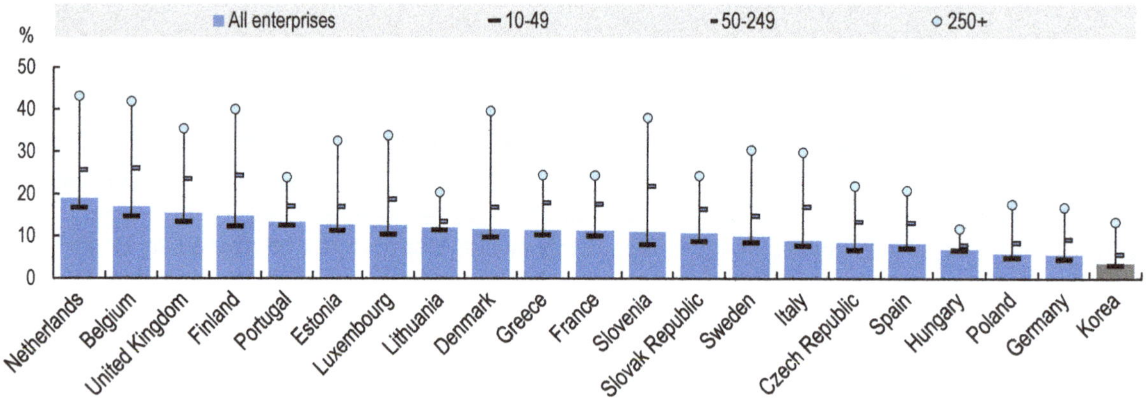

Note: For Korea, data relate to the year 2015.
Source: OECD (2017[15]), OECD Digital Economy Outlook 2017, OECD Publishing, Paris.

Many SMEs are not stepping up efforts to invest more in IT technology, either. OECD elaborations based on the Workplace Panel Survey show that 58.8% of small firms and 47.2% of medium-sized firms do 'not at all' or 'not much' agree that the company significantly expanded investments in IT in 2015. This compares to 44.3% of larger companies (Figure 1.23).

Figure 1.23. Firms' investments in IT

Percentage of firms significantly expanding investments on IT, by firm size

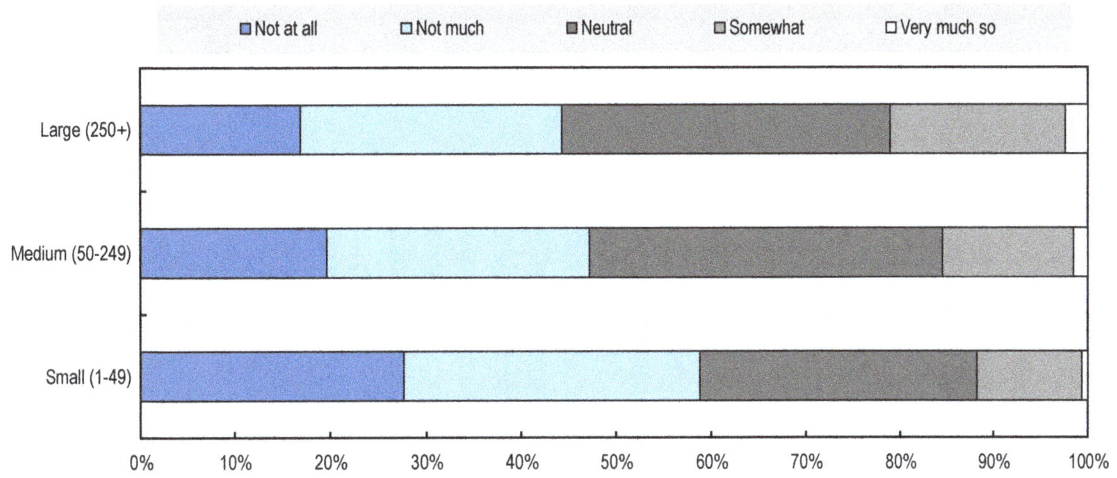

Note: data refers to the percentage of firms agreeing with the statement 'Our workplace significantly expanded investments on IT' by firm size.
Source: OECD elaborations based on the Workplace Panel Survey (6th wave, 2015).

Low levels of adoption of new technologies in SMEs means that many routine jobs that could be partially/completely automated are still performed by workers. In this context, the potential for Korean SMEs to improve their technology base and introduce automation practices is high. If new technologies are adopted by SMEs in the future, and more tasks are automated, many SMEs may go through significant transformations, a situation which may require many SME workers to retrain.

1.2.2. Globalisation and participation in Global Value Chains (GVCs)

An increasingly globalised world has a profound impact on the skills that are in demand in the labour market. Globalisation can lead to greater specialisation and hence different skill-sets needed by firms. In fact, evidence from advanced economies suggests that increasing participation in global value chains (GVCs) raises the demand for those high-level skills which are needed to specialise in high-tech manufacturing industries and in complex business services (OECD, 2017[16]; OECD, 2016[17]). Increasingly GVCs can also lead to jobs being offshored, especially at the low-end of the skills spectrum.

Korean SMEs have not yet become major players in GVCs. This leaves an opportunity to Korea to act early and anticipate potential disruptions. Indeed, although in Korea SMEs account for more than 80% of total business employment, their contributions to overall exports is just 20%, the second lowest in the OECD after Mexico (Figure 1.24).

Even though this share does not take into account the role that SMEs play as suppliers of inputs to larger direct exporters, SMEs' indirect contribution to exports also appears limited: value added from domestic services, where SMEs account for 90% of employment, accounted for only 26% of gross exports over 2010-14, well below the 40% OECD average (OECD, 2018[3]).

Figure 1.24. SME export activity by country, 2015 or latest available year

As a percentage of exports, total business economy

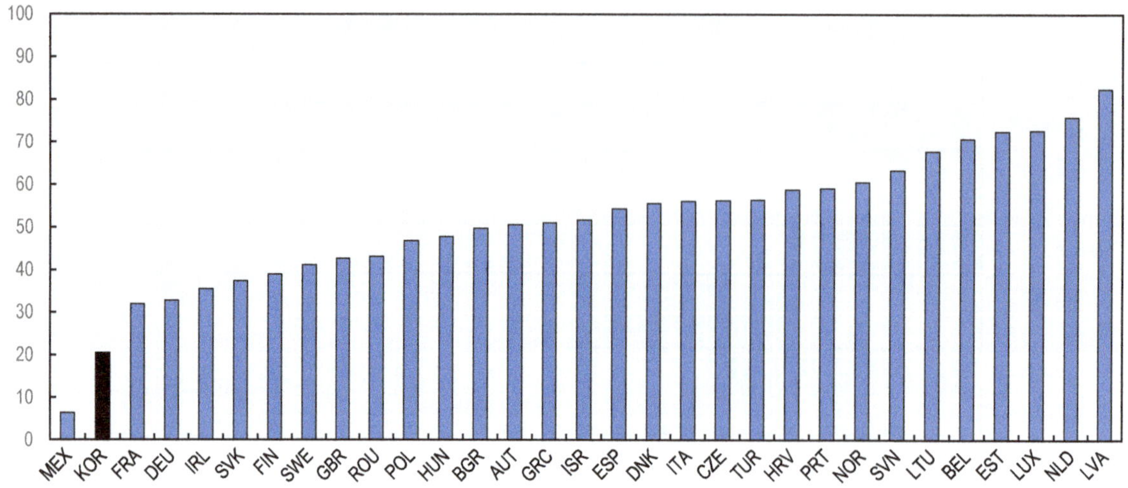

Source: OECD Structural and Demographic Business Statistics Database, 2018 (http://dx.doi.org/10.1787/sdbs-data-en) and Trade by Enterprise Characteristics Database, 2018 (https://doi.org/10.1787/eeefdd40-en).

The propensity to engage in international markets is also low among Korean SMEs. Compared to OECD countries for which data are available, Korean SMEs have the third lowest reported participation in international markets (i.e. percentage of firms selling goods or services abroad) after Japan and Chile, among both innovative and non-innovative SMEs (Figure 1.25).

Figure 1.25. SMEs participating in international markets, by innovation status, 2010-12

As a percentage of firms in the relevant group

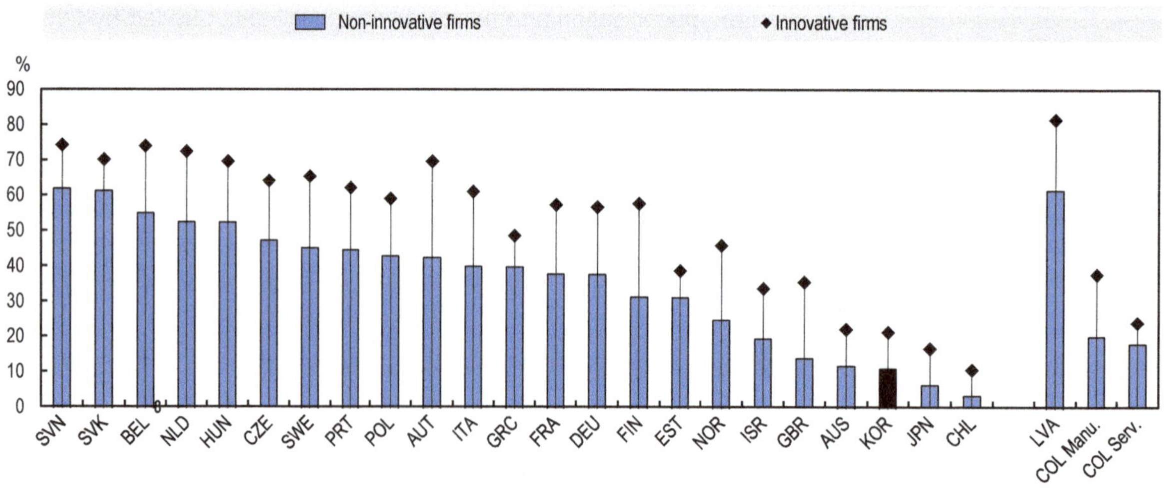

Note: Participation in international markets is defined as firms selling goods or services abroad. International comparability may be limited due to differences in innovation survey methodologies and country-specific response patterns. European countries follow harmonised survey guidelines with the CIS.

Source: OECD (2015[18]), *OECD Sciences, Technology, and Industry Scoreboard*, https://doi.org/10.1787/sti_scoreboard-2015-en.

1.2.3. Population ageing

One mega-trend that could, in the future, have large implications for skill needs in Korean firms – and particularly SMEs – is population ageing. According to the UN world population prospects, the old-age dependency ratio is expected to increase very sharply from just 17.7% in 2015 to 66.3% in 2050. This means that Korea will move from having the third lowest to the fifth highest old-age dependency ratio in the OECD in only 35 years, by far the largest increase in the OECD (Figure 1.26).

Figure 1.26. Population ageing

Population aged 65+ as percentage of population aged 15-64

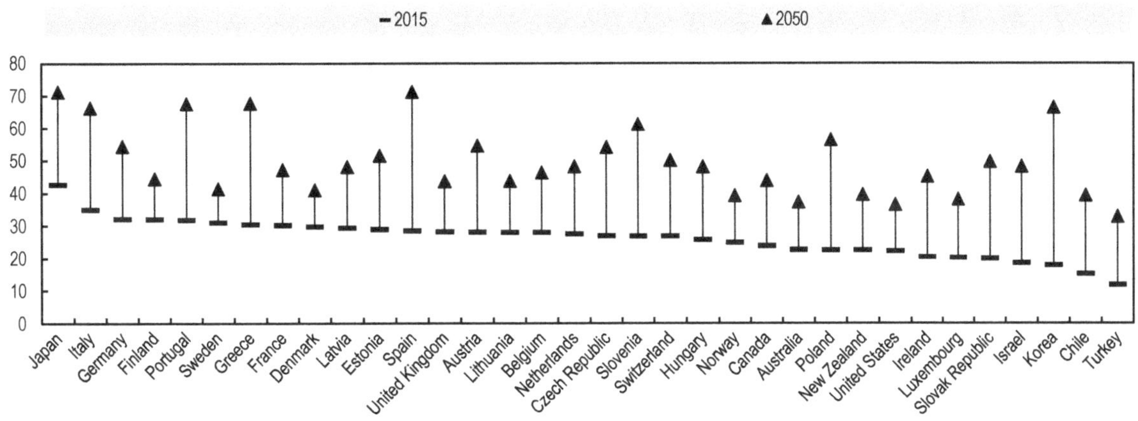

Note: Projections are based on the medium scenario of possible future growth of the world population.
Source: UN world population prospects (2017).

Population ageing impacts skill and training needs in a number of ways. First of all, it increases the need for individuals to maintain and update their skills over longer working lives. Recent policy measures in Korea already include plans to extend working lives to cope with rapid population ageing: the standard eligibility age for public pension is currently 61 years and it is set to rise to 65 by 2033.

Second, the retirement of large cohorts can lead to significant shortages of labour, a gap that can (partially) be filled through training of the existing workforce. Finally, population ageing is likely to contribute to further shifts in the structure of the economy, as demand for goods and services changes. For example, population ageing may result in an increased demand for health and elderly care services/personnel – requiring more individuals to be trained for these professions.

While the implications of population ageing on skills and training needs is likely to affect the Korean labour market as a whole, the consequences for SMEs may be even more marked. First of all, population ageing is expected to increase competition for workers, which can be particularly challenging for SMEs which already struggle to offer attractive working conditions.

Secondly, most older workers are concentrated in SMEs – which is a challenge considered that skills and education gaps between youth and older generations are among the widest in the OECD (OECD, 2019[19]; OECD, 2019[20]; OECD, 2018[21]). According to PIAAC data, some 40.7% of all older employees (ages 50-65) in Korea work in micro firms, 26.8% work in small firms, 17.2% work in medium-sized firms, and only 15.2% work in larger companies (Figure 1.27). Unless these skills gaps are closed, SMEs may face a competitive disadvantage vis-à-vis larger firms.

Third and last, when they are not employed in an SME, many older people often launch a second career that involves self-employment or business ownership. However, few have the necessary business skills to achieve high productivity and business success (OECD, 2018[21]). This means that, unless they are adequately trained, many older workers may end up setting up and running unproductive small and medium businesses. According to PIAAC data, about 20% of older people (50-65) in Korea are business-owners (i.e. self-employed with employees), the second highest share in the OECD after Greece, and another 22% are own account workers (i.e. self-employed without employees) (Figure 1.27).

Figure 1.27. Older workers in SMEs and larger companies, OECD and Korea

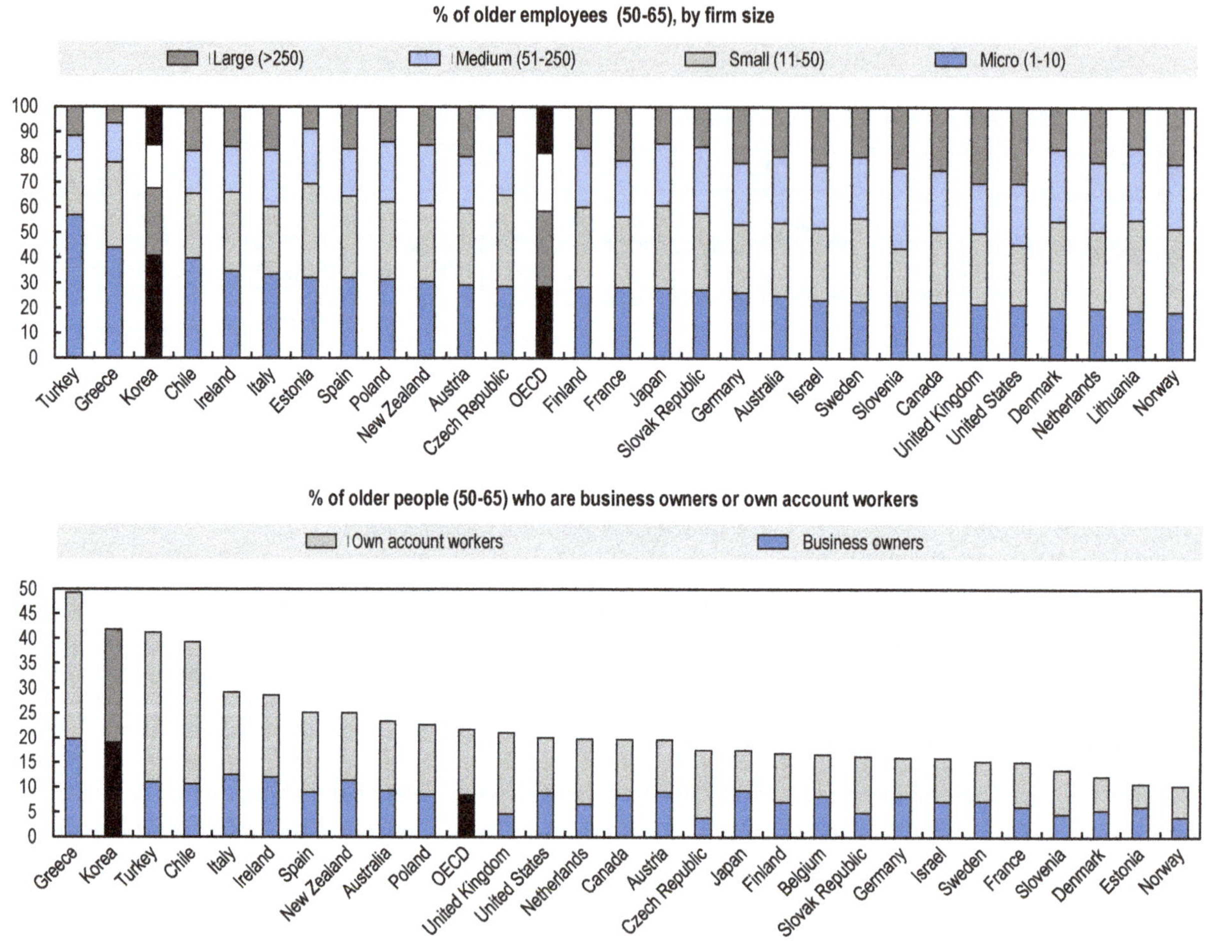

Note: OECD average refers to the weighted average of OECD countries that have participated to the Survey of Adult Skills. Business owners are self-employed with employees. Own account workers are self-employed without employees.
Source: OECD elaborations based on PIAAC (2012; 2015).

1.3. Skills imbalances in the Korean labour market

The labour market and economic context discussed in Sections 1.1 and 1.2 is generating imbalances between the demand and supply of skills. While many SMEs struggle to find employees, jobseekers have a hard time finding jobs that are a good match for their skills. Drawing from national and international data sources, this section looks at skills imbalances in the Korean labour market, focussing particularly on SMEs.

1.3.1. Korean SMEs face chronic labour shortages

Despite the fact that the Korean adult population is highly educated, Korean SMEs face significant labour shortages. For example, a recent poll by the Korea Small Business Institute reported that 80.5% of SMEs are experiencing difficulty finding employees (OECD, 2018[3]).

Results of the latest *Occupational Labour Force Survey at Establishment* point to similar findings and show that during the second half of 2018, there were 77 000 unfilled vacancies in SMEs[15] (12.9% of job openings), compared to 7 000 in large firms (4.4% of job openings).[16]

In the same period, SMEs reported to need 240 000 additional workers[17] – compared to only 29 000 in large firms – in order to operate the business and production facility normally and to respond to customer orders.[18] As shown in Table 1.3, in the second half of 2018, the labour shortage rate of SMEs (2.5%) was over twice that of large firms (1.2%).

Table 1.3. Labour shortage rate in Korea by firm size (%)

	2017 (second half)	2018 (first half)	2018 (second half)
Total (5+)	2.3	2.4	2.2
5-299	2.6	2.8	2.5
5-9	3.5	3.6	2.9
10-29	2.6	2.6	2.2
30-99	2.2	2.4	2.3
100-299	2.3	2.6	2.6
300+	1.1	1.1	1.2

Note: The Occupational Labour Force Survey at Establishment asks employers for the current number of workers and the number of persons needed (more than current staff) in order to operate the business and production facility normally, and to respond to customer orders. Labour shortage rate is defined as follows: the number of persons needed / (the number of current workers + the number of persons needed).
Source: MOEL, Occupational Labour Force Survey at Establishment.

Different data sources and studies all suggest that chronic labour shortages in SMEs are not due to a lack of available workers, but reflect low wages and poor working conditions (OECD, 2018[3]). They could also reflect poor HR processes, as SMEs are typically less efficient in looking for and recruiting talent.

Indeed, Korea displays high levels of educational attainment and the highest share of young adults with tertiary qualifications among OECD countries (OECD, 2019[19]). However, as discussed in Section 1.1.3, SMEs are often unable to attract younger high-skilled talents likely because – compared to larger companies – they offer less attractive jobs.[19]

In this context, it is not surprising that many Korean high-skilled adults simply do not wish to work for an SME. For example, a 2016 survey of university students by the Federation of Korean Industries reported that 32% wanted to work for a big company and another 25% preferred state-run institutions. Only 5% said they wanted to work at an SME (FKI, 2016[22]).

University graduates often prefer to wait for an attractive job opportunity than run the risk of being "trapped" in a small firm. Many of them spend time preparing for entry exams needed to enter large companies. In this context, it is not surprising that Korea is one of the few OECD countries in which young university graduates (aged 15-29) are most likely to be neither in employment, education, or training (NEET) than their lower-educated peers (OECD, 2019[20]; Fernandez et al., 2020[23]).

When adults do take up a job in an SME, it is often out of necessity rather than for the opportunities that the job itself can offer. According to Workplace Panel Survey data, 36.3% of workers in micro-firms in 2015 said that the main reason for taking up their current job was that they needed urgent money to pay for expenses, a share that decreases evenly to 12.3% of workers in larger firms. Unsurprisingly, compared to workers in large firms, SME workers less often cite work conditions (e.g. work hours, wages) and job stability as a reason for taking up their job (Figure 1.28).

Figure 1.28. Reasons for taking up a job in Korea

Percentage of workers by firm size

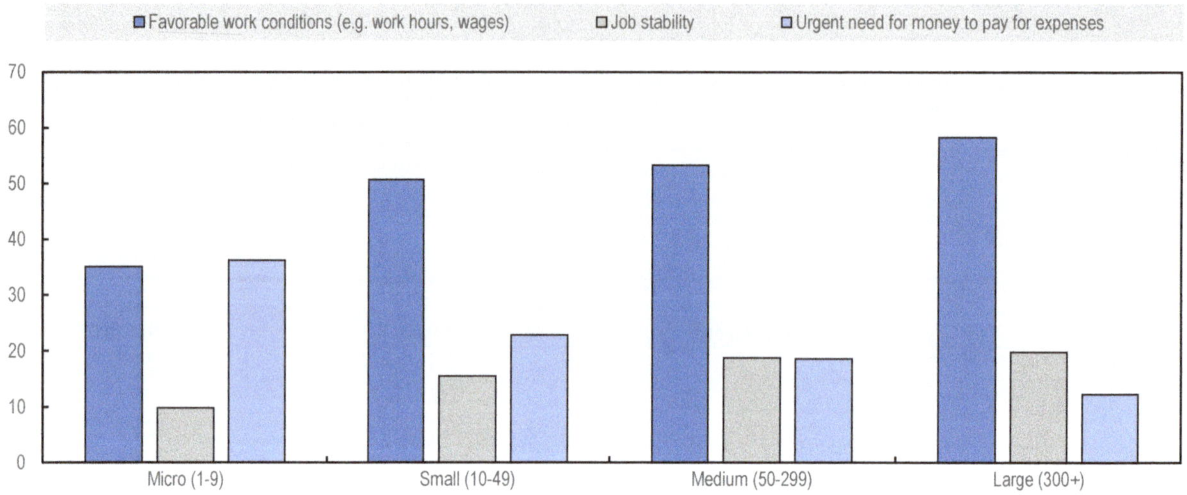

Note: The graph includes only the three most frequently reported reasons. Other responses contained in the questionnaire include 'Couldn't find a job in desired field'; 'Couldn't find a job suiting my major or area of experience'; 'In order to gain the experience needed to move onto a better job'; 'In order to balance housework/ childcare with work'; 'In order to balance studies with work'; 'Because pay at this job depends on effort'; 'Flexible work hours'; and 'Other'.

Source: OECD elaborations of the Korean Workplace Panel Survey (6th wave, 2015).

SMEs are well aware of these challenges. Results of the *Occupational Labour Force Survey at Establishment* show that, during the second half of 2018, 23.3% of SMEs reported that the main reason for not hiring new staff was that 'the working conditions (such as the wage level) did not match the expectations of the job seeker'. Another 18.5% reported that they could offer only 'jobs that job seekers avoid' (Figure 1.29).

Figure 1.29. Most important reasons for not hiring new staff in Korea

Percentage of firms, by firm size

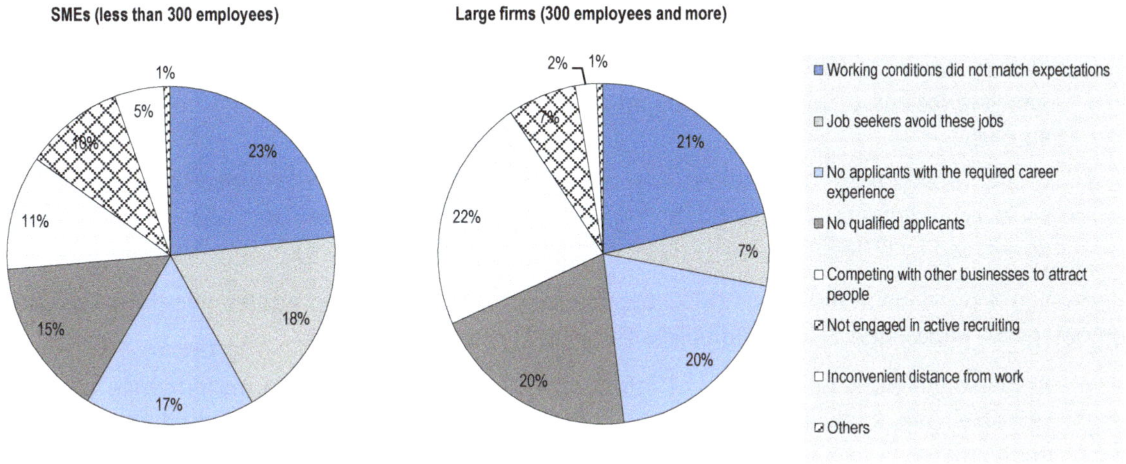

Note: responses reflect the answers mentioned as first priority.
Source: Occupational Labour Force Survey at Establishment, second half of 2018.

1.3.2. OECD Skills for Jobs database

The *OECD Skills for Jobs* database provides timely information for Korea and other OECD and emerging countries, about skills shortages (i.e. when adequate skills are hard-to-find in the current labour market) and skills surpluses (i.e. when certain skills are in excess in the labour market relative to the demand).

Unlike employer surveys,[20] the *OECD Skills for Jobs* indicators are based on quantitative data from large-scale household surveys, and are constructed using a multidimensional set of quantitative signals of skills pressure, including wage growth, employment growth and unemployment. Box 1.1 provides a detailed description of the methodology behind the OECD Skills for Jobs database, as well as the specificities of the methodology used to construct the indicators for Korea.

Box 1.1. The OECD Skills for Jobs database

The OECD Skills for Jobs database provides timely information about skills shortages – i.e. when skills sought by employers are not available in the pool of potential recruits – and skills surpluses – i.e. when the supply of certain skills is higher than the demand. It covers 40 countries among OECD and emerging economies.

The database has key innovative features compared to existing measures of skills shortages/surpluses. By looking at skills – i.e. the set of competences mobilised to perform the tasks related to a job – rather than occupations or fields of study, the new indicators go beyond the traditional measures of imbalances. Furthermore, unlike the generally subjective information available from employer surveys, the OECD Skills for Jobs database draws from quantitative data derived from household surveys. Finally, the indicator is constructed using a multidimensional set of quantitative signals on skills pressure (i.e. five sub-indices, including wage growth, employment growth and unemployment), which provides a holistic interpretation of skill imbalances in the labour markets.

Skill needs indicator

The skill needs indicator is constructed in two consecutive steps:

- In the first step, sub-indices for hourly wage growth, employment growth, unemployment rate, hours worked and under-qualification are used to provide a quantitative indication of the extent of the labour market pressure on each one of the occupations analysed. The result of this analysis returns a ranking of occupations ordered from the one most in shortage to most in surplus.
- In the second step, occupations that are in shortage/surplus are mapped into the underlying skills requirements associated to those occupations, using the occupation-skills taxonomy developed by O*NET.

Information is provided at the 2-digit ISCO occupation level and is disaggregated into three domains of competence – knowledge, skills, and abilities:

- Knowledge refers to the body of information that makes adequate performance on the job possible (e.g. knowledge of plumbing for a plumber; knowledge of mathematics for an economist).
- Skills refer to the proficient manual, verbal or mental manipulation of data or things (e.g. complex problem solving; social skills)
- Ability refer to the competence to perform an observable activity (e.g. ability to plan and organise work; attentiveness; endurance).

Qualification mismatch

The qualification mismatch index calculates the share of workers in each economy/occupation that are under- or overqualified to perform a certain job. This is done by computing the modal (i.e. most common) educational attainment level for each occupation in each country and point in time, and use this as a benchmark to measure whether individual workers' qualifications match the "normal" education requirement of the occupation.[21] Thus, over-qualification (under-qualification) depicts a situation for which the highest level of education achieved by an individual worker in an occupation is above (below) the modal level for all workers in that occupation.

Methodology used to construct the Skills for Jobs database indicators for Korea

The data source used to develop the indicators for Korea is the Korean Labor & Income Panel Study (KLIPS), from the Korean Labor Institute (KLI). The occupational shortage indicator is calculated for 35 occupational groups at the ISCO-08 2-digit level. In the case of Korea, the unemployment rate sub-component was not used to calculate the occupational shortage indicator, the reason being that there were too few observations on the unemployed with available information on occupations in the previous job. The self-employed workers are excluded from the analysis, because KLIPS survey does not include information on wages and hours worked for the self-employed, which is needed to construct the indicators. For Korea, the Skills for Jobs indicators are disaggregated by the size of the firm – an exercise which was not done for other countries contained in the OECD Skills for Jobs database. These indicators are constructed by calculating the weighted average of the occupational shortage index, aggregated by firm size. It is important to note that in the KLIPS survey, information on firm size is missing for a substantial number of observations.

Source: OECD (2018[24]), *Skills for Jobs*, https://www.oecdskillsforjobsdatabase.org/data/Skills%20SfJ_PDF%20for%20WEBSITE%20final.pdf; OECD (2017[25]), *Getting Skills Right: Skills for Jobs Indicators*, https://doi.org/10.1787/9789264277878-en.

Mismatches in the Korean labour market

OECD *Skills for Jobs* results at the occupational level show that in Korea shortages can be found in a large variety of occupations, such as skilled agricultural, forestry, and fishery workers, as well as health associate professionals, electrical and electronics trade workers, and assemblers. On the other hand, surpluses – i.e. where signals suggest that supply exceeds demand – are observed in occupations like managers, agricultural forestry, and fishery labourers, as well as protective service workers (Figure 1.30).[22]

Figure 1.30. Imbalances by occupation, Korea, 2017

Hard-to-fill (+) and easy-to-fill (-) occupations

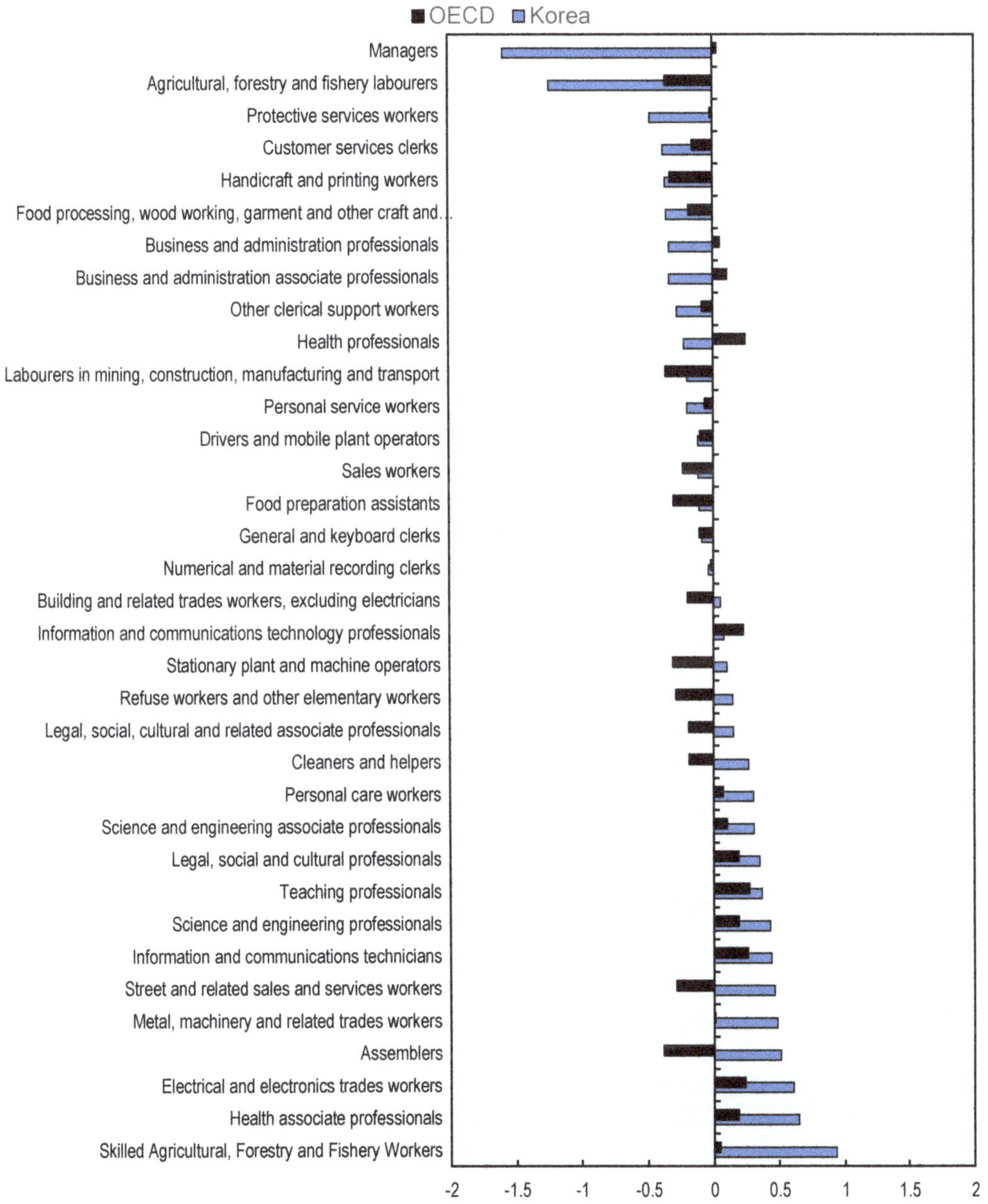

Note: ISCO-08 occupations. The degree of imbalances ranges from -2.5 (easy-to-find) to +2.5 (hard-to-find).
Source: OECD Skills for Jobs database.

The OECD *Skills for Jobs* database goes beyond occupational imbalances and also provides detailed information on skills imbalances. Figure 1.31 shows that in Korea – like in the OECD area on average – certain high-level cognitive skills are in shortage (reasoning and verbal abilities). There are also observed shortages in basic skills and complex problem solving skills. Physical and manual skills (physical strengths; visual abilities) seem to be rather at an equilibrium level – unlike what can be observed in the OECD area on average where these skills are in surplus. The only surpluses in Korea can be observed for knowledge of Law and Public Safety, and Business and Management.

Figure 1.31. Imbalances by skills, 2017

Hard-to-find (+) and easy-to-find (-) skills, knowledge types and abilities

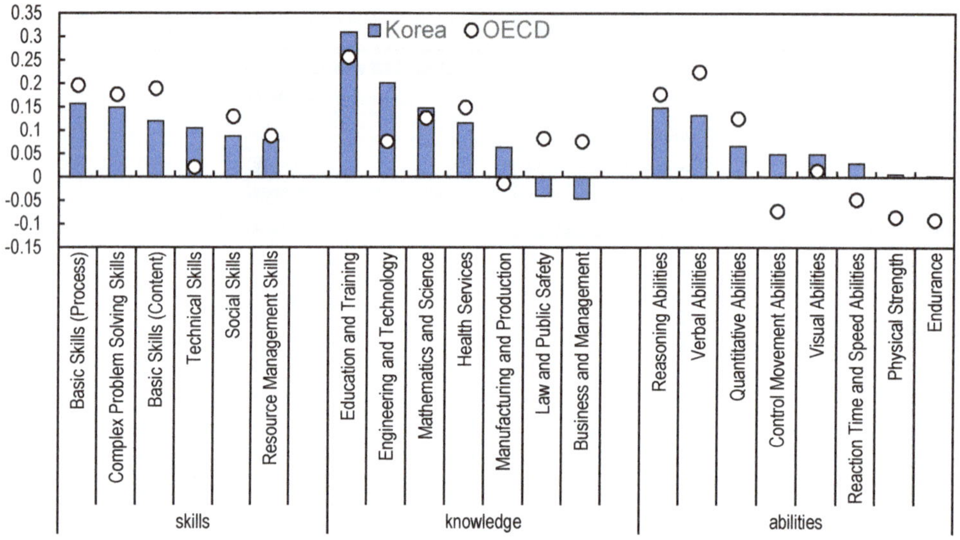

Source: OECD Skills for Jobs database.

Results from the OECD *Skills for Jobs* database also provide a detailed picture of shortages and surpluses at the sector level, based on the occupational composition of each sector. Figure 1.32 reveals that, in Korea, sectoral/industry shortages are the strongest in the agriculture, forestry and fishing sector, as well as in the education sector – meaning that a large share of workers in those sectors is employed in occupations that are in shortage. Conversely, surpluses are found in the sectors of Public administration and defence, Financial and insurance activities, and Accommodation and food service activities, where a large share of those sectors' employment is in occupations in surplus or that face weak demand. Notably, weak demand rather than excess supply seems to be an issue in the public administration sector which is unusually small in Korea by international standards.[23]

Figure 1.32. Imbalances by industry, 2017

Concentration of easy-to-fill (+) and hard-to-fill (-) occupations by industry

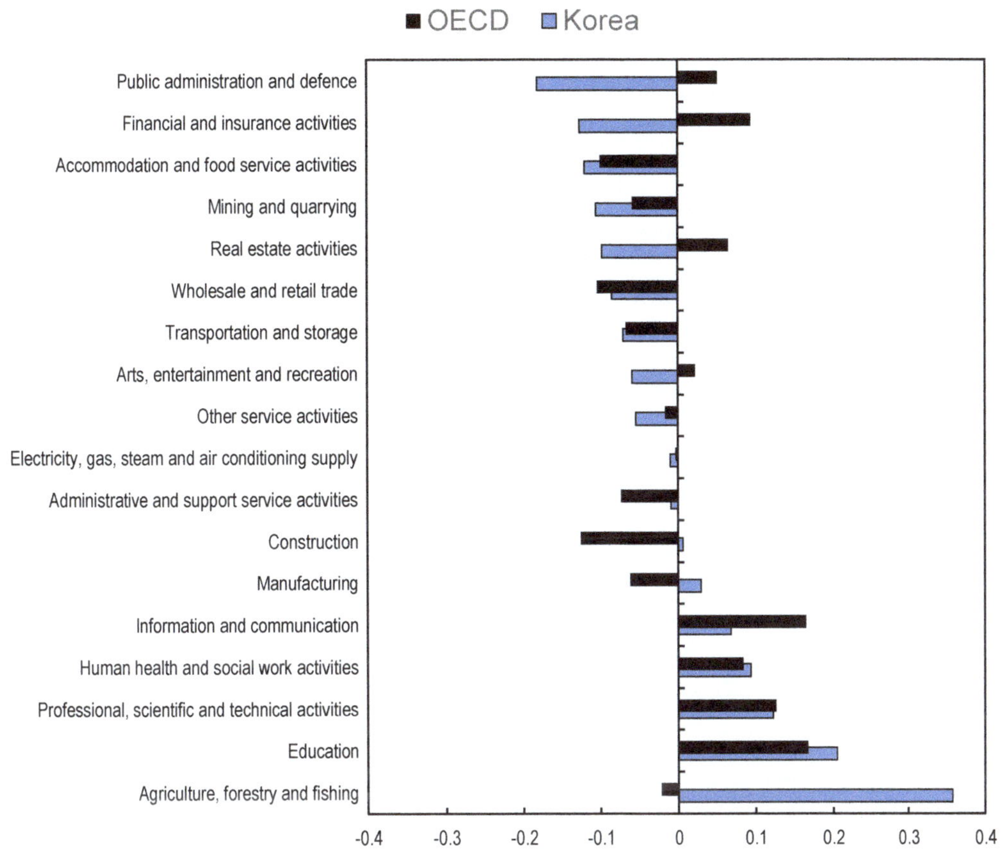

Note: The degree of imbalances ranges from -2.5 (easy-to-find) to +2.5 (hard-to-find). The industry results are employment-weighted averages of the occupation results, using information of the occupational composition within industries. Electricity, gas, steam and air conditioning supply also include "water supply; sewerage, waste management and remediation activities". Wholesale and retail trade also include "repair of motor vehicles and motorcycles". Public administration and defence also include "compulsory social security".
Source: OECD Skills for Jobs database.

In addition to substantial shortages and surpluses, the Korean labour market also has a significant share of workers who are mismatched in terms of qualification level.[24] According to the OECD Skills for Jobs data, in 2017, 21% of Korean workers were under-qualified for their occupation, and an additional 12% were over-qualified (Figure 1.33, Panel A).[25] This is lower than mismatch levels observed in other OECD countries, where 19% of workers were under-qualified and 17% over-qualified on average. Another positive feature of the Korean labour market is that mismatches are on a downward trend, as rates of over- and under-qualification have decreased by 10 percentage points in the period 1998-2017 (Figure 1.33, Panel B).

Despite relatively low and declining levels of under/over-qualifications, Korea still performs less well than several OECD countries in Europe (e.g. Czech Republic, Poland, and Slovak Republic). The presence of some degree of over-qualification in the Korean workforce is consistent with the inability of the labour market to absorb the high share of young university graduates. Under-qualification, on the other hand, might reflect that employers have difficulties finding workers with the right qualification level and resort to hiring under-qualified workers.[26] It could also reflect that older workers often do not have qualifications although they may have the skills (acquired through experience) needed to perform the job.

Figure 1.33. Share of workers mismatched by qualification level

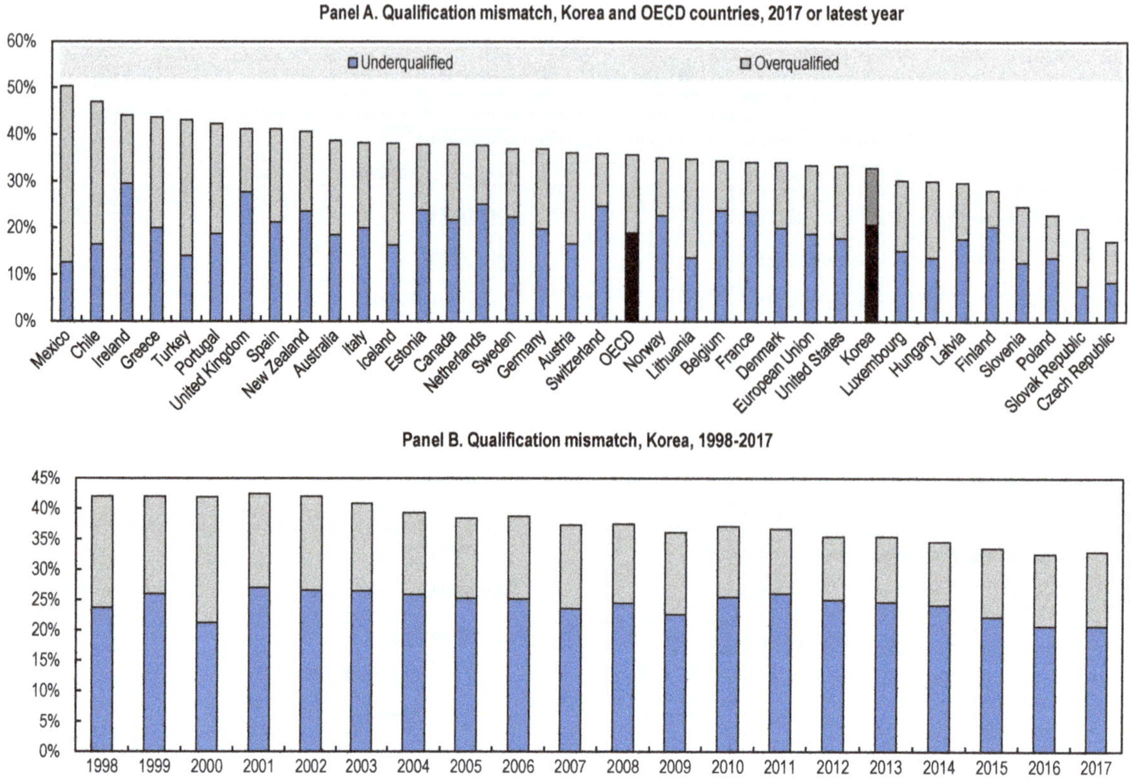

Note: In Panel A, OECD average excludes Korea. Differences between countries also reflect differences in the occupational classification used.
Source: OECD Skills for Jobs database.

Mismatches in Korean SMEs

Looking at occupational shortages and surpluses at firm size level suggests that, in Korea in 2017, small firms were facing the most intensive shortages, followed by medium sized-firms /very small firms, and large firms. On the other hand, micro-firms were facing surpluses on average (Figure 1.34).

As explained in Box 1.1, these disaggregated indicators are a weighted average of the occupational shortages, and therefore they simply reflect the occupation structure by firm size. The only reason for a certain firm size category to have stronger shortages is that they employ more workers in occupations in shortage and fewer in occupations in surplus. These data do not reflect whether a certain firm size category faces more difficulties finding workers for a specific occupation than other firm size categories. For example, the reason why small firms with 30-49 employees experience more shortages is that their workforce is made up disproportionately with occupations in shortage. Likewise, surpluses in micro-firms reflect the fact that these firms use occupations in surplus more intensively.

Figure 1.34. Imbalances by firm size, 2017

Hard-to-fill (+) and easy-to-fill (-) occupations

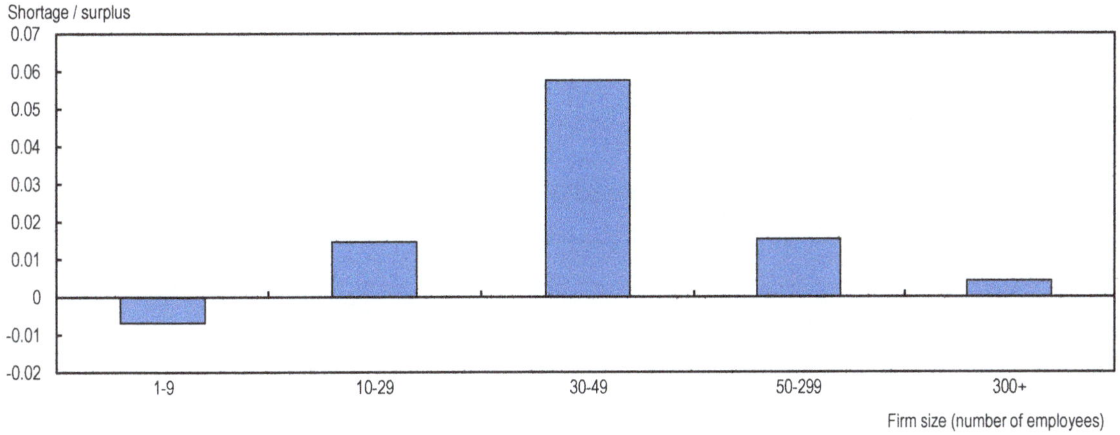

Note: The degree of imbalances ranges from -2.5 (easy-to-find) to +2.5 (hard-to-find). In the data source used to calculate this indicator (i.e. the Korean Labor and Income Panel Study) information on firm size is missing for a substantial number of observations.
Source: OECD elaborations based on the OECD Skills for Jobs database.

More detailed results for skills, abilities, and knowledge types, broadly confirm this patterns. Apart from two notable exceptions (reaction time and speed abilities; and control movement abilities), small firms with 30-49 employees experience the greatest shortages in all the broad skills, abilities and knowledge types presented in Figure 1.35.

Figure 1.35. Imbalances by skills and firm size, 2017

Hard-to-find (+) and easy-to-find (-) skills, knowledge types and abilities

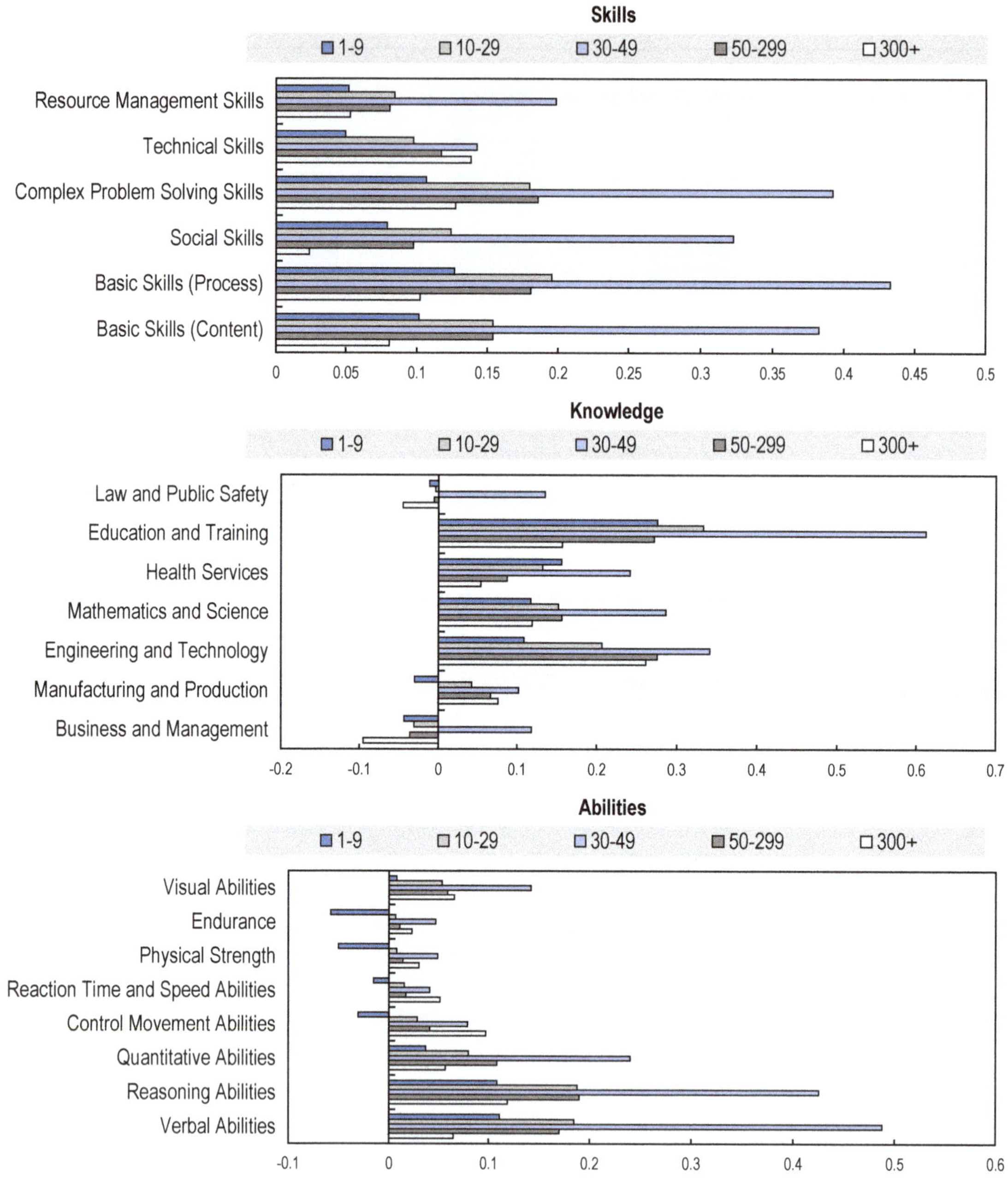

Note: In the data source used to calculate this indicator (i.e. the Korean Labor & Income Panel Study) information on firm size is missing for a substantial number of observations.
Source: OECD elaborations based on the OECD Skills for Jobs database.

Over the past two decades, qualification mismatches have decreased across firms of all sizes in Korea, but today they remain more prominent among the smallest firms. Almost 45% of workers in micro-firms are either under or overqualified for their job, compared to only about 25% of workers in large firms (Figure 1.36).

Figure 1.36. Share of workers mismatched by qualification level and firm size

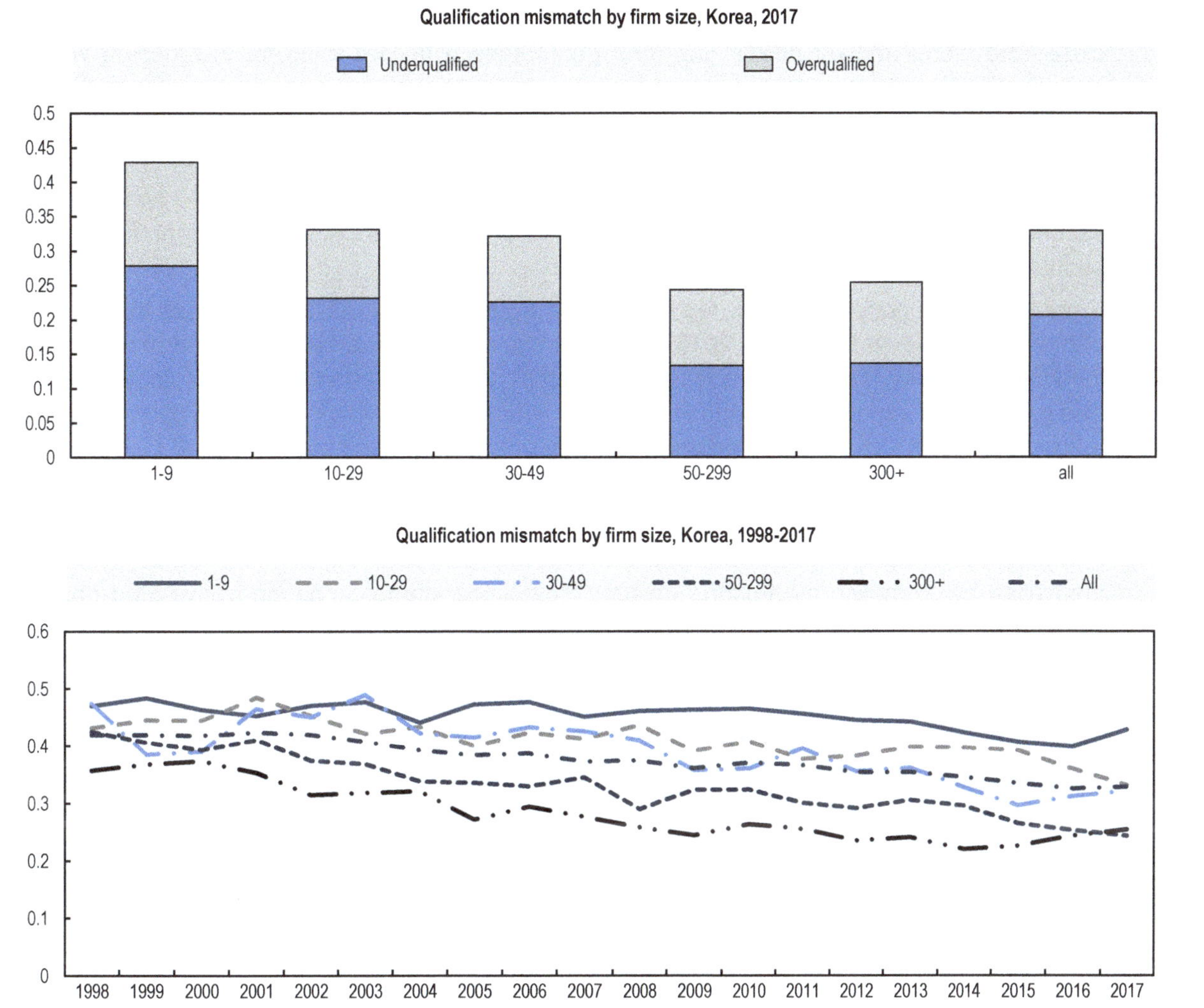

Note: In the data source used to calculate this indicator (i.e. the Korean Labor & Income Panel Study) information on firm size is missing for a substantial number of observations.

Source: OECD elaborations based on the OECD Skills for Jobs database.

1.4. Context conditions to tackle skills imbalances in SMEs

As will be discussed in Chapters 2 to 5, Korea has already implemented many adult learning measures to enhance training participation in SMEs. Yet, there is only so much that adult learning programmes can do to reduce skills shortages. For example, wide differences in working conditions between SMEs and large companies – largely driven by productivity gaps, the virtual inexistence of trade unions in SMEs, and a widespread subcontracting culture – may hamper SMEs' ability to attract and retain high skilled workers, which in turn may undermine their ability to train their staff (see Chapter 2).

In this context, complementary policies that go beyond the scope of adult learning (e.g. labour market, industrial policies) need to be put in place to promote an adult learning-friendly environment. Recently, the government has put in place several policy measures that go in this direction. These policies revolve around:

- *Improving working conditions in SMEs*, in a view to help SMEs attract high-skilled workers. For example, the government's recent decision to significantly increase the minimum wage (see Chapter 2) reflects an effort to achieve an "income-led growth" that fosters workers' productivity, closes the labour market duality gap, and guarantees a decent living for low-income workers including SME workers.
- *Linking performance more closely to wages*. Recent efforts to move away from seniority wages and promote better links between workers' productivity and wages – such as the introduction of the "wage peak" system, and efforts to promote the use of objective wage grids[27] – could motivate workers to train to advance and progress in their career. These are steps in the right direction that should be scaled-up more widely.
- *Speeding up the adoption of new technologies in SMEs* – which will likely increase their demand of high-level skills. In December 2018 the Korean government has set up a smart manufacturing innovation strategy. The objective is to have 30 000 plants converted to smart factories by 2022. The government expects that SMEs in the manufacturing sector would create 66 000 new jobs by automating 50% of their manufacturing facilities and increase KRW 18 trillion (about EUR 14.1 billion) of sales. Recognising that adequate manpower is needed to make full use of new technologies, the government is planning to train 100 000 smart manufacturing workers.
- *Pursuing innovation growth*. In particular, the government is trying to make SMEs a driver of innovation by promoting the Fourth Industrial Revolution and fostering innovative start-ups (see Chapter 4). To accomplish this, the government established the Ministry of SMEs and Start-ups in 2017 and launched a range of new initiatives to promote a favourable business environment. These include measures to build an innovative ecosystem and infrastructure for future industries, boost financial support to SMEs and venture start-ups, and expand support for SME exporters.
- *Strengthening employment services to improve job matching*. For example, the government will increase the number of employment service offices, including Employment-Welfare Plus Centers, to ensure that jobseekers can find an employment service help desk close to where they live. From July 2020, the government plans to establish 70 additional mid-sized job centres and branch offices in regions that currently do not have an Employment-Welfare Plus Centers. This measure may improve job matching for all firms, including SMEs.
- *Supporting jobseekers with their independent job-search efforts*. The government is strengthening the use of job information online platforms such as WorkNet. Since August 2019, WorkNet has more innovative features such as the "Theme-based Recruitment Section" where jobseekers can find the businesses they want to work for more easily. Going forward, WorkNet will also offer an online 24/7 automated counselling (*chatbot*), as well as AI-based job information recommendation based on jobseekers' profile. This measure could help all jobseekers to find a job, and could indirectly improve job matching in all firms, including SMEs.

References

Arntz, M. et al. (2016), *The Risk of Automation for Jobs in OECD Countries: A Comparative Analysis*, OECD Publishing, Paris, https://doi.org/10.1787/5jlz9h56dvq7-en. [11]

Chang, H. and Y. Lee (2017), *Survey of the Actual Situation of the Competitiveness of Small and*, Trade Focus, No. 32, Korea International Trade. [13]

Fernandez, R. et al. (2020), "Identifying and addressing employment barriers in Belgium, Korea and Norway: Implementing the OECD Jobs Strategy", *OECD Social, Employment and Migration Working Papers*. [23]

FKI (2016), *A Survey on the Employment Perceptions of University Students in 2016*. [22]

Kim, J. (2015), "Promoting Good-Quality Job Creation in the Sector of SMEs", *KDI Focus*, Vol. 29. [4]

MoEL (2017), *MOEL (2017), Survey Report on Labor Conditions by Employment Type*, Korean Ministry of Employment and Labor, http://laborstat.molab.go.kr/newOut/renewal/menu05/menu05_search_popup.jsp. [8]

Nedelkoska, L. and G. Quintini (2019), *Automation, skills use and training*, OECD Social, Employment and Migration Working Papers, No. 202, https://doi.org/10.1787/2e2f4eea-en. [10]

OECD (2019), *Education at a Glance: OECD indicators*, OECD Publishing, Paris, https://doi.org/10.1787/f8d7880d-en. [19]

OECD (2019), *Getting Skills Right: Future-Ready Adult Learning Systems*, OECD Publishing, Paris, https://doi.org/10.1787/9789264311756-en. [9]

OECD (2019), *Investing in Youth: Korea*, OECD Publishing, Paris, https://doi.org/10.1787/4bf4a6d2-en. [20]

OECD (2019), *OECD SMEs and Entrepreneurship Outlook 2019*, OECD Publishing, Paris, https://doi.org/10.1787/34907e9c-en. [1]

OECD (2018), *Connecting People with Jobs: Towards Better Social and Employment Security in Korea*, OECD Publishing, Paris, https://doi.org/10.1787/9789264288256-en. [5]

OECD (2018), *OECD Economic Surveys: Korea 2018*, OECD Publishing, Paris, https://dx.doi.org/10.1787/eco_surveys-kor-2018-en. [3]

OECD (2018), *Skills for Jobs*, OECD Publishing, Paris, https://www.oecdskillsforjobsdatabase.org/data/Skills%20SfJ_PDF%20for%20WEBSITE%20final.pdf. [24]

OECD (2018), *Working Better with Age: Korea*, OECD Publishing, Paris, https://doi.org/10.1787/9789264208261-en. [21]

OECD (2017), *OECD Digital Economy Outlook 2017*, OECD Publishing, Paris, https://doi.org/10.1787/9789264276284-en. [15]

OECD (2017), *Entrepreneurship at a Glance 2017*, OECD Publishing, Paris, https://doi.org/10.1787/entrepreneur_aag-2017-en. [2]

OECD (2017), *Getting Skills Right: Skills for Jobs Indicators*, OECD Publishing, Paris, https://doi.org/10.1787/9789264277878-en. [25]

OECD (2017), *OECD Skills Outlook 2017: Skills and Global Value Chains*, OECD Publishing, Paris, https://doi.org/10.1787/9789264273351-en. [16]

OECD (2016), *Getting Skills Right: Assessing and Anticipating Changing Skill Needs*, OECD Publishing, Paris, https://dx.doi.org/10.1787/9789264252073-en. [26]

OECD (2016), *OECD Employment Outlook 2016*, OECD Publishing, Paris, https://doi.org/10.1787/empl_outlook-2016-en. [17]

OECD (2015), *OECD Sciences, Technology, and Industry Scoreboard*, OECD Publishing, Paris, https://doi.org/10.1787/sti_scoreboard-2015-en. [18]

OECD (forthcoming), *Economic Survey of Korea 2020*, OECD Publishing, Paris. [6]

OECD (forthcoming), *Inclusive Growth in Korea*, OECD Publishing, Paris. [14]

Seol, G. (2019), *The Fourth Industrial Revolution and Workers in SMEs: Korean case*, Korea Research Institute for Vocational Education and Training (KRIVET). [12]

Statistics Korea (2018), *Supplementary Results of the Economically Active Population Survey by Employment Type in August 2018*, Statistics Korea. [7]

Notes

1 This report focuses on adult learning that is job-related, i.e. adult education and training that is expected to have some effect on performance and productivity at work.

2 Small and medium-sized enterprises (SMEs) are non-subsidiary, independent firms which employ less than a given number of employees. This number varies across countries. In this report, the upper limit designating an SME is 250 employees, unless otherwise specified. The self-employed and unpaid family workers are excluded from the analysis. If a different definition is used, this is because the data source does not allow to use such breakdowns.

3 Micro-firms are defined as firms with less than 10 employees.

4 34.4% in the manufacturing sector.

5 Labour market segmentation has important implications for working conditions because compared to regular workers, non-regular workers have precarious job contracts, are less likely to be coved by social insurance, and have lower access to training (OECD, 2018[5]).

6 The working hours in micro-firms (1-29 employees) are less or similar to those of large firms (+300). This can be explained by the high prevalence of temporary and daily workers with short working hours in micro-

firms. Indeed, the share of those workers in micro-firms (13.2%) is more than double that of large firms (5.5%).

[7] Compared with 24.3% in the OECD on average.

[8] Levels 3, 4 or 5.

[9] The difference between SMEs and large firms can be due to several factors, such as: a different occupational and industrial composition of employment; differences in the content of the jobs (all else being equal) e.g. tasks of a given occupation in an SME might be different from the tasks of the same occupation in a large firm.

[10] This is partly due to the fact that SME high-risk workers tend to persist in their employment situation: only few of them lost (11.6%) or changed (5.1%) jobs in the first half of 2017 (against 12.3% and 5.3% of workers in large firms respectively).

[11] This refers to the share of firms reporting a level of standardisation of 80%-100%. Data refers to main products / delivered services.

[12] This refers to the share of firms reporting a level of automation of 80%-100%. Data refers to main products / delivered services.

[13] Low technology adoption could also explain productivity gaps in SMEs.

[14] For Australia, data refer to the fiscal year 2014/2015, ending 30 June, instead of 2016. For industrial classification, ANZSIC06 division is used instead of ISIC rev.4 division. Data include agriculture, forestry and fishing. For Canada, data refer to 2012 and to enterprises that have made expenditures on software as a service (e.g. cloud computing). The North American Industry Classification System (NAICS) is used instead of ISIC Rev.4. Medium-sized enterprises have 50-299 employees. Large enterprises have 300 or more employees. For Iceland, data refer to 2014. For Japan, JSIC Rev.13 division is used instead of ISIC Rev.4, data refer to 2015 and to businesses with 100 or more employees. Medium-sized enterprises have 100-299 employees. Large enterprises have 300 or more employees. For Brazil and Korea, data refer to 2015. For Mexico, data refer to 2012. For Switzerland, data refer to 2015 and to firms with five or more employees.

[15] In this survey, SMEs are defined as firms with less than 300 employees. Large firms are defined as firms with 300 employees or more.

[16] 91.7% of all unfilled vacancies were in SMEs.

[17] In addition to the current workforce.

[18] Some 89.2% of all additional workers needed in Korea were in SMEs.

[19] SMEs report difficulties in hiring middle-skilled workers. The Occupational Labour Force Survey at Establishment shows the number of unfilled vacancies by skill level and firm size. Results show that SMEs face shortages of workers with education level 2-1 (educational attainment of high school graduate), level 1 (no requirement) and level 2-2 (2-year college graduate). By contrast, large firms face shortages of level 2-2 (2-year college graduate) and level 3 (university graduate or master degree).

[20] Employer surveys, like the *Occupational Labour Force Survey at Establishment*, provide a direct source of information on skill shortages, and therefore they are very useful to give an indication of firms' hiring

challenges. However, these surveys are usually subjective. Instead of representing true skill shortages (e.g. lack of skills in the available workforce), they may reflect hiring difficulties resulting from poor working conditions, inadequate remuneration, or poor HR policies (OECD, 2017[25]).

[21] The modal educational attainment level is calculated for each 3-digit ISCO occupation that has at least ten observations, and different modes are calculated for each country and year.

[22] Some of the results need to be taken with caution, because they may reflect some biases in the data sources used. For example, the surpluses observed in agricultural forestry, and fishery labourers, presented Figure 1.30, may reflect the fact that the data source used (KLIPS) is sampled over mainly urban households while rural households are under-represented. Moreover, it is well recognised in Korea that labour shortages are common in the agricultural sector, and the government tries to fill these gaps through foreign workers. In this context, surpluses observed in agricultural forestry, and fishery labourers could be due to the fact that domestic shortages are filled by foreign workers.

[23] Because the self-employed are excluded from the analysis (see Box 1.1), results need to be taken with caution for sectors with high shares of self-employment. This is the case for the Real Estate Activities. Shortages presented in Figure 1.32 may reflect the fact that in Korea the real estate business sector is mostly dominated by self-employed and freelancers.

[24] Qualification mismatch measures the misalignment between a workers' occupation and his/her qualification level. Workers are said to be underqualified when their highest educational attainment is below the usually observed qualification level in the worker's occupation. In the opposite case, when a worker's qualification level is above the standard qualification level in his/her occupation, this worker is overqualified.

[25] There are many ways to measure over-qualification and under-qualification mismatches (OECD, 2016[26]). Differences with the results reported in this report are mostly linked to the use of a different methodology.

[26] The fact that under-qualification mismatches are higher than over-qualification mismatches may reflect the fact that the sample is biased towards older generations, who are less likely to hold qualifications and are more likely to be under-qualified for their job.

[27] Korean government submitted a bill that promotes the adoption of objective wage grids through labour-management agreement, in the construction workforce (skills) grading system. The bill was presented to the National Assembly but has not yet passed.

2 Enhancing SMEs' training efforts

Adult learning is key to allow SMEs to close the productivity gap with larger companies, strengthen their position in global value chains, and tackle demographic changes. However, relatively few SMEs support the acquisition of skills. Indeed, Korean SMEs face great difficulties to provide training to their workers. Some of the challenges they are facing, such as lack of training facilities or the lack of a dedicated HR department, are commonly observed across SMEs in the OECD area. Other challenges, like fear of poaching, or the lack of personnel, are particularly pressing in the Korean context and relate to structural factors. The chapter analyses the key barriers that SMEs are facing in providing training to their workers.

In Brief

SMEs in Korea should support the skills of their workers

Adult learning is crucial in Korea to help SMEs to close the gaps with larger companies, strengthen their position in global value chains, and tackle demographic changes. However, in Korea few SMEs provide training to their employees. This chapter analyses the barriers that Korean SMEs are facing in providing training to their workers. The key findings of this chapter can be summarised as follows:

- Korean SMEs provide far less training opportunities to their workers compared to large firms. In 2015, only 42.6% of micro and small firms provided training to their workers, against 52.8% of medium-sized firms and 64.2% of large firms. The remainder of firms provided either only legally mandatory training or no training at all.
- Partly as a result of low training provision by SMEs, Korea has the second largest training gap between workers in micro and large firms in the OECD (after Chile). Only 30.3% of workers in micro-firms participate in job-related formal or non-formal adult learning in a given year, compared to 52.5% in small firms, 63.2% in medium-sized firms, and 69.6% in large firms. Training duration also tends to be short for SME workers. The median hours spent on (non-formal) job-related training is 32 hours per year for SME workers, compared to 48 hours for workers in larger firms.
- Participation to informal learning at work is also low among SME workers. Only 41.5% of workers in micro-firms participate in informal learning (i.e. learning by doing the job, learning from others, or learning new things at work at least once a week) – a rate that progressively increases to 51.8% in large companies. These rates place Korea at the very bottom of the OECD ranking.
- Lack of staff (i.e. lack of time of employees, shortages of labour) is the most important reason for not implementing or supporting training, cited as the key training barrier by 30% of SMEs in Korea.
- Fear of poaching – i.e. the fear that the worker would leave the company shortly after training – is another barrier to training provision among Korean SMEs. This is not surprising considering that Korean SMEs typically offer less attractive working conditions, job turnover is generally high, and workers are often looking for better employment opportunities in larger firms.
- Lack of financial resources is also a key reason for not providing training. Many SMEs are not able to use the plethora of financial incentives available to cover training costs, either because they are not aware of these schemes, or because they do not meet eligibility criteria (e.g. enrolment in Employment Insurance; minimum training hours).
- SMEs managers and business owners are not always supportive of training. This is due to a number of reasons, including SMEs' low demand for high-level skills, poor perception of training quality, lack of awareness of the benefits of training, as well as poor entrepreneurship skills among managers/business owners.
- In Korea like in other OECD countries, SMEs typically lack HR departments/staff and training facilities – which put them at a disadvantage *vis-à-vis* large companies when it comes to training provision.

Introduction

Adult learning can help SMEs to close the productivity gap with large firms. It can also strengthen SMEs' position in global value chains (GVCs) by helping them to specialise in high value-added activities (e.g. technologically advanced industries, complex business services). Adult learning is also valuable for SMEs going through changes due to company transitions, such as growth, restructuring, introduction of new technologies, or exporting for the first time. Despite the benefits of skills investments, relatively few SMEs in Korea support the acquisition of skills. To improve training provision, it is important for policy makers to fully understand the key obstacles that SMEs are facing, and put in place policy measures that remove such barriers.

This chapter is structured as follows. Section 2.1 depicts training participation patterns in SMEs, highlighting the extent to which SMEs offer adequate training opportunities to their workers, as well as how much SME workers participate to job-related formal, non-formal, and informal training. Section 2.2 highlights the key barriers that SMEs are facing in offering training to their workers. Section 2.3 investigates how recent labour market policies – e.g. the increase in the minimum wage and the new 52-hour workweek policy – could indirectly affect SMEs training efforts.

2.1. Training participation patterns in SMEs

In Korea SMEs offer little training opportunities to workers compared to large companies. Partly as a result of this, the gap in training participation between workers in SMEs and workers in larger firms is among the widest in the OECD. This section highlights training participation patterns in SMEs, investigating whether Korean SMEs provide adequate training to their workers, whether SME workers (including vulnerable workers) have adequate access to training, and the extent to which SME workers are exposed to informal learning opportunities at the workplace.

2.1.1. Do Korean SMEs provide adequate training to their workers?

Much like in other OECD and European countries (OECD, 2019[1]),[1] smaller firms in Korea provide far less training opportunities to their workers compared to larger companies. In 2015, only 42.6% of micro and small firms provided training[2] beyond legally mandatory course to their workers, against 52.8% of medium-sized firms and 64.2% of large firms – according to the Korean Workplace Panel Survey data (Figure 2.1).The remainder of firms provided either only legally mandatory training or no training at all.

The duration of the training programmes offered by SMEs is also much shorter. In 2015, the average annual training time per person[3] was 15.8 hours in micro and small firms, 17.6 hours in medium-sized firms, and 20.4 in larger companies (Figure 2.1).

Figure 2.1. Training provision by firms, Korea, 2015

Percentage of firms providing training and annual training time per person (hours), by firm size

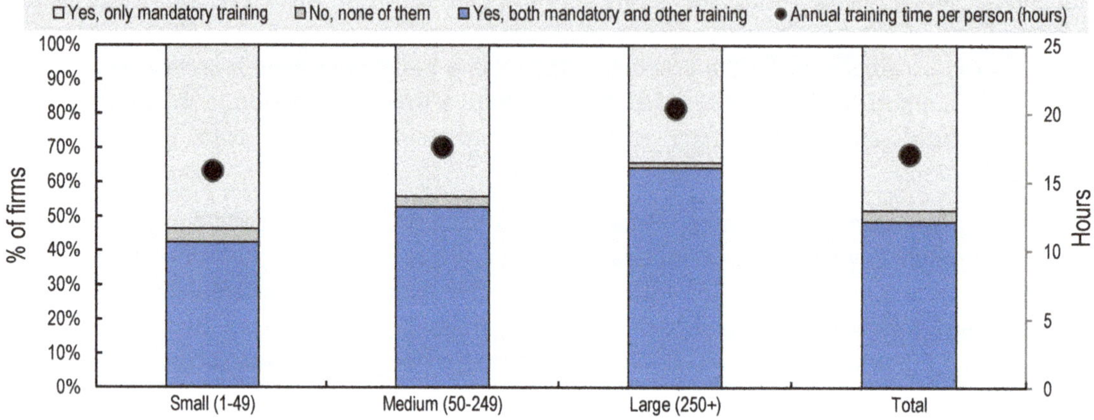

Note: Average annual training time per person is the total training hours of the trained employees divided by the total number of employee in the year preceding the survey. Annual training time per person (hours) excludes legally mandatory training.
Source: OECD Secretariat calculations based on the Workplace Panel Survey (6th wave, 2015).

2.1.2. Do SME workers in Korea have adequate access to training?

Similarly to what can be observed in other OECD countries, in Korea SME workers train much less than workers in larger firms. Analysis of the Survey of Adult Skills (PIAAC) shows that participation in training increases with the size of the firm in Korea. Only 30.3% of workers in micro-firms participate in job-related formal or non-formal adult learning in a given year, compared to 52.5% in small firms, 63.2% in medium-sized firms, and 69.6% in large firms (Figure 2.2).

Korea has the 7th lowest participation rate in the OECD among workers in micro-firms. The combination of extremely low training rates among workers in micro-firms and above-average training among workers in large firms, results in the highest training gap between workers in micro and large firms (39.3 percentage points) in the OECD after Chile, and well above the OECD average (25 percentage points).[4]

Figure 2.2. Participation in training, by firm size, OECD countries

Percentage of workers who participated in (formal or non-formal) job related adult learning in the last 12 months

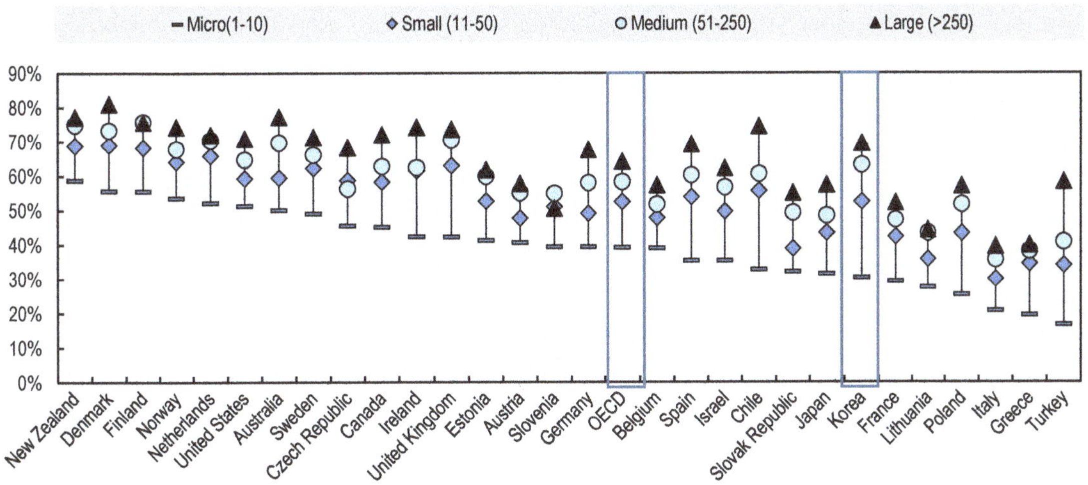

Source: OECD Secretariat calculations based on the Survey of Adult Skills, PIAAC (2012, 2015).

Even when SME workers do train, the duration of their training tends to be short. According to PIAAC data, in Korea the median hours spent on (non-formal) job-related training is 32 hours per year for SME workers, compared to 48 hours for workers in larger firms. Gaps in training hours across firms of different sizes can be found in almost all OECD countries[5] but they are higher in Korea than in any other OECD country with the exception of Denmark (Figure 2.3).

Figure 2.3. Training hours, by firm size, OECD countries

Median number of hours participants spend on non-formal job-related adult learning per year

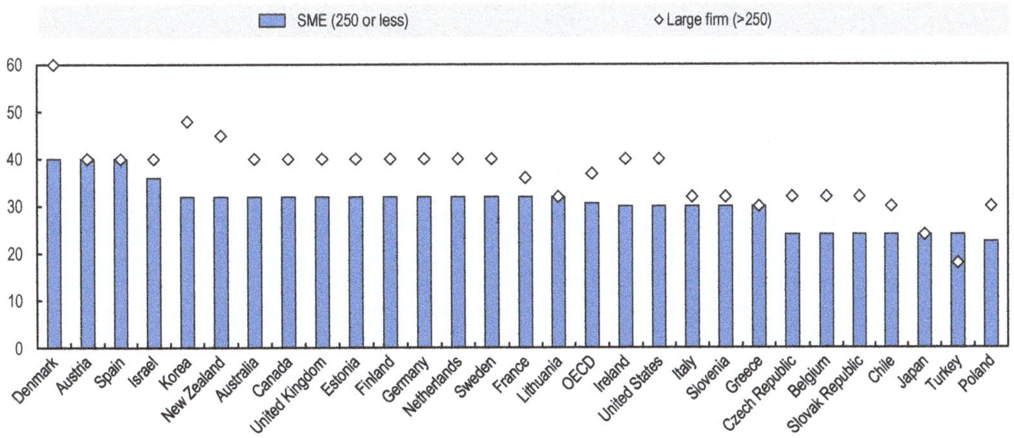

Source: OECD Secretariat calculations based on the Survey of Adult Skills, PIAAC (2012, 2015).

2.1.3. Do vulnerable groups in SMEs train?

Like in other OECD countries, in Korea vulnerable workers – such as older workers, women, the low-skilled, low-wage earners, or temporary workers – are less likely to train. These are the workers who arguably need training the most, yet they are typically less likely to take part in adult learning.

In Korea, vulnerable workers lag behind in firms of all sizes, but their participation in training is particularly low if they work in an SME. This is a challenge because vulnerable workers represent a considerable share of the SMEs workforce (Chapter 1). Similarly and equally worrying, often SME workers with a more privileged socio-economic status train much less than vulnerable workers in large companies. This may suggest that firm size is an issue beyond workers' socio-demographic characteristics.

Looking at age differences, PIAAC data shows that older workers (ages 54-65) in Korean SMEs are much less likely to train compared to older workers in large firms, as well as compared to prime age workers (ages 25-53) in both SMEs and large firms (Figure 2.4). These gaps are much larger in Korea than in the OECD area on average, and compared to best performing OECD countries such as New Zealand and Finland.

Figure 2.4. Gap in participation between older and prime age workers, by firm size, selected OECD countries

Percentage of adults participating in formal and non-formal job-related learning

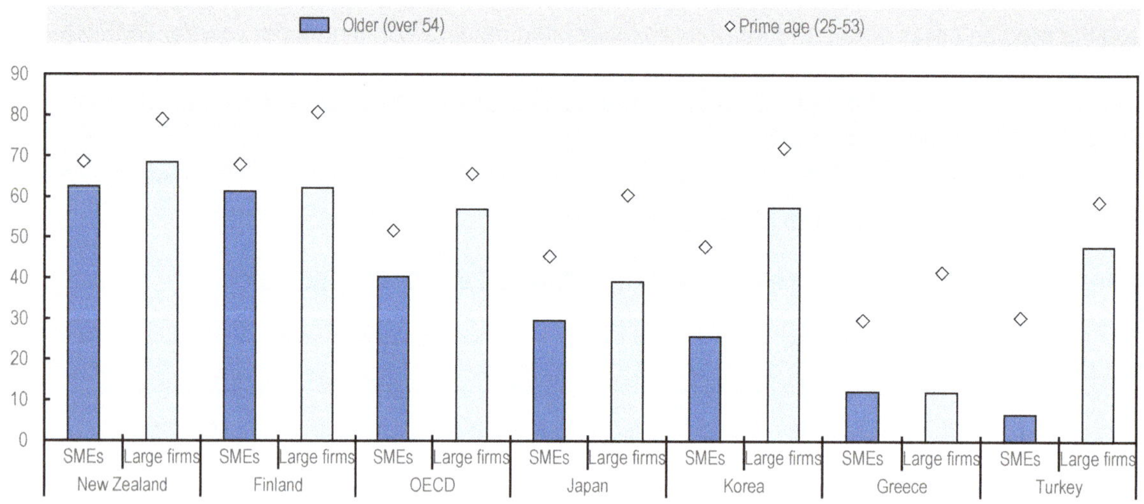

Note: Belgium refers to Flanders only, United Kingdom to England and Northern Ireland. SMEs are firms with 250 employees or less. Large firms have more than 250 employees.
Source: OECD Secretariat calculations based on the Survey of Adult Skills, PIAAC (2012, 2015).

Looking at gender differences shows a slightly more positive picture. Gaps in training participation between men and women are small in Korean SMEs (3 percentage points) yet they remain higher than the OECD area where gaps are virtually inexistent on average. In large firms, gaps are quite substantial in Korea: 13.8 percentage points compared to an OECD average of 4.2 (Figure 2.5).

Figure 2.5. Gap in participation between women and men, by firm size, selected OECD countries

Percentage of adults participating in formal and non-formal job-related learning

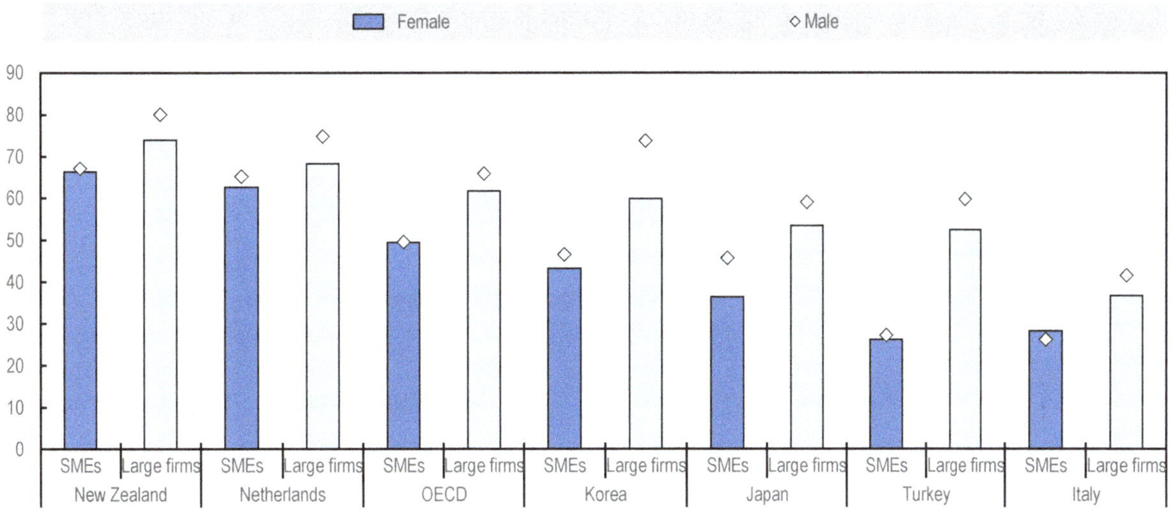

Note: Belgium refers to Flanders only, United Kingdom to England and Northern Ireland. SMEs are firms with 250 employees or less. Large firms have more than 250 employees.
Source: OECD Secretariat calculations based on the Survey of Adult Skills, PIAAC (2012, 2015).

Figure 2.6. Gap in participation between low-skilled and medium/high-skilled workers, by firm size, selected OECD countries

Percentage of adults participating in formal and non-formal job-related learning

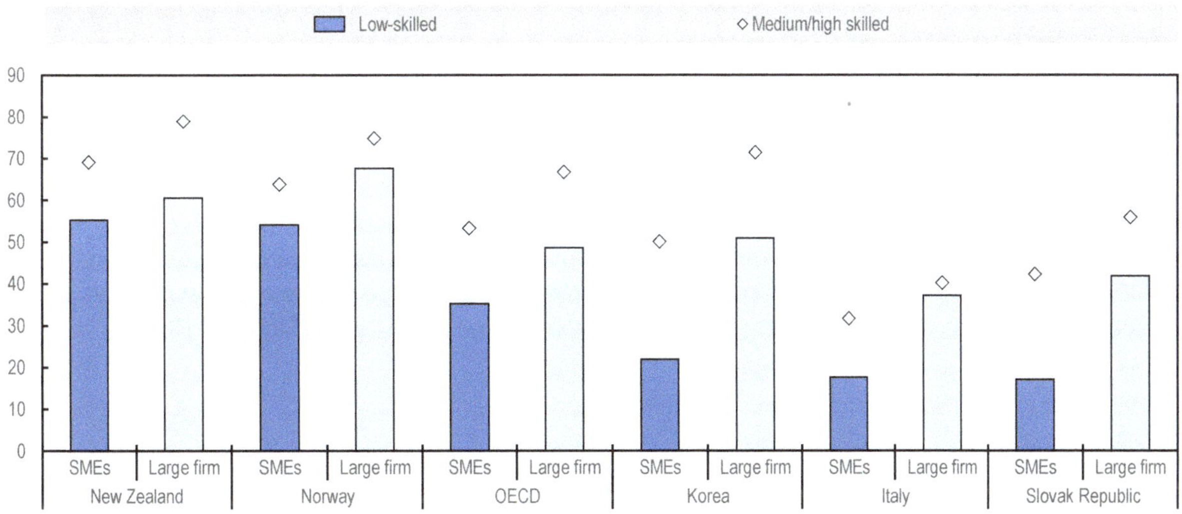

Note: Countries with less than 10 observations (Japan) were removed from the analysis. The low skilled are adults with numeracy or literacy scores equal to 1 or below. Belgium refers to Flanders only, United Kingdom to England and Northern Ireland. SMEs are firms with 250 employees or less. Large firms have more than 250 employees.
Source: OECD Secretariat calculations based on the Survey of Adult Skills, PIAAC (2012, 2015).

Working for an SME in Korea seems to compound the disadvantage in training opportunities already faced by the low-skilled. Indeed, in Korea low-skilled workers, i.e. adults with low numeracy or literacy skills according to PIAAC, in SMEs train much less than similarly low-skilled workers in large firms. Patterns across OECD countries vary considerably (Figure 2.11).

Beyond socio-demographic characteristics, the employment situation of workers – including their earnings and contract type – is also related to the take-up of adult learning opportunities. For instance, in Korean SMEs, low-wage workers (i.e. earning at most two third of the national median wage) are less likely to take part in adult learning compared to better paid workers in both SMEs and large firms, as well as compared to similarly low-paid workers in larger companies (Figure 2.7).

Figure 2.7. Gap in participation between low-wage and medium/high-wage workers, by firm size, selected OECD countries

Percentage of adults participating in formal and non-formal job-related learning

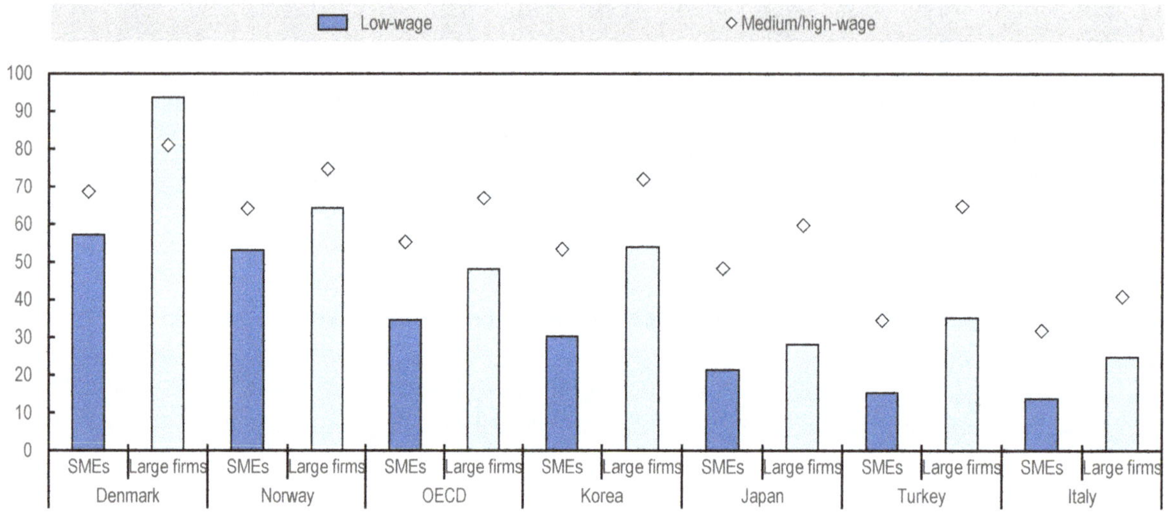

Note: Belgium refers to Flanders only, United Kingdom to England and Northern Ireland. Low-wage workers are defined as workers earning at most two third of the national median wage. SMEs are firms with 250 employees or less. Large firms have more than 250 employees.
Source: OECD Secretariat calculations based on the Survey of Adult Skills, PIAAC (2012, 2015).

Access to training also varies across workers with different types of contract. In Korea, gaps in adult learning participation rates between temporary and permanent workers are less than 3 percentage points in SMEs, but they are more marked in large companies (6 percentage points), just above the OECD average (5 percentage points). The situation is more mixed in the OECD area (Figure 2.13).

Figure 2.8. Gap in participation between temporary and permanent workers, by firm size, selected OECD countries

Percentage of adults participating in formal and non-formal job-related learning

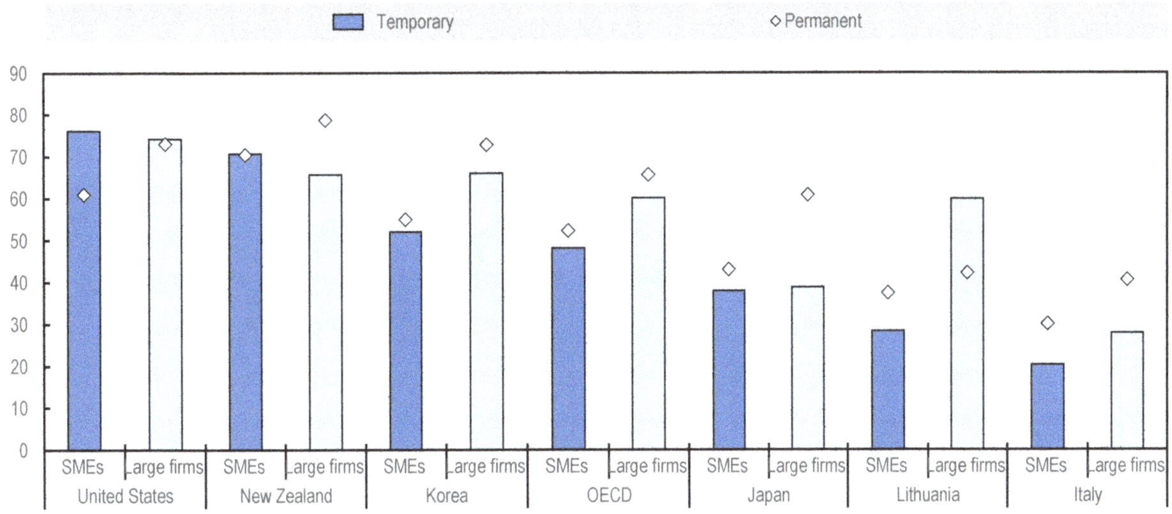

Note: Belgium refers to Flanders only, United Kingdom to England and Northern Ireland; formal and non-formal job-related education and training. SMEs are firms with 250 employees or less. Large firms have more than 250 employees.
Source: OECD Secretariat calculations based on the Survey of Adult Skills, PIAAC (2012, 2015).

2.1.4. Expanding informal learning opportunities for SME workers

On top of improving access to formal and non-formal learning, Korea also needs to give further opportunities to SME workers to learn new skills through informal learning, i.e. learning that is less organised and structured and includes learning by doing, learning from colleagues (co-workers or supervisors), or learning new things.

Informal learning could accommodate training around work demands and minimise time spent off-site – which is particularly important for SMEs that struggle to free workers' time for training (see Chapter 2). Informal learning could also help save money, by increasing workers' skills at little or no direct training costs for firms, workers, and the government. It could also improve the skills of workers who would otherwise have little access to training.

Unfortunately, participation to informal learning is exceptionally low in Korea by OECD standards – and particularly so in smallest firms. PIAAC data shows that only 41.5% of workers in micro-firms participate to informal learning at least once per week (67.4% in the OECD), against 44.7% in small firms (70.2% in the OECD), 46.2% in medium-sized firms (70.8% in the OECD), and 51.8% in large companies (73.7% in the OECD). These rates place Korea at the very bottom of the OECD ranking (Figure 2.9).

Korea is also one of the few OECD countries where the incidence of informal learning is significantly below that of non-formal training (Fialho, Quintini and Vandeweyer, 2019[2]). This means that the many workers who miss out on non-formal training are not able to compensate with more opportunities for informal learning at work.

SME workers in Korea do poorly – compared to other OECD countries – on all types of informal learning, i.e. learning by doing, learning from others, or learning new things at work. About 30% of Korean SME workers learn by doing their job at least once a week, 30% learn from others, and 24% learn new things (well below the OECD average of 56%, 56%, and 38% respectively) (Figure 2.10). Interestingly, there is not so much overlap between the three forms of informal learning. Only about 12% of SME workers experience all three in Korea, against the OECD average of 21%.

Figure 2.9. Participation to informal learning, by firm size

Percentage of workers who regularly participate in informal learning (at least once per week)

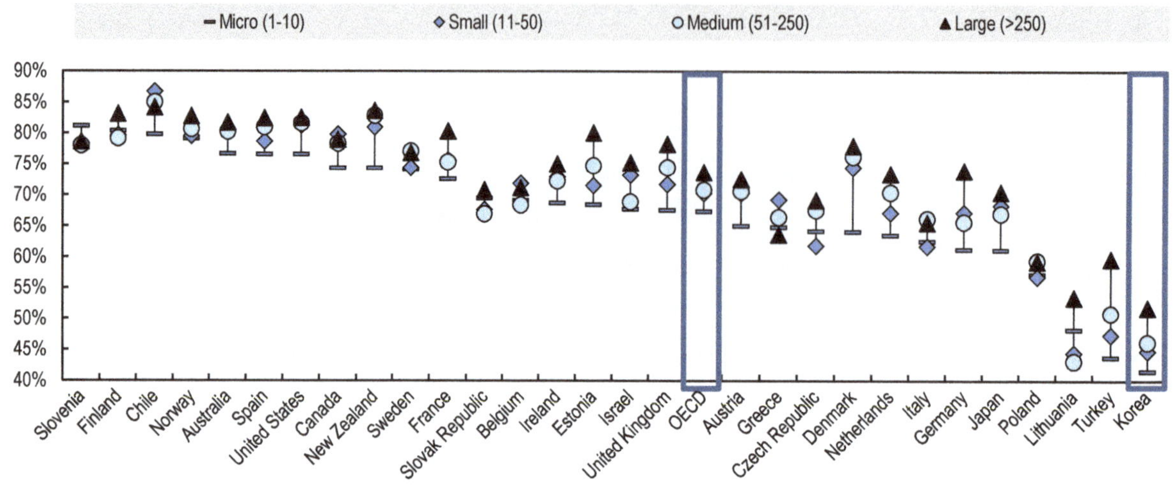

Note: informal learning is defined as learning by doing the job, learning from others, or learning new things at work at least once a week.
Source: OECD Secretariat calculations based on the Survey of Adult Skills, PIAAC (2012, 2015).

Figure 2.10. Incidence of informal learning in SMEs

Percentage of SME workers who experienced learning-by-doing, learning-from-others and learning new things at work at least once a week

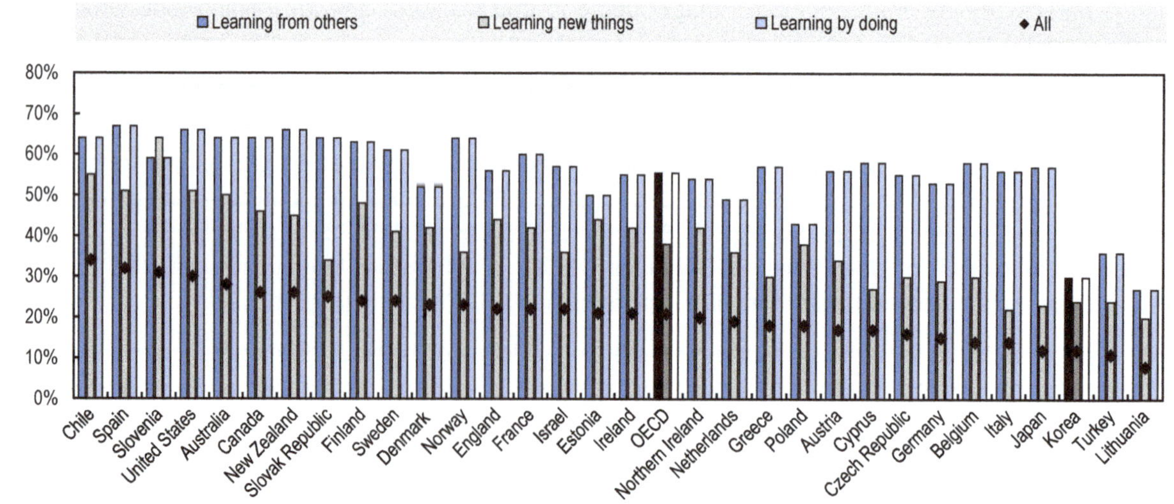

Note: Percentage of SME workers who experienced each form of informal learning and all three at least once a week. OECD refers to the unweighted average of the OECD countries shown. Results refer to SME workers only, i.e. workers who work in firms with 250 employees or less.
Source: OECD Secretariat calculations based on the Survey of Adult Skills, PIAAC (2012, 2015).

Another key challenge is that even when SME workers learn informally, they spend little time doing so by international standards. Using the methodology developed by Fialho, Quintini and Vandeweyer (2019[2]), Figure 2.11 shows that SME workers spend an average of 59.7 hours a year in learning by doing (110.1 hours in the OECD on average), 55.8 hours in learning from others (83 in the OECD) and 47.9 hours in learning new things (77.8 in the OECD).

Figure 2.11. Hours spent on informal learning in SMEs

Hours spent learning-by-doing, learning-from-others and learning new things at work per year

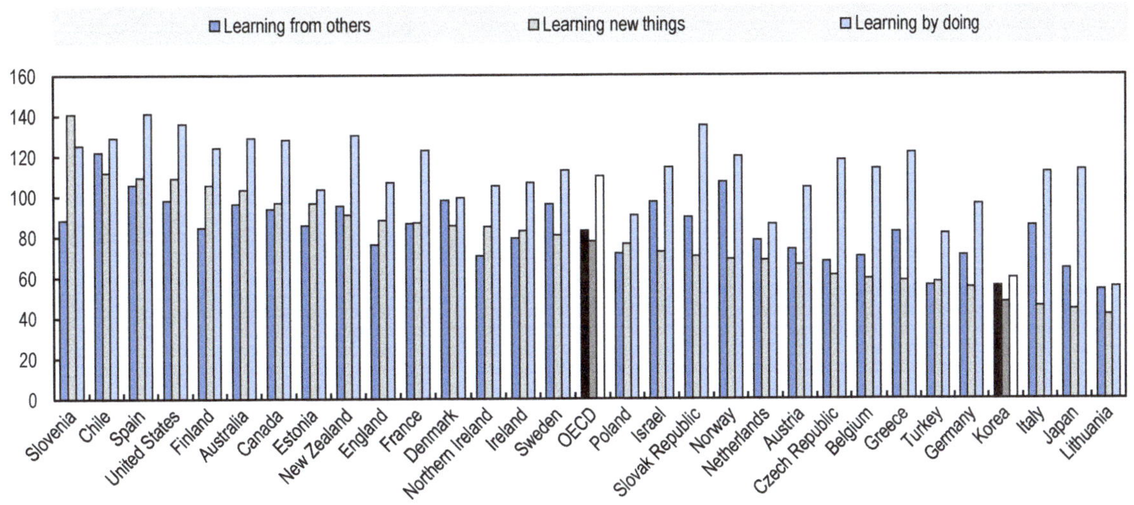

Note: Number of hours spent in each of the informal learning activities. The average value is attributed to the response categories to obtain the number of hours of informal training and hours are adjusted for part-time work. OECD refers to the unweighted average of the OECD countries shown. Results refer to SME workers only, i.e. workers who work in firms with 250 employees or less.
Source: OECD Secretariat calculations based on the Survey of Adult Skills, PIAAC (2012, 2015).

Looking at the distribution of responses on the frequency of informal learning also reveals that Korea performs very poorly compared with other OECD countries (Figure 2.12). About 26% of SME workers report never learning from others, the highest value in the OECD and double the OECD average of 13%. Similar average distributions are observed for learning by doing and learning new things.

Figure 2.12. Frequency of learning from others in the workplace, in SMEs

Share of respondents in each answering category

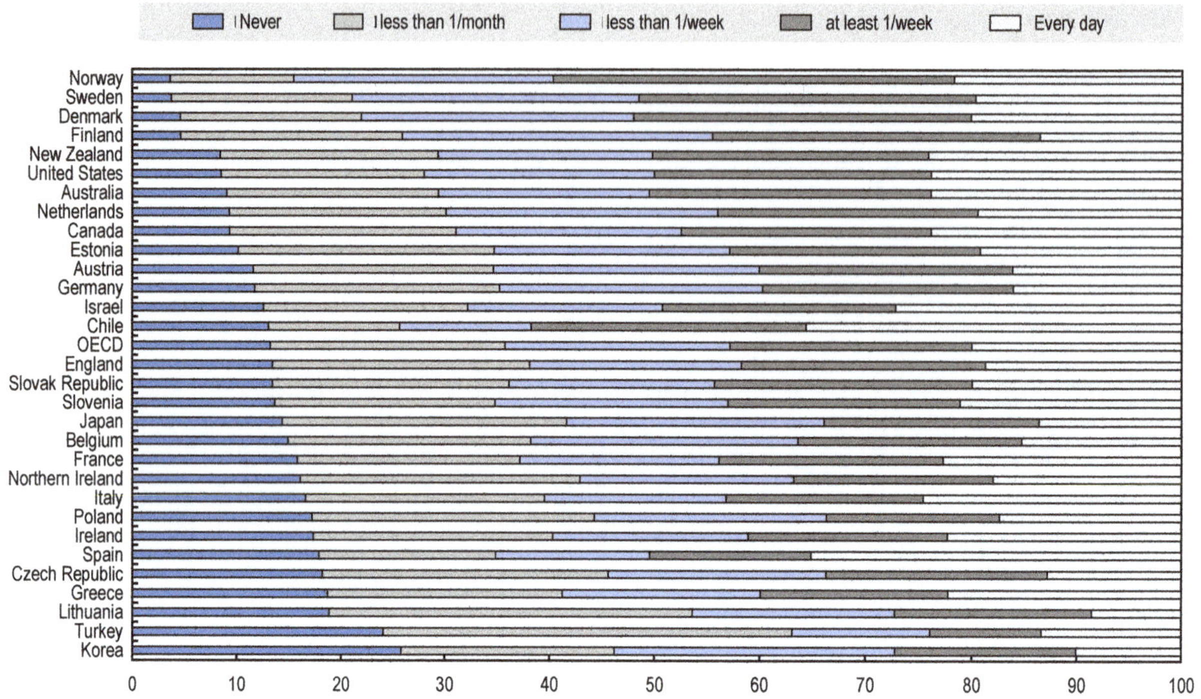

Note: OECD refers to the unweighted average of the OECD countries shown. Results refer to SME workers only, i.e. workers who work in firms with 250 employees or less.
Source: OECD Secretariat calculations based on the Survey of Adult Skills, PIAAC (2012, 2015).

Low engagement in informal learning seems to be in stark contrast with the fact that many SME workers consider informal learning as being a valuable learning option. Elaborations of the Human Capital Corporate Panel Survey (2017) show that between 60 and 70% (depending on the size of the firm) of workers in Korea believe that informal learning – defined in this survey as 'learning through interactions between co-workers, seniors and subordinates' – have a great or considerable effect on job performance (Figure 2.13).

Figure 2.13. Workers' opinion on informal learning, Korea, 2017

Effect of informal learning on job performance (percentage of workers, by firm size)

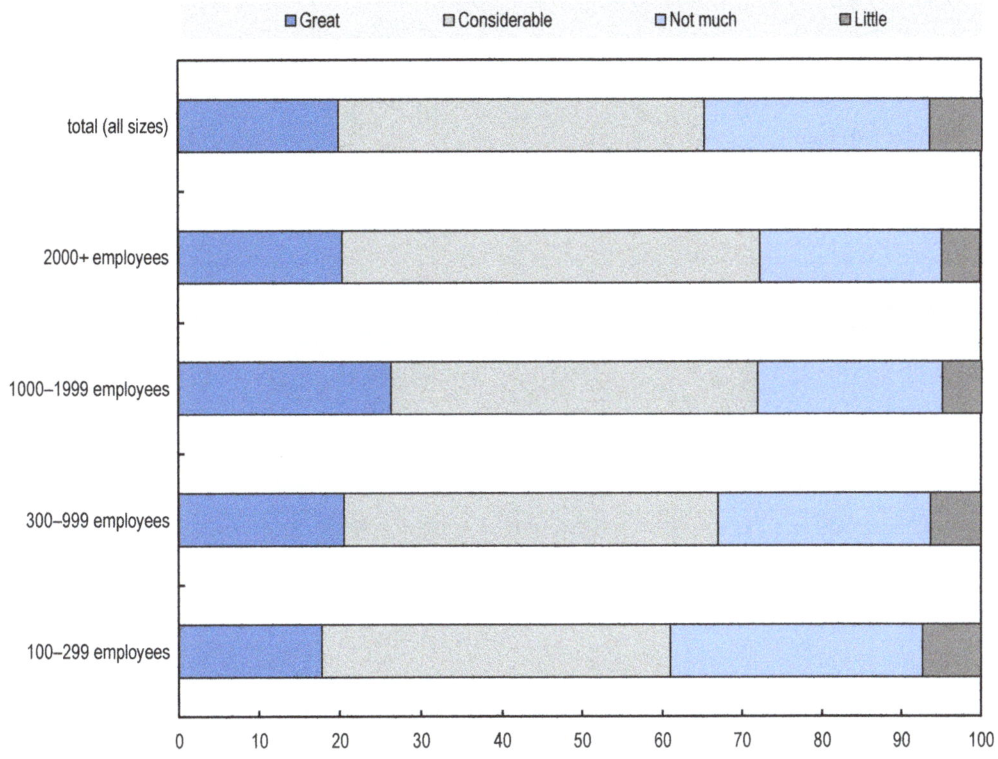

Note: Informal learning is defined in this survey as 'learning through interactions between co-workers, seniors and subordinates'.
Source: KRIVET elaborations of the Human Capital Corporate Panel Survey (7th wave, 2017).

There are several potential reasons behind limited informal learning practices among Korean SMEs. According to some observers, workers in Korea seem to prefer formal or non-formal learning situations in which learning is delivered by an instructor rather than informally. Moreover, rigid hierarchical structures may weaken individual autonomy to choose collaboration and peer-learning and therefore inhibit informal learning. Finally, high job turnover, especially in SMEs, may inhibit effective knowledge transfer from tenured colleagues to newer workers (Jeong, McLean and Park, 2018[3]).

2.2. What are the barriers that SMEs are facing?

SMEs face greater difficulty in providing training to their workers compared to larger firms. Some of the challenges they are facing are commonly observed across SMEs in the OECD area, while others are peculiar to the Korean context and relate to structural factors. The next sections investigate the most important barriers that are undermining SMEs' ability to train their workers, such as lack of personnel, fear of poaching, financial barriers, lack of HR department/staff, lack of training facilities, as well as the mind-set of managers and business owners.

2.2.1. Lack of personnel

According to several observers, lack of personnel (i.e. lack of time of employees, shortages of labour) is probably the most important factor behind low training provision in SMEs. National surveys seem to corroborate these arguments: the Workplace Panel Survey (2015) suggests that lack of manpower (i.e. lack of personnel) is the most frequently cited reason for not implementing or supporting training, cited as the key training barrier by 30% of SMEs (Figure 2.14). This is also the most frequently cited reason for large firms.

Figure 2.14. Most important reason for not implementing or supporting training, Korea

Percentage of firms by firm size

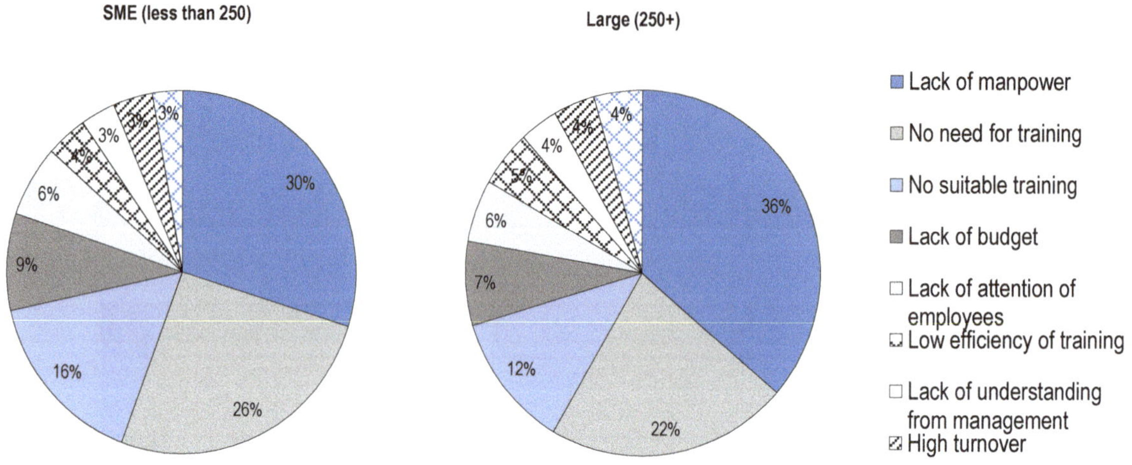

Note: Data refers to the most important reason for not implementing or supporting training during the year before the survey.
Source: OECD elaborations based on the Workplace Panel Survey (6th wave, 2015).

Indeed, in Korea SMEs experience great difficulties in freeing up time for their employees to take training. Because SMEs often face labour shortages and struggle to secure staff (see Chapter 1), management of workers is very tight and leaves little space for workers' skills development. SMEs also tend to be more oriented towards immediate goals, notably survival and maintaining business operations, and operate to shorter horizons than larger companies.

Lack of personnel may not only reduce SMEs' training efforts, but could also discourage SME workers to undertake voluntary training (see Chapter 3). Moreover, it could potentially undermine SMEs' ability to use the adult learning programmes put in place by the government. The next sections discuss two policy measures that could help SMEs tackle lack of staff: i) job rotation schemes and ii) structured on-the-job training (S-OJT).[6]

Job rotation scheme

Job rotation schemes – i.e. an arrangement for the replacement of absent workers (by an unemployed person or worker), which also covers the cost of replacement – offer a valuable solution to the problem of worker absence during training. Job rotation schemes have already been implemented by some OECD countries, including Korea (OECD, 2019[1]).

Korea offers financial support to SMEs that use job rotation schemes. More specifically, when SMEs grant paid education and training leave to their staff for at least 120 training hours for 30 continuous days, and when they hire a replacement, they can receive a training subsidy that covers the wages of the replacement (capped at the minimum wage and not included in the annual ceiling of each firm) (see Annex 2.A). A new pilot project launched in August 2018 allows SMEs to receive additional funding beyond annual ceilings.

Unfortunately, the take-up of the subsidy is extremely low: the programme counted only six participants in 2016.[7] This is mainly because SMEs struggle to secure high-quality replacement workers. Indeed, SMEs either cannot find any replacements, or find replacements who cannot work as effectively as previous employees (Chae, Choi and Yang, 2018[4]).

Good practice examples from OECD countries show that job rotation schemes are more successful when they operate in coordination with the Public Employment Service (PES) and/or existing adult learning programmes. This can help firms secure potential candidates (either unemployed people or workers). For example, in Denmark, firms can set up a training plan for their workers in cooperation with the municipal job centre, benefit from assistance in recruiting replacement workers, and receive a public subsidy for hiring a long-term unemployed person to replace the employee on training. The employment period should go from a minimum of 10 hours to a maximum of 26 weeks (Eurofound, 2019[5]; OECD, 2018[6]).[8]

The international experience also suggests that it is important for replacement workers to receive adequate training before taking up the position, so that they can be productive as soon as they start the job. This includes training to get the replacement worker acquainted with employer-specific practices/tools. In Germany, for example, some localities have developed a substantial support infrastructure orientated to the needs of small firms, where replacement workers are carefully prepared in advance of taking up a position (Stone, 2010[7]). Similarly, in Denmark replacement workers can receive a short training before starting work (OECD, 2018[6]). This approach assumes that the duration of the replacement is relatively long, to ensure that training efforts are worth the investment.

Korea is in a good position to improve the current job rotation scheme to raise it to the standards of international best practices. In particular, Korea needs to rely on the PES and/or existing adult learning programmes to find and train a replacement worker. The PES is already supporting firms with the recruitment of replacements in case a worker goes on maternity or childcare leave, so its role could be expanded to also tackle absences related to training. Another possible policy option is to link the Korean job rotation scheme to the CHAMP programme (see Annex 2.A) to encourage temporary transfers of employees from large firms to SMEs. This policy was already suggested by a recent OECD report on older workers (OECD, 2018[6]).

To increase the take-up of job rotation schemes, Korea should:

- *Assist SMEs to secure replacement workers.* This could be done by operating job rotation schemes in coordination with the PES and/or existing adult learning programmes (e.g. CHAMP).
- *Ensure that replacement workers receive adequate training* before taking up the position. In this way, replacement workers can be productive as soon as they start the job.

Structured on-the-job training

Structured on-the-job training (S-OJT) can offer another viable solution to the problem of lack of staff and to the difficulty of finding a replacement worker. Through S-OJT, training providers send teachers to the company, where they perform a task analysis, they evaluate the expertise of workers, identify workers' training needs, and then offer training programmes accordingly (Choi, Lee and Jacobs, 2015[8]).

As such, the key feature of S-OJT is that training is delivered at the workplace rather than in a classroom or some other off-the-job setting. This type of training allows workers to train while minimising the time spent not working (e.g. commuting). Because of its features, it is especially relevant for SMEs, which may not have the capacity to send employees to outside training.

Recognising its potential, in 2012 the MoEL and HRD Korea implemented *SME structured on-the-job training programme*. The programme provides a subsidy that covers the cost of training, job analysis/module development, training delivery, and assessment of results. The average annual support for each company is KRW 24 million in 2019 (approximately EUR 18 500) per company. Despite its potential, however, the programme is still at an early stage of development and today remains quite small, with only 122 participating firms in 2018.[9]

Expanding S-OJT is one of the priorities of the '3rd Basic plan for vocational skills development', the national adult learning strategy developed by the MoEL. Under this strategy, the Korean government will analyse the contexts under which S-OJT is implementable, identify good practice examples, and scale up best practices. To operationalise this strategic direction, perhaps Korea could learn from the experience of OECD countries (e.g. France; Singapore) that have already implemented a similar S-OJT system in SMEs (Box 2.1).

To tackle lack of personnel in SMEs, Korea should further invest in on-the-job training. Korea should evaluate the pilot "SME structured on-the-job training programme" and scale it up if considered successful.

Box 2.1. Strengthening on-the-job training in SMEs: the experience of France and Singapore

France

The *Formation en Situation de Travail* (FEST) is the on-the-job training programme targeted to SMEs promoted by the French Ministry of Labour and social partners since 2014. In order to formalise FEST, the French Ministry of Labour launched a call to training funds (*Opérateurs de Compétences* – OPCO) to develop FEST experiments. In total 24 projects from 13 organisations have been selected. The selected projects were able to implement their FEST experiments with support of the Ministry. The experiments had a few common characteristics: only applied in firms with less than 300 employees; priority given to low-skilled individuals; diverse profile of participants, including new hires, experienced workers and unemployed; training including normal work activities and "learning elements" (e.g. moments of reflection). Small firms with less than 50 employees were reimbursed by their training fund (OPCO) for implementing FEST. A recent evaluation of the programme showed that the project was successful in helping participants to develop the skills demanded by the firm. The project also had positive indirect effects on participants' confidence and autonomy at completing tasks, and contributed to consolidate their working relations with managers (Case and Freundlieb, 2018[9]).

Singapore

The National Centre of Excellence for Workplace Learning (2018) aims to help companies set up on-the-job training structures. Companies can apply for grants from SkillsFuture Singapore, and SMEs can receive up to 90% of the cost of training in-house trainers. It is expected to help more than 1 000 companies, especially SMEs, in the next five years.

Source: OECD (2017[10]) *Getting Skills Right: France*, https://doi.org/10.1787/9789264284456-en; Case and Freundlieb (2018[9]), *Experimentation Afest: Action de Formation En Situation de Travail*, Ministère du Travail, https://travail-emploi.gouv.fr/IMG/pdf/rapportfinalafest.pdf.; OECD (2019[11]), OECD SMEs and Entrepreneurship Outlook 2019, https://dx.doi.org/10.1787/34907e9c-en.

2.2.2. *Fear of poaching*

Fear of poaching is another key factor undermining training provision in Korean SMEs. When workers leave the company shortly after training, firms cannot reap the benefits of their skills investments. If they fear poaching, firms may be reluctant to provide training in the first place. Or, they may be willing to provide only firm-specific training (which produces skills that are less transferable to other companies) in a view to minimise poaching risks (Kuczera, Kis and Wurzburg, 2009[12]; Jeong, McLean and Park, 2018[3]).

While this is a challenge that Korea shares with other countries (OECD, 2019[11]), fear of poaching is particularly pressing in Korean SMEs, which on average offer less attractive working conditions, where job turnover is generally high, and where workers are often looking for better employment opportunities in larger firms (see Chapter 1).

Evidence confirms that poaching is quite widespread among Korean SMEs. In Korean small firms (5-29 employees), workers are more likely to leave the firm one year after training than workers who did not train, even after controlling for workers' observable characteristics – a pattern that is not observed in larger companies (Yoo et al., 2009[13]).

Similarly, the Ministry of Trade, Industry and Energy (MoTIE) estimates that 49% of SMEs reported skills poaching in 2013 (OECD, 2017[14]). In a similar vein, the HCCP survey shows that, in 2017, 14% of SMEs (100-299 employees) 'slightly' or 'fully' agreed that turnover of trained personnel is high, a share that gradually decreases with firm size (Figure 2.15). It is likely that fear of poaching is even more common among smaller companies (with less than 100 employees), which are not covered by this survey.

Figure 2.15. Turnover of trained staff, Korea, 2017

Percentage of firms agreeing that turnover of trained personnel is high, by firm size

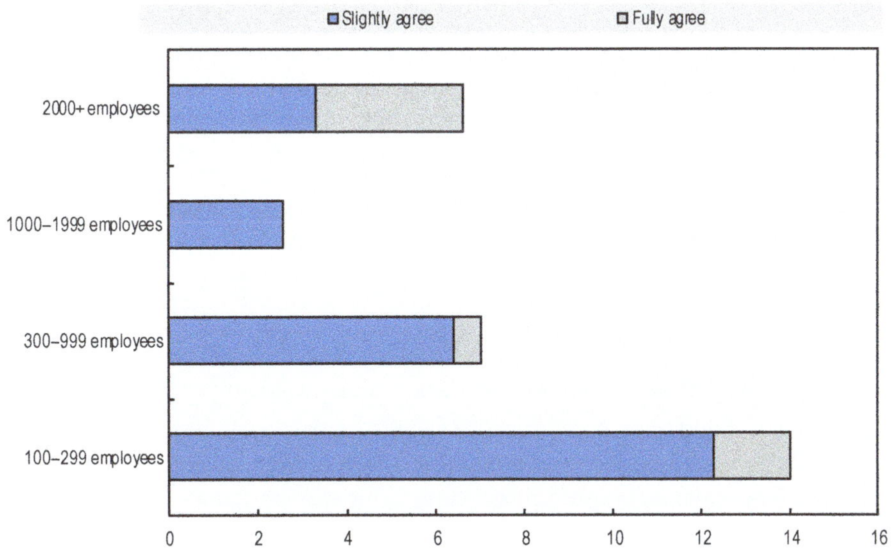

Source: KRIVET elaborations of the Human Capital Corporate Panel Survey (7th wave, 2017).

In order to help SMEs overcome fear of poaching, Korea needs to reduce the gap in working conditions – e.g. wages, job protection – between smaller and larger firms (Chapter 1). This would make SME workers less willing to look for a better job elsewhere, and ultimately mitigate SMEs' fear of poaching. Reducing the gap in working conditions across firms of different sizes relies upon a number of structural policies (e.g. industrial and labour market policies) that fall outside the scope of adult learning.[10]

2.2.3. Financial barriers to training

In Korea, like in other OECD countries, SMEs typically face important financial barriers to provide training to their workers. These barriers relate to both the direct costs of training (e.g. training fees) and the indirect costs of training (e.g. workers' wages; foregone productivity during worker absence).

The direct costs of training are higher for SMEs than for large firms: while large firms can distribute the fixed training costs over a larger group of employees, smaller firms cannot benefit from economies of scale, and as a result they generally incur a higher training cost per worker compared with large enterprises (Lee, 2016[15]).

The indirect costs of training are also often greater in SMEs than in larger firms: releasing workers from revenue-generating activities for training is particularly costly for SMEs, who have fewer employees to rely upon to maintain business activities and for which work reallocation and recruitment is typically more difficult or costly (OECD, 2019[11]) (see Section 2.2.1).

On top of higher direct and indirect training costs, smaller firms are also particularly sensitive to business cycles and are more likely to respond to economic downturns by cutting investments in training. In 2017, according to the Human Capital Corporate Panel Survey data, 28.9% of Korean SMEs (100-299 employees) reported that they did not have sufficient funds to invest in training due to management crises (e.g. sales reduction) – higher than the country average (firms of all sizes) of 22.6%.[11] Although data for smaller companies is not available, it is likely that an even greater share of micro- and small firms faced similar financial constraints.

In this context, it is not surprising that Korean SMEs invest much less financial resources in the training of their workers compared to larger companies. In 2018, according to the Enterprise Labour Cost Survey, the average monthly education and training expenditure of SMEs (10-299 employees) was KRW 6.3 thousand (about EUR 5) per worker, compared to KRW 42.9 thousand (about EUR 34) in larger companies (300 or more employees).

The international experience shows that financial incentives can be very useful policy tools to help firms (including SMEs) to overcome financial barriers to training. Depending on their design, financial incentives can reduce firms' direct and indirect cost of training, help them overcome liquidity constraints, and encourage them to set aside resources for future training (OECD, 2017[16]; OECD, 2019[1]).

Recognising their potential, Korea has already put in place a plethora of financial incentives – e.g. training subsidies, loans, reimbursement of training expenses – to help firms overcome financial barriers to training. These benefits are all fully funded by the Employment Insurance, and their generosity and eligibility criteria often vary with firm size, with more generous benefits and looser access requirements offered to SMEs (Paik, 2016[17]). Annex 2.A provides a detailed description of financial incentives available to Korean SMEs.

Research evidence shows that the subsidies for employer-provided training have increased SME's investments in adult learning and have had a positive impact on wages and productivity. For example, Ban (2013[18]) found that SMEs have experienced a positive effect of training subsidies on corporate training investment and productivity, while large enterprises have not experienced a significant increase. Similarly, Yun and Park (2017[19]) showed that workers undertaking training organised by their employers through the subsidy scheme have longer tenure than workers who did not receive any training. Participating workers also experienced a 4.8% wage increase in the year following the training.

While efforts to reduce the cost of training for SMEs have been remarkable in Korea (in terms of the quantity and generosity of financial incentives programmes available, see Annex 2.A), in practice these programmes are often under-used. To give an example, in 2016 only six participants benefited from the job rotation scheme subsidy (see Section 2.2.1). Information collected through employers' surveys corroborates that the use of available financial support is rather low. The Human Capital Corporate Panel Survey data shows that in 2017, the share of SMEs reporting that they rarely used government-supported training programmes varied between 35% and over 70% (depending on the programme considered) (Figure 2.16). These rates are, in the vast majority of cases, higher in SMEs than in larger firms (Figure 2.16).

Figure 2.16. Use of government-supported training programmes, Korea, 2017

Percentage of firms responding that the programme is rarely used and that high improvement is needed, by training programme and firm size

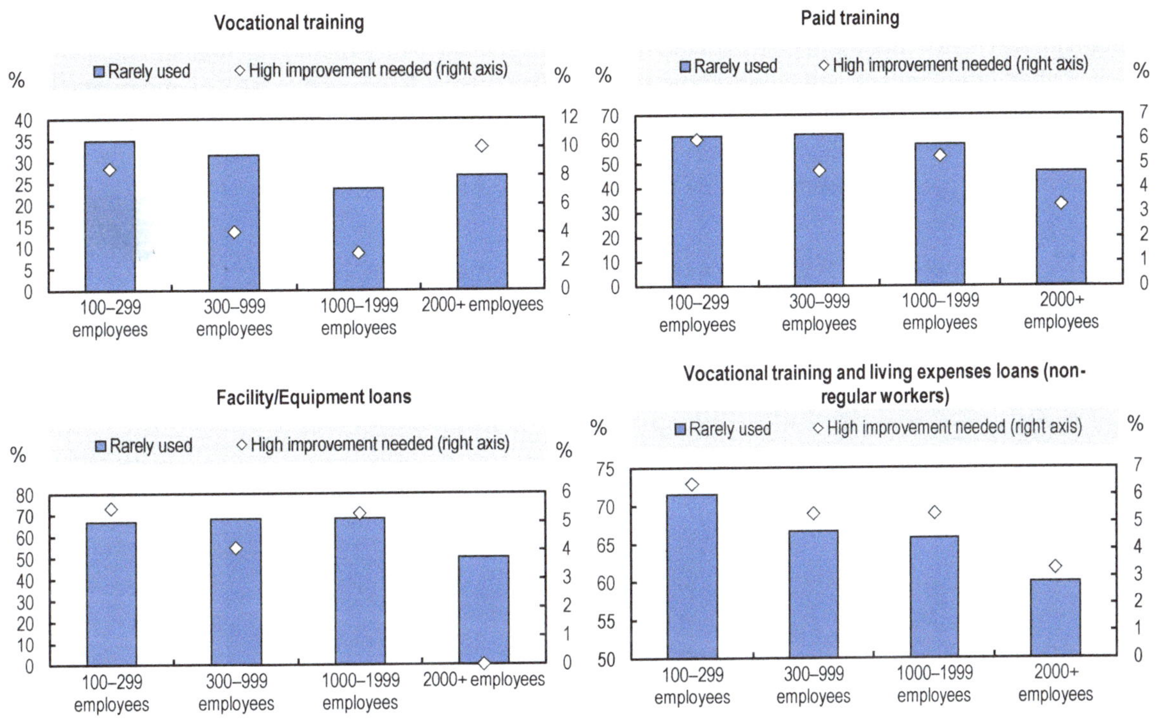

Note: Government-supported training programmes are programmes financially supported by the MoEL.
Source: KRIVET elaborations of the Human Capital Corporate Panel (HCCP) Survey (7th wave, 2017).

One reason for low take-up relates to strict eligibility criteria. To benefit from financial incentives, SMEs need to meet certain minimum criteria, e.g. they have to prove that they have offered, or plan to offer, a minimum number of training hours. For instance, in order to access subsidises for on-site training, SMEs need to provide a minimum of 8 hours of training (Paik, 2016[17]). To give another example, in order to be able to access the subsidy for education and training leave, SMEs need to provide a minimum of 20 training hours (for a minimum of 5 days) (see Annex 2.A). According to several stakeholders, these minimum training hour requirements can hardly be met by an SME that is often unable to release the worker for extended periods (see Section 2.2.1).

Another key explanation for low take-up is that financial incentives do not cover the breadth of training options that SMEs could potentially be interested in.[12] Often, subsidies finance training programmes that reflect the government's skills priorities but that are not necessarily aligned to SMEs' training needs (see Chapter 4) (Paik, 2016[17]).

Little awareness of financial incentives among SMEs could also partly explain low take-up. As discussed in Section 2.2.4, SMEs often lack a dedicated HR department/staff that could identify financial incentives available as well as existing government-supported adult learning programmes. In this context, the government could take action to promote awareness around financial incentives available, along the lines of what is already being done in other OECD countries. For example, Ireland has developed the *Irish Government's Supporting SMEs campaign*, which aims at increasing awareness of the range of government financial supports available for start-ups and small businesses. In the context of this campaign, the government has developed an online guide ("*Supporting SMEs Online Tool*") conceived to help Irish start-ups and small businesses navigate the range of government financial supports.

Finally, another potential reason for low take-up of financial incentives is the unequal access to Employment Insurance across firms of different sizes. Many SMEs do not enrol in Employment Insurance although they should, and therefore they are not eligible for financial support (see Chapter 5). In this context, it is not surprising that large firms often get the bulk of EI-reimbursements.

Recent estimates show that the top ten conglomerates receive 21% of the funds to finance training (SBS, 2013[20]). Other more recent estimates show that in 2017, large firms with 1 000 or more employees received 17.4% of the Employment Insurance fund to finance training (MoEL, 2018[21]). Similarly, the Workplace Panel Survey highlights that in 2015 around 40% of training SMEs did not receive any reimbursements for training expenditures by the EI, double the share of large firms (Figure 2.17).

Figure 2.17. Reimbursement of training expenditures by employment insurance, Korea, 2015

Percentage of training firms that receive reimbursements of training expenditures, by reimbursements rates and firm size

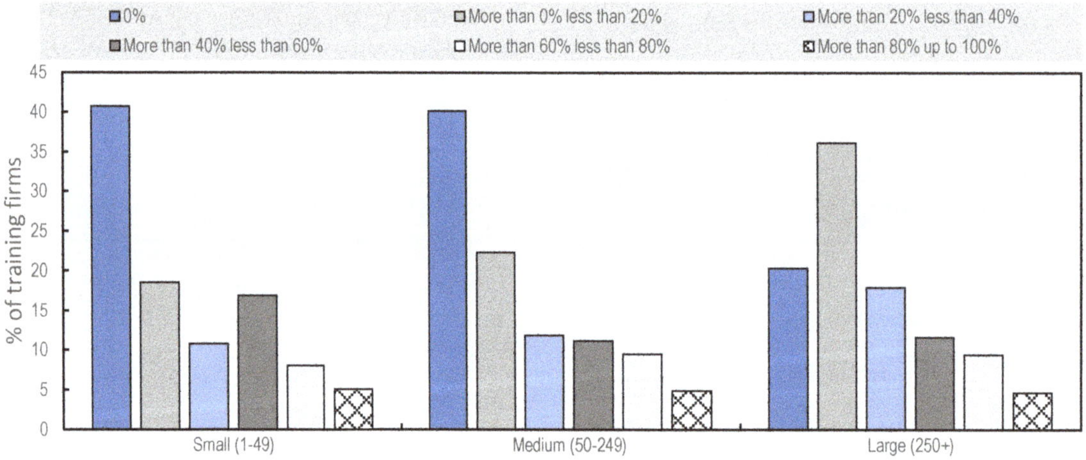

Note: Data includes only training firms that report data on training expenditures.
Source: OECD elaborations based on the Workplace Panel Survey (6th wave, 2015).

It is important to note that financial incentives will be fully used by SMEs only if complementary action is taken to address other training barriers that SMEs are facing – e.g. lack of staff, fear of poaching. If these additional barriers are not tackled, it is unlikely that SMEs will be able to make full use of financial incentives and to ultimately increase training provision.

Korea could implement several policy measures to increase take-up of financial incentives. These include efforts to:

- *Continue ongoing efforts to increase the coverage of Employment Insurance across SMEs*. This would allow more SMEs to be eligible to receive government-supported subsidies for training.

- *Reduce or eliminate the minimum training hours for eligibility for financial incentives*. Because short-duration training is harder to monitor, when minima are dropped, complementary action should be taken to strengthen the monitoring of potential fraud.
- *Raise awareness of existing financial incentives available*, for example through public campaigns and/or online guides. This is crucial to ensure that SMEs can take informed decisions on how to finance the training of their workers.

2.2.4. Lack of a dedicated HR department/staff

Another key factor behind low training provision is that SMEs typically lack a Human Resources (HR) department/staff dedicated to organising and co-ordinating training (OECD, 2019[11]; Lee, 2016[15]). Elaborations of the Workplace Panel Survey show that, in 2015, 24% of small firms (1-49 employees), 17% of medium-sized firms (50-249), and 9% of large firms (250+) had no training department nor a person solely dedicated to training (Figure 2.18).

The lack of a dedicated HR department/staff means that there is no staff dedicated to planning suitable training, monitoring training processes, evaluating training effectiveness, and/or handling the cumbersome administrative processes for reimbursement of training expenses. It also means that there is no staff in charge of exploring and benefiting from the many adult learning programmes in place (e.g. financial incentives) (see Section 2.2.3).

Indeed, according to Workplace Panel Survey data, about 40% of small firms in Korea pre-planned annual training, compared to about 50% in medium-sized firms and 65% in large firms (Figure 2.18). Similar results are found regarding pre-approved annual budgets for training costs. Other national surveys confirm these findings.[13]

Figure 2.18. HR department/staff and related activities, Korea, 2015

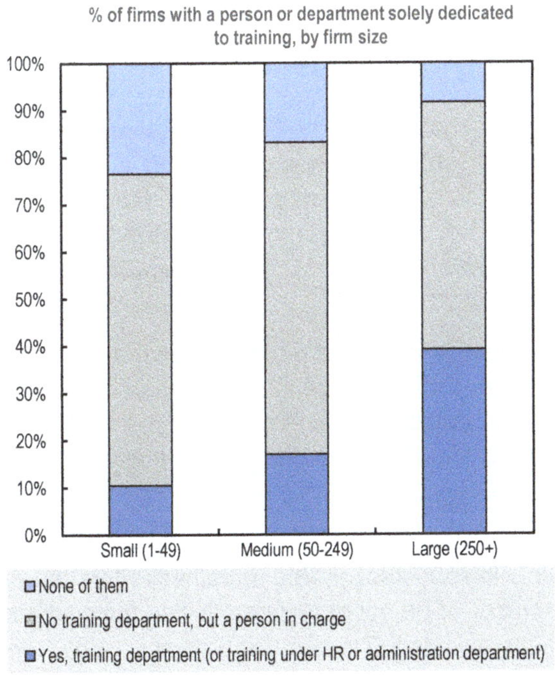

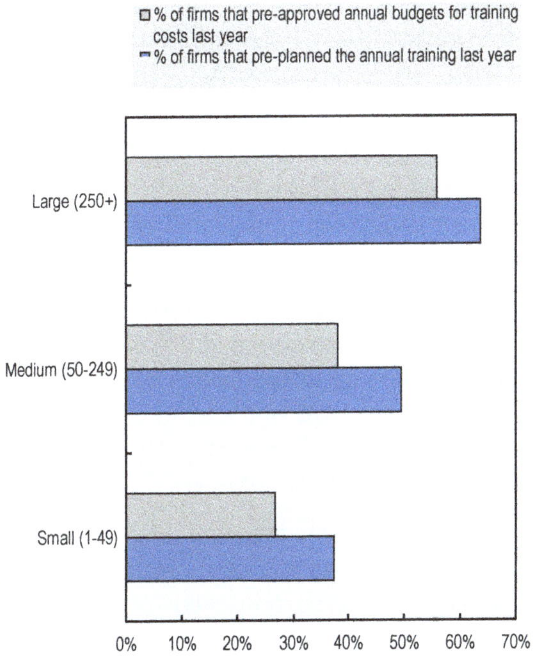

Source: OECD elaborations based on the Workplace Panel Survey (6th wave, 2015).

Korea has already taken steps to solve this issue. The most important policy measure recently implemented is the *SMEs training support centres*. Implemented in 2018 as a pilot, the programme was recently scaled-up and today includes five centres throughout Korea. It aims to tackle the lack of Human Resources (HR) capabilities of SMEs, by supporting business guidance, company diagnosis, as well as training programme design in SMEs. The amount of support per centre is KRW 600 million (approximately EUR 460 000) (see Annex 2.A for a full description).

2.2.5. Lack of training facilities

Another key challenge is that SMEs, unlike larger companies, often do not have their own training facilities. This puts SMEs at a disadvantage vis-à-vis larger companies who have their own training infrastructures. Elaborations of the Human Capital Corporate Panel Survey (2017) show that 85.5% of SMEs (100-299 employees) have no training facility, compared to 16.7% of very large firms (2000+ employees). When they do have training facilities, SMEs are also more likely to share them with affiliates (Table 2.1). Data for micro- and small firms are not available, but it is likely that most if not all of these firms do not have any HRD facility at all.

Table 2.1. Human Resource Development training facilities, 2017

Percentage of firms, by firm size

	100-299 employees	300-999 employees	1000-1999 employees	2000+ employees	Total
Percentage of firms with independent HRD facilities in the company	6.8%	17.5%	28.9%	56.7%	15.6%
Percentage of firms with HRD facilities shared with affiliates	7.7%	9.9%	13.2%	26.7%	10.1%
Percentage of firms with no facility	85.5%	72.5%	57.9%	16.7%	74.3%

Source: KRIVET elaborations of the Human Capital Corporate Panel Survey (7th wave, 2017).

The main programme implemented in Korea to address this challenge is the National Human Resources Development Consortium (National HRD Consortium, or CHAMP), which is considered a case of best practice internationally. Under the programme, launched in 2001, large firms, employers' associations and universities are encouraged (through financial incentives) to set up consortiums with SMEs to share their training facilities and equipment, as well as experience and knowhow in vocational training (OECD, 2018[6]) (see Annex 2.A for a description).

The National HRD Consortium addresses many of the organisational and technical constraints faced by SMEs. This programme also provides a good opportunity to form and strengthen partnerships between large firms and their subcontractors, firms in the same industry and region, and universities and businesses. In particular, because training courses are organised on the basis of this partnership, they can respond more closely to business needs (OECD, 2018[6]).

According to research studies that analyse the performance of the National HRD Consortium, the completion rate of training courses is high at 90.6%, as is the satisfaction rate of trainees (4.21 out of 5), and the level of the practical application of skills in workplaces (4.08 out of 5). In particular, the cost benefit ratio is quite high: for every KRW 1 in costs, the programme yields 3.5 in benefits (Lee et al., 2012[22]).

Despite these achievements, the National HRD Consortium can be still be improved. First, training in the new technology areas in response to the Fourth Industrial Revolution is limited. Indeed, only 5.3% of trainees[14] took training in new fields in 2018, according to national data. Another challenge is that joint training centres could be operated more efficiently. In particular, Korea needs to conduct rigorous performance evaluations for each joint training centre and manage the centres with underperforming or overlapping functions by imposing penalties (e.g. suspending or reducing subsidies).

Improve the National HRD Consortium programme by: encouraging training in new fields (4th industrial revolution); conducting rigorous performance evaluations of each joint training centre; and sanctioning centres with underperforming or overlapping functions. This will reduce the administrative burden involved for SMEs to take advantage of adult learning programmes and financial incentives.

2.2.6. Mind-set of managers and business owners

Managers and business owners are those who ultimately decide on training strategies, especially in smaller firms. Therefore, ensuring that they are supportive of workers' training is a key prerequisite for making adult learning a reality in smaller firms.

Research studies from Korea and other OECD countries show that managers and business owners with the right mind-set are key for training. For example, Bae and Lawler (2000[23]) show that firms in Korea that value Human Resource Management (HRM) and people as a source of competitive advantage are more likely to have high-involvement in training strategies. Jeon and Kim (2012[24]) find that top management leadership in human resources, e.g. managers/owners that have a clear vision about HRD and emphasise the importance of competent staff,[15] are positively associated with the effectiveness of informal learning. Research from other OECD countries shows similar results. For example, in Japan studies show that the attitudes of the owner/manager is the most influential factor in determining the intensity of training in SMEs (Gamage and Sadoi, 2008[25]).

Despite this evidence, much remains to be done to shape a positive learning culture among managers and business owners in Korean SMEs. There are several underlying reasons behind this lack of a learning culture.

One relates to the low demand for skills among SMEs, which inevitably translates into a low demand for training. Korean SMEs often employ low-skilled workers and produce low value-added goods (e.g. in the service sector), and therefore they do not consider training to be a revenue-generating activity (OECD, 2019[11]).

Indeed, elaborations of the Workplace Panel Survey (2015) show that in Korea, 26% of SMEs (less than 250 employees) report 'no need for training due to work characteristics/simplicity of tasks' as the most important reason for not implementing or supporting training, the 2nd most frequently cited reason after lack of personnel (see Figure 2.14).

In this context, low-valued-added production strategies and low skill levels become locked into a self-reinforcing cycle and result in a low skills equilibrium. Breaking the vicious cycle and fostering a learning culture will partly rely upon efforts to shift the productive system towards the use of new and high value-added technologies (see Chapter 4).

Another reason behind the lack of a learning culture is the perception, among managers and business owners, which available training is of low quality or low relevance. Indeed, government-sponsored training programmes are not always perceived as being aligned with the needs of SMEs (Chapter 4). This potentially generates reluctance and doubts about the usefulness of training among managers and business owners. Elaborations of the Workplace Panel Survey (2015) show that in Korea, 16% of SMEs (less than 250 employees) report that the most important reason for not implementing or supporting training is that there was 'no suitable training reflecting one's workplace', and another 3.8% report that 'training offers little benefits due to low efficiency of training' (see Figure 2.14). Efforts to improve training quality and offer more tailored courses targeted to the needs of SMEs could help to convince managers about the effectiveness and relevance of training.

Another related challenge is that managers and business owners in SMEs often lack awareness of the benefits of training, and therefore are not always convinced about the value of workers' continuous learning. According to the Human Capital Corporate Survey (2017) data, some 24% of SMEs (100-299 employees) in 2017 'slightly' or 'fully' agreed that management lack awareness for education and training issues. This share decreases to only 17% in firms with 300-999 employees, 13.1% of firms with 1000-1999 employees, and 6.6% of firms with 2000+ employees (Figure 2.19).[16] In this context, making the business case for training – by building and sharing the evidence on the links between skills and firms' performance – could change managers' mind-sets towards learning and can ultimately be expected to raise training levels.

Figure 2.19. Awareness for education and training among managers, Korea

Percentage of firms reporting that management lacks awareness for education and training, by firm size

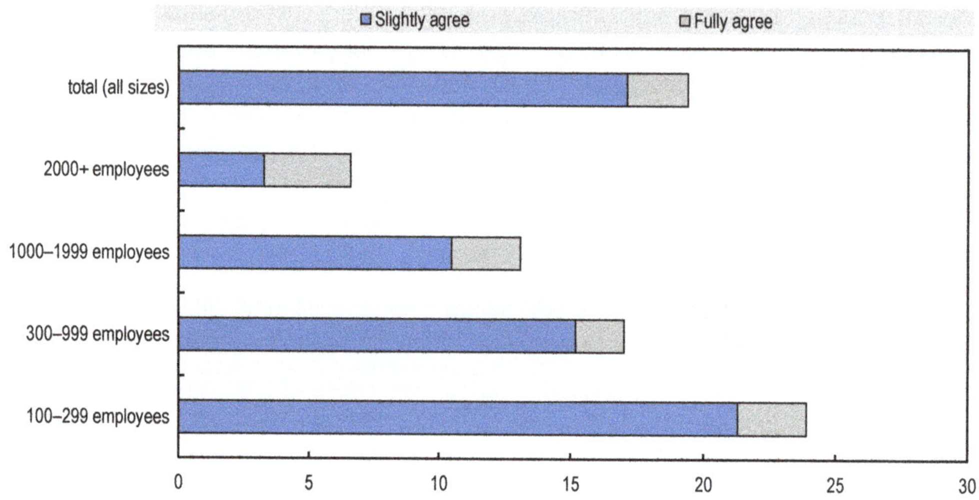

Source: KRIVET elaborations of the Human Capital Corporate Survey (7th wave, 2017)

Another key issue is that – given that SMEs often lack HR departments/staff (see Section 2.2.4) – managers themselves may not be aware of all the adult learning policies available to SMEs and could find it difficult to navigate the numerous programmes available (Kim, 2019[26]). Supporting managers of SMEs to understand what programmes are available and how to use them is key.

On top of raising the demand for high-level skills, improving training quality and relevance, and making the business case for training, going forward, Korea will also need to ensure that entrepreneurs are adequately trained to start and run a business that nurtures its talents. Enhancing the skills of entrepreneurs – e.g. by expanding education and training programmes on entrepreneurship – may lay the foundations for more training opportunities for SME workers. Well-trained entrepreneurs are also more likely to implement High Performance Workplace Practices (HPWPs), which could improve the quality of the work environment and therefore the attractiveness of jobs in SMEs.

Although the government has been extending entrepreneurship-related education programmes in recent years, Korea still has a long way to go to catch up with better performing countries. For example, experts interviewed in the context of the Global Entrepreneurship Monitor (GEM) survey considered that entrepreneurship education is unsatisfactory in Korea – in both primary, secondary, and post-secondary education. Korea performed particularly poorly on post-secondary education programmes in entrepreneurship, ranking 37th out of 54 countries (GEM, 2018[27]).[17]

In Korea, adults are less likely than peers in the OECD area to feel that they have the skills, knowledge and experience to start a business. In Korea, 43% of men and 29% of women indicated that they had sufficient skills, knowledge and experience to start a business over the 2013-17 period, among the lowest levels in the OECD area (Figure 2.20). These results need to be taken with caution, because they reflect subjective perceptions of skills.[18]

Figure 2.20. Adult perception of their entrepreneurship skills

Proportion of adults who report having the skills and knowledge to start a business, 2013-17, by gender

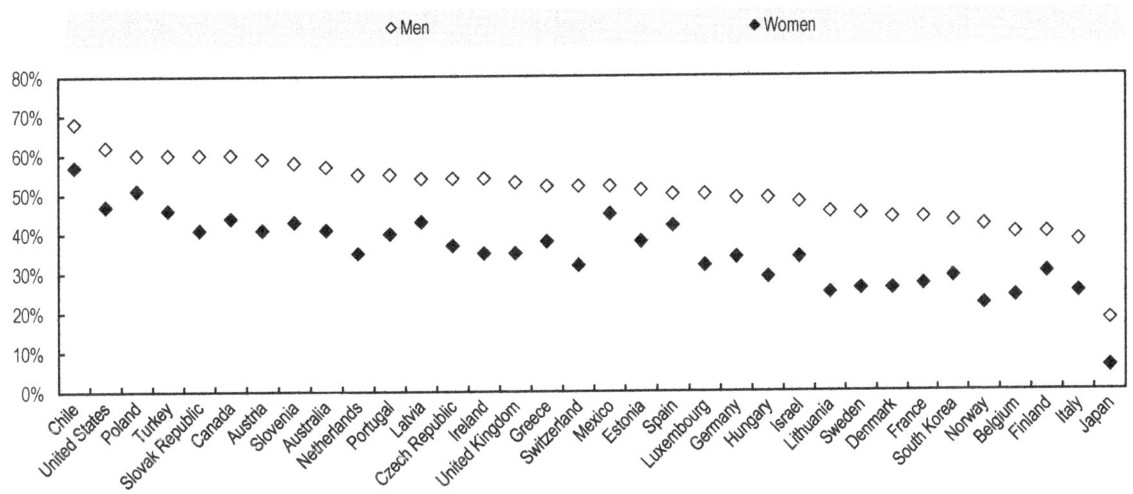

Source: Global Entrepreneurship Monitor (GEM) (2018[27]), Special tabulations of the 2013-17 adult population survey from the Global Entrepreneurship Monitor.

Moreover, in Korea many adults have no access to training on starting and growing a business, compared to other OECD countries. Figure 2.21 shows that in Korea 36% of men and 29% of women reported having access to training on how to start a business in 2013, rates that are well below the majority of OECD countries.

Figure 2.21. Access to entrepreneurship training

Proportion of adults who report that they can access to training on how to start a business, by gender, 2013

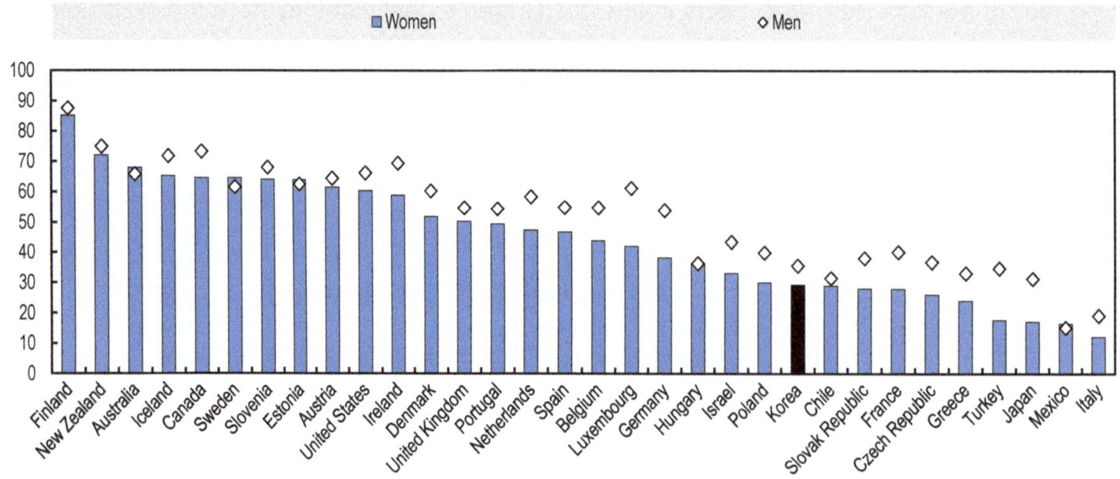

Source: OECD (2019[1]), "Entrepreneurship: Access to training and money to start a business, by sex", OECD Gender Portal, OECD, Paris.

Another challenge worth mentioning is that many older people, after retirement, decide to start and run a business, but few of them have the necessary business skills to achieve high productivity and business success (see Chapter 1). This means that, unless they are adequately trained, these older people may set up and run unproductive businesses.

In addition to poor initial education options to become entrepreneurs, few continuous training opportunities are offered to established business owners. In Korea like in other OECD countries, lost working time is an especially important constraint with respect to owner-manager training, and many small business owners consider that undergoing training themselves will not enhance their ability to operate the firm.

Indeed, elaborations of the Survey of Adult Skills (PIAAC) show that only 40.5% of business owners (self-employed with employees) in Korea participate to formal or non-formal learning in a given year. While this is in line with the OECD average (39.6%), Korea lags well behind best performing countries such as Finland, Germany, the Netherlands and Norway where over half of business owners participate to job-related training in a given year (Figure 2.22).

Figure 2.22. Training of business owners, Korea and OECD countries

Percentage of business owners who participated in (formal or non-formal) job related adult learning in the last 12 months

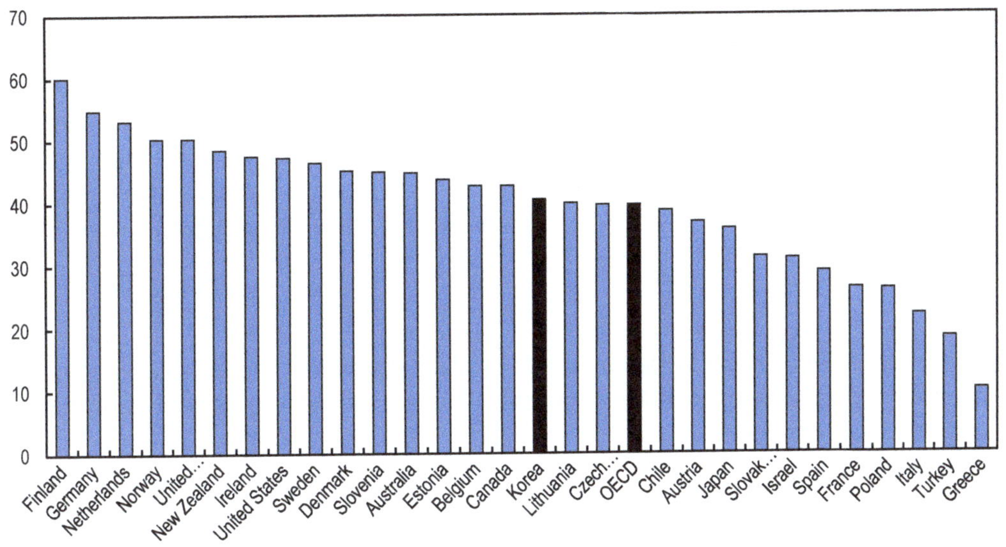

Note: Business owners are self-employed adults with employees.
Source: OECD Secretariat calculations based on the Survey of Adult Skills, PIAAC (2012, 2015).

Korea has already recognised these challenges and has put in place several programmes specifically aimed at creating a learning culture among managers and business owners. These efforts aim to build future entrepreneurs through entrepreneurship and start-up education; train managers and business owners through targeted adult learning programmes; and make them aware of the importance of training, through awareness campaigns. These programmes are described in Annex 2.A. Examples from OECD countries are provided in Box 2.2.

To improve the mind-set of managers and business owners in SMEs and ensure that they are supportive of workers' training, Korea should:

- *Make the business case for training*. For example, building and sharing the evidence on the links between skills and firms' performance, could change managers and business owners' mind-sets towards learning and can ultimately be expected to raise training levels.
- *Enhance the skills of entrepreneurs and ensure that they are adequately trained* to start and run a business that nurtures its talents. This could be done by expanding initial education programmes on entrepreneurship as well as by providing more adult learning programmes targeted to managers/business owners.
- *Raise the demand for high-level skills in SMEs*. Encourage larger firms to engage in greater transfer of technological and organisational know-how with smaller companies in their supply chains. This will of course require action in a number areas beyond adult learning measures.
- *Develop a knowledge-sharing platform* where business owners and managers can exchange on how they implement training.

Box 2.2. Building the skills of managers and business owners in SMEs: international good practice examples

United Kingdom

The Small Business Leadership Programme (2018) looks to provide management training to 2000 small business leaders in its first year and to scale-up to reach 10 000 beneficiaries by 2025. The Small Business Leadership Programme is part of a package of measures to assist businesses in improving their productivity. This also includes the strengthening of local networks focused on business improvement, getting the UK's leading businesses signed-up to mentoring programmes, and promoting "Knowledge Transfer Partnerships" whereby postgraduates are placed in small businesses to translate their research insights into business growth.

Mexico

The Business incubators for basic enterprises (2015) encourages the upgrading of managerial skills and ICT adoption in micro-enterprises. Micro-enterprise owners receive six hours of basic management training as part of this programme.

New Zealand

Lightning Lab XX is a four-month mentorship-driven business acceleration programme. Based in Wellington, Lightning Lab XX makes a seed investment of NZD 20 000 (approximately EUR 12 600) in each company in return for a small equity stake, and offers support services that are delivered through mentors. The programme receives funding from the science and innovation arm of the Ministry of Business, Innovation and Employment and private sponsors.

Australia

Women in STEM and Entrepreneurship (2016) aims to increase awareness and participation of girls and women in STEM and entrepreneurship education and careers, increase participation of girls and women throughout the innovation ecosystem, and stimulate an increase in the number of women in senior leadership and decision making positions in government, research organisations, industry and businesses. This programme supports projects that seek to increase girls' and women's interest in STEM fields and entrepreneurship, develop their skills and knowledge, build their professional networks, or other activities consistent with the programme's objectives. The government has allocated AUD 8 million (approximately EUR 5 million) for 2016-20.

Source: OECD (2019[11]), OECD SMEs and Entrepreneurship Outlook 2019, OECD Publishing, Paris.

2.3. Recent labour market policies and their implications for training

Korea is implementing major labour market reforms that could potentially have significant implications for SMEs training. These measures include the recent increase in the minimum wage and the gradual introduction of the 52-hour workweek. Although it is early to assess the impact of these policies, the next sections explore their potential implications for adult learning.

2.3.1. The increase in the minimum wage

The Korean Minimum Wage Council decided to raise the hourly minimum wage (MW) by 16.4% in 2018 and 10.9% in 2019[19] - with plans to increase it by an additional 2.9% in 2020. These increases are part of the "income-led growth" that the government aims to achieve to address worsening income inequality, close the labour market duality gap, and guarantee a decent living for low-income workers (OECD, forthcoming[28]).

Stakeholders interviewed in the context of this project have expressed conflicting views on what could be the implications of the MW hike on training. According to some observers, the increase in labour costs could reduce firms' budgets for training. Other stakeholders point to the fact that increased labour costs will generate a drop in the rate of return on education, which may lead employers to invest less in training. It is also possible that the increase in the MW could increase firms' reliance on informal workers, leading to under-investments in training as these workers are not bound by a long-term employment relationship.

Other more optimistic observers argue that there might be indirect effects that generate an increase in training provision. Because training programmes are often subsidised by the government, the MW hike is unlikely to reduce firms' training efforts. Rather the opposite, companies will likely try to meet the cost of higher MWs by investing in training to make their workers more productive. Moreover, workers benefiting from MW hikes may decide to stay longer with their employers, and the resulting lower job turnover could incentivise both firms and workers to engage in training.

While evidence on the impact of MW increases on training is not available in Korea, the international experience shows that in some OECD and developing countries, the rise or introduction of the minimum wage had negative implications for workers' training. In Japan, Hara (2017[29]) finds that a 1% increase in the minimum wage causes a 2.8% decline in formal training. In China, Haepp and Lin (2016[30]) find significant negative effects of the introduction of minimum wages on firms' human capital investment rates. In Germany, Bellman, Gerner and Hübler (2017[31]) show that the introduction of the new statutory minimum wage was associated with a slight reduction in the intensity of training (although no impact on the incidence of training was found).

Going forward, it is important that Korea carefully monitors the impacts of the MW hike on training provision, and especially in SMEs, which could be particularly affected by this policy.

2.3.2. The 52-hour workweek policy

The tradition of long working hours in Korea may take time away from workers' training. Indeed, working time in Korea was the third longest in the OECD in 2018 at 1967 hours per year, 13% above the OECD average.[20] While long working hours is an issue for firms of all sizes, working time is even longer in SMEs, which typically face labour shortages (see Chapter 1) (OECD, 2018[32]).

To address this challenge, several actions have been taken in Korea. In June 2010, a tripartite agreement was reached to cap maximum working time at 1 800 hours by 2020. To achieve this goal, the government is gradually cutting the statutory limit on weekly working hours from 68 to 52. The policy was implemented in July 2018 for firms with 300 or more employees, and is gradually being rolled out to firms with 50 to 299 employees as of January 2020 and firms with 5 to 49 employees as of July of 2021 (SMEs with less than 5 employees will not be affected).

In order to smooth the implementation process, the government plans to publish a '*Flexible working hours guide*' and hold industry-specific and regional briefing sessions for businesses and keep them informed. For example, in preparation for the implementation of the 52-hour workweek system, the government will establish a 'field support group' in 48 local employment offices to provide customised support to SMEs that are facing troubles preparing for the change.

Thanks to this measure, Korea's working time legislation has become more in line with OECD practice. But while the policy is a much-needed step in the right direction for improving work-life balance, it is too early to tell what will be the implications of the 52-workweek measure on training. Several stakeholders expressed concerns on the potential unintended negative consequences that the policy could have on workers' participation to training programmes.

Because the time workers spend on training is counted as working hours in Korea, firms may decide to cut their training efforts in a view to comply with the 52-workweek measure. This may be particularly true for SMEs that already struggle with labour shortages and face difficulties to free up time for their employees to take training (see Section 2.2.1). This is similar to what happened in France with the 35-workweek measure, whereby firms cut lunchbreak, time for putting on uniforms and protective gears that were previously part of the working time.

At the same time, in Korea the 52-workweek measure could free up workers' time for pursuing training that is voluntarily initiated and that typically takes place *outside* of working hours. This includes training that would prepare the worker for a career shift, in a different firm or a different sector.

Recent evidence suggests that the first phase of the 52-hour workweek policy reform (applying to large firms with 300 or more employees) has been effective in reducing the incidence of very long working hours (Hijzen and Thewissen, 2020[33]). Evidence on previous policy efforts to reduce working time legislation showed that the measure increased productivity per hour worked (Park and Park, 2019[34]). Going forward, it will be important for Korea to monitor the impact of the 52-workweek measure on SMEs and workers' attitudes towards training. Moreover, the government should capitalise on the briefing sessions and field support groups to guide SMEs on matters related to training, for example by increasing awareness of existing flexible work systems and adult learning programmes.

Korea should carefully evaluate the impact that new labour market policies may have on training. These measures include the recent increase in the minimum wage and the 52-hour workweek policy.

References

Bae, J. and J. Lawler (2000), "Organizational and HRM strategies in Korea: impact on firm performance in an emerging economy", *Academy of Management Journal*, Vol. Vol. 43, No. 3, 502-517, https://www.jstor.org/stable/1556407. [23]

Ban, G. (2013), "Do Training Subsidies Have the Positive Effects on Corpoate Training?", *Korean Journal of Labor Economics*, Vol. 36/2, pp. 95-124. [18]

Bellmann, L., M. Gerner and O. Hübler (2017), *Training and minimum wages: first evidence from the introduction of the minimum wage in Germany*, IZA Journal of Labor Economics, https://doi.org/10.1186/s40172-017-0058-z. [31]

Case, F. and I. Freundlieb (2018), *Experimentation Afest: Action de Formation En Situation de Travail*, Ministère du Travail, https://travail-emploi.gouv.fr/IMG/pdf/rapportfinalafest.pdf. [9]

Chae, C., Y. Choi and J. Yang (2018), *Action Plan for Facilitating Paid Leave Training*, Korea Research Institute for Vocational Education and Training. [4]

Choi, Y., C. Lee and R. Jacobs (2015), "The hierarchical linear relationship among structured on-the-job training activities, trainee characteristics, trainer characteristics, training environment characteristics, and organizational characteristics of workers in small and medium-sized enterpris", *Human Resource Development International*, Vol. 18/5, pp. 499–520, https://doi.org/10.1080/13678868.2015.1080046. [8]

Eurofound (2019), *Job rotation: Denmark*, European Monitoring Centre on Change, https://www.eurofound.europa.eu/observatories/emcc/erm/support-instrument/job-rotation. [5]

Fialho, P., G. Quintini and M. Vandeweyer (2019), "Returns to different forms of job related training: Factoring in informal learning", *OECD Social, Employment and Migration Working Papers, No. 231*, https://dx.doi.org/10.1787/b2180. [2]

Gamage, A. and Y. Sadoi (2008), "Determinants of Training and Development Practices in SMEs: A Case of Japanese Manufacturing Firms", *Sri Lankan Journal of Human Resource Management*, Vol. Vol.2, No.1, http://dx.doi.org/10.4038/sljhrm.v2i1.5104. [25]

GEM (2018), *Global Entrepreneurship Monitor: Korea*, Global Entrepreneurship Monitor, https://www.gemconsortium.org/economy-profiles/south-korea. [27]

Haepp, T. and C. Lin (2016), *How Does the Minimum Wage Affect Firm Investments in Fixed and Human Capital? Evidence from China*, IZA Discussion Papers, No. 10332, http://hdl.handle.net/10419/149191. [30]

Hara, H. (2017), "Minimum wage effects on firm-provided and worker-initiated training", *Labour Economics*, Vol. 47, pp. 149-162, https://doi.org/10.1016/j.labeco.2017.05.011. [29]

Hijzen, A. and S. Thewissen (2020), "The 2018-2021 working time reform in Korea: A preliminary assessment", *OECD Social, Employment and Migration Working Papers*. [33]

HRD Korea (2018), *Employer Vocational Competency Development Training Manual*. [36]

Jeong, S., G. McLean and S. Park (2018), "Understanding informal learning in small- and medium-sized enterprises in South Korea", *Journal of Workplace Learning*, Vol. Vol. 30 No. 2, 2018/Emerald Publishing Limited, http://dx.doi.org/10.1108/JWL-03-2017-0028. [3]

Jeon, K. and K. Kim (2012), "How do organizational and task factors influence informal learning in the workplace?", *Human Resource Development International*, Vol. Vol. 15/No. 2, http://dx.doi.org/10.1080/13678868.2011.647463. [24]

Kim, C. (2019), *Skills Development Perceptions of SME CEOs in Korea*, Korea Research Institute for Vocational Education and Training (KRIVET). [26]

Kuczera, M., V. Kis and G. Wurzburg (2009), *OECD Reviews of Vocational Education and Training: A Learning for Jobs Review of Korea 2009*, OECD Reviews of Vocational Education and Training, OECD Publishing, Paris, https://dx.doi.org/10.1787/9789264113879-en. [12]

Lee, C. et al. (2012), "Performance Analysis of National Human Resource Development Consortium Project Using Logic Model", *The Journal of Vocational Education Research*, Vol. 31/1, pp. 195-216. [22]

Lee, K. (2016), "Skills Training by Small and Medium-Sized Enterprises: Innovative Cases and the Consortium Approach in the Republic of Korea", *Asian Development Bank Institut*, Vol. ADBI Working Paper 579/No. 579, http://: http://www.adb.org/publications/skills-trainingsmall-and-medium-sized-enterprises-innovative-cases-consortium-approach-korea/. [15]

MoEL (2019), *Employment Insurance White Paper.* [35]

MoEL (2018), *The Employment Insurance White Paper*, Korean Ministry of Employment and Labor. [21]

OECD (2019), *Education at a Glance: OECD indicators*, OECD Publishing, Paris, https://doi.org/10.1787/f8d7880d-en. [1]

OECD (2019), *OECD SME and Entrepreneurship Outlook 2019*, OECD Publishing, Paris, https://dx.doi.org/10.1787/34907e9c-en. [11]

OECD (2018), *Working Better with Age: Korea*, OECD Publishing, Paris, https://doi.org/10.1787/9789264208261-en. [32]

OECD (2018), *Working Better with Age: Korea*, Ageing and Employment Policies, OECD Publishing, Paris, https://dx.doi.org/10.1787/9789264208261-en. [6]

OECD (2017), *Entrepreneurship at a Glance 2017*, OECD Publishing, Paris, https://doi.org/10.1787/entrepreneur_aag-2017-en. [16]

OECD (2017), *Getting Skills Right: France*, OECD Publishing, Paris, https://doi.org/10.1787/9789264284456-en. [10]

OECD (2017), *OECD Skills Strategy Diagnostic Report: Korea 2015*, OECD Skills Studies, OECD Publishing, Paris, https://dx.doi.org/10.1787/9789264300286-en. [14]

OECD (forthcoming), *Inclusive growth review of Korea*, OECD Publishing, Paris. [28]

OECD/EU (2017), *The Missing Entrepreneurs 2017: Policies for Inclusive Entrepreneurship*, OECD Publishing, Paris, https://dx.doi.org/10.1787/9789264283602-en. [38]

Paik, S. (2016), *Financing Skills Development– Korean Experience*, KDI School of Pub Policy & Management Paper No. 16-27, http://dx.doi.org/doi.org/10.2139/ssrn.2891527. [17]

Park, J. et al. (2018), *Performance Diagnosis and Performance Management of Work-Study Dual System*. [37]

Park, W. and Y. Park (2019), *When Less is More: The Impact of the Regulation on Standard Workweek on Labor Productivity in South Korea*, Association for Public Policy Analysis and Management. [34]

SBS (2013), *Employment Insurance Vocational Training Corporate Support Fund*, https://cnbc.sbs.co.kr/article/10000594596. [20]

Stone, I. (2010), "Encouraging small firms to invest in training:", *UK Commission for Employment and Skills* Issue No. 5, https://core.ac.uk/download/pdf/4151307.pdf. [7]

Yoo, G. et al. (2009), *An Empirical Analysis on the Performance of Vocational Training and a Study on the Reform Direction of Government Support Projects*, Korean Labor Economic Association, http://www.prism.go.kr/homepage/entire/retrieveEntireDetail.do;jsessionid=9352FF20E58FF9F95C7C4639943461B7.node02?cond_research_name=&cond_research_start_date=&cond_research_end_date=&research_id=1490000-200900077&pageIndex=2504&leftMenuLevel=160. [13]

Yun, J. and S. Park (2017), *Analysis of Vocational Training Performance of Employees: Focusing on the Performance of Individual Workers*. [19]

Annex 2.A. Adult learning programmes for SMEs

This annex describes the adult learning programmes put in place in Korea to encourage SMEs to offer training to their employees.

Subsidies for employer-provided training

When employers provide vocational training to their current and prospective workers, they can recover all or part of the training costs through the Employment Insurance (EI), the national compulsory social insurance scheme (see Chapter 5).[21]

Human Resources Development Service of Korea (HRD Korea) – a public agency under the Ministry of Employment and Labor (MoEL) that supports workers' lifelong education – is responsible for the approval of training courses and the reimbursement of employer-provided training.

In order to receive training subsidies, companies need to meet certain eligibility criteria (e.g. minimum training hours). These eligibility criteria are typically more flexible for SMEs. For example, in case of collective (i.e. classroom) training and on-the-job training, the course should last at least 2 days or 16 hours for large firms and at least 1 day or 8 hours for SMEs (eligible for preferential support). Remote training requires a minimum of 8 hours of training, regardless of firm size (Annex Table 2.A.1).

The amount of the subsidy also varies depending on the size of the firm (see Annex Table 2.A.1). As of 2018, SMEs eligible for preferential supports (see Box 2.3) have 100% of training costs subsidised. This compares to a 60% subsidy for large firms with less than 1 000 employees and 40% for large firms with 1 000 or more employees. In addition, Korea provides wage subsidies to firms that train non-regular workers. SMEs receive 120% of the minimum wage (MW) during the training period, while large firms receive 100% of the MW.

Annex Table 2.A.1. Subsidies for employer-provided training

Eligibility criteria and subsidy, by training type and firm size (2018)

Training type	Firm size	Eligibility criteria (minimum training time)	Subsidy	
			Training cost (Percentage of training unit cost)	Wage for non-regular workers (Percentage of minimum wage)
Collective / On-the-job training	SMEs (eligible for preferential support)	1 day and 8 hours	100%	120%
	Large firms with less than 1 000 employees	2 days and 16 hours	60%	100%
	Large firms with 1 000 or more employees	2 days and 16 hours	40%	100%
Remote training	SMEs (eligible for preferential support)	8 hours	100%	Not available
	Large firms with less than 1 000 employees	8 hours	80%	Not available
	Large firms with 1 000 or more employees	8 hours	40%	Not available
Mixed training	All firms	Mix of collective (or on-the-job) and remote training		

Note: SMEs refer to the Preferentially Supported Enterprises defined in the Employment Insurance Act. Collective training refers to the training in which a group of trainees are gathered and trained in a suitable (certified) facility (except for industrial production facilities and workplaces). On-the-job training refers to the training in which workers acquire knowledge and skills related to their jobs from their supervisors or seniors in the same environment as the actual place of work. Remote (smart) training refers to the training conducted using information and communication media, and management of trainees is conducted on the web. Mixed training is a combination of two or more types of training in the midst of collective training, on-the-job training and remote (smart) training.
Source: MoEL (2019[35]), Employment Insurance White Paper; HRD Korea (2018[36]), Employer Vocational Competency Development Training Manual.

Box 2.3. Definition of SMEs eligible for preferential supports

Under the Employment Insurance system, the government gives priority to SMEs when providing financial support through employment security and vocational skills development projects. The definition of Preferentially Supported Enterprises is based on Article 19 of the Employment Insurance Act and Article 12 of its enforcement decree. The definition is solely determined by the number of ordinarily employed workers and varies by industry. To meet the criteria of the Preferentially Supported Enterprises, the number of ordinarily employed workers is 500 or less in the manufacturing sector, 300 or less in mining, construction, and telecommunications sectors, 200 or less in wholesale and retail trade, and 100 or less in other industries (Table 2.2).

Table 2.2. Definition of Preferentially Supported Enterprises

Number of ordinarily employed workers, by industry

Industrial classification	Number of ordinarily employed workers
1. Manufacturing	500 workers or fewer
2. Mining / 3. Construction / 4. Transportation / 5. Publishing, motion picture, broadcasting, telecommunications and information services / 6. Business facilities management and business support service / 7. Professional, scientific and technical services / 8. Health and social work services	300 workers or fewer
9. Wholesale and retail trade / 10. Accommodation and food services / 11. Financial and insurance activities / 12. Arts, sports and recreation related services	200 workers or fewer
13. Other industries.	100 workers or fewer

Source: Enforcement Decree of the Employment Insurance Act.

In recent years, the number of workers taking employer-provided training funded under the Employment Insurance Act has increased rapidly from 2.47 million in 2015 to 4.58 million in 2018.[22] In parallel, the gap in training opportunities between large firms and SMEs has been gradually decreasing. During the 2015-18 period, the number of trainees in SMEs (1-299 employees) increased by 2.3 times while that of large companies (+300) increased by 1.5 times. As a result, the share of SMEs in total training participation increased from 46% in 2015 to 57.3% in 2018. In particular, the share of small businesses (1-49) increased significantly from 18.2% to 27.3% (Annex Figure 2.A.1). This increase in training is mainly due to the increase in distance training.

Employer-provided training funded under the Employment Insurance Act takes different forms, including collective training (i.e. classroom), on-the-job training, and remote training (e.g. by correspondence, internet, or smartphone). Although collective training was used most often in 2016, the use of remote training is on the rise, reflecting recent development of IT technology and changing learning patterns of workers (Annex Figure 2.A.2) (see Chapter 4). The use of on-the-job training is extremely low, accounting for only 0.04% of the total training.

Annex Figure 2.A.1. Trends in employer-provided training under the Employment Insurance, by firm size

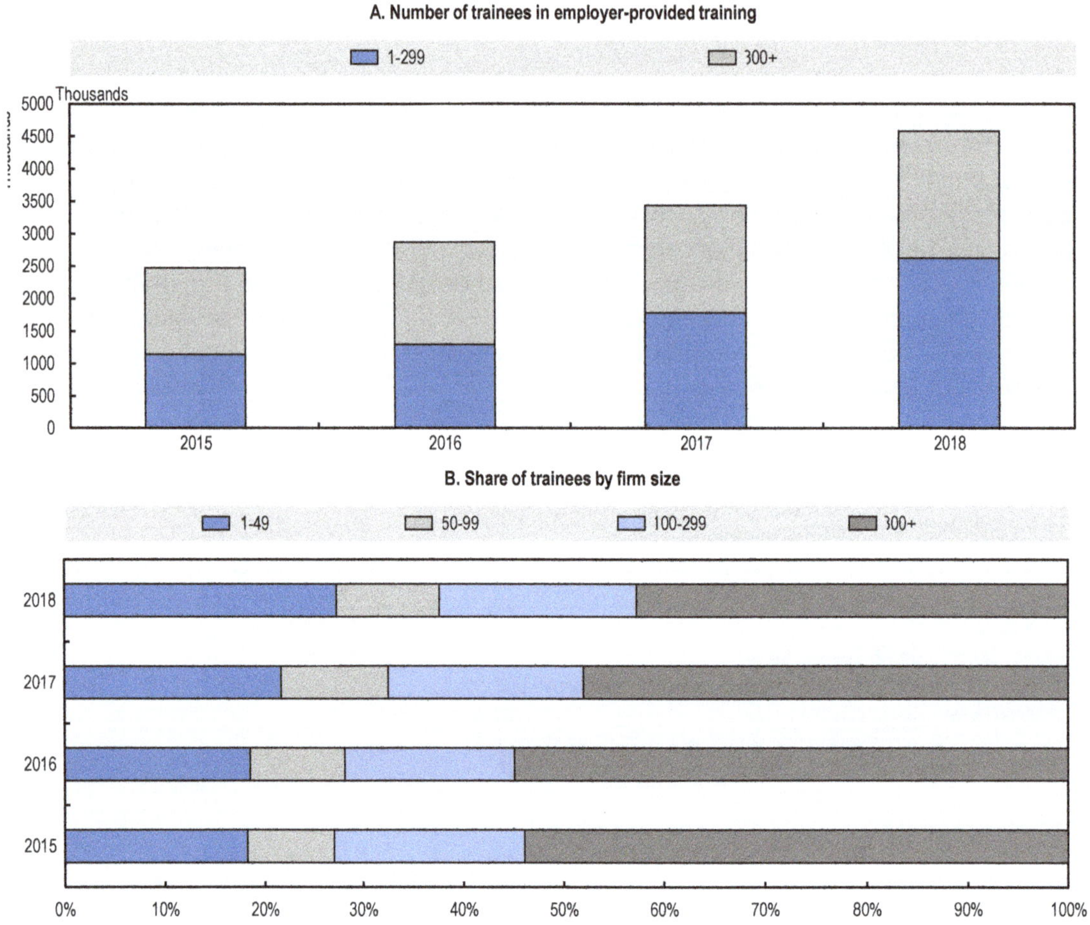

Note: Employer-provided training refers to the programmes that provide training subsidies to employers. It includes the following programmes: (1) subsidy for employer-provided training, (2) National HRD consortium, (3) region-industry tailored training, (4) Work and Study dual system (5) Stepping stone to employment programme.
Source: Administrative data provided by the Ministry of Employment and Labor.

Annex Figure 2.A.2. Employer-provided training, by training type

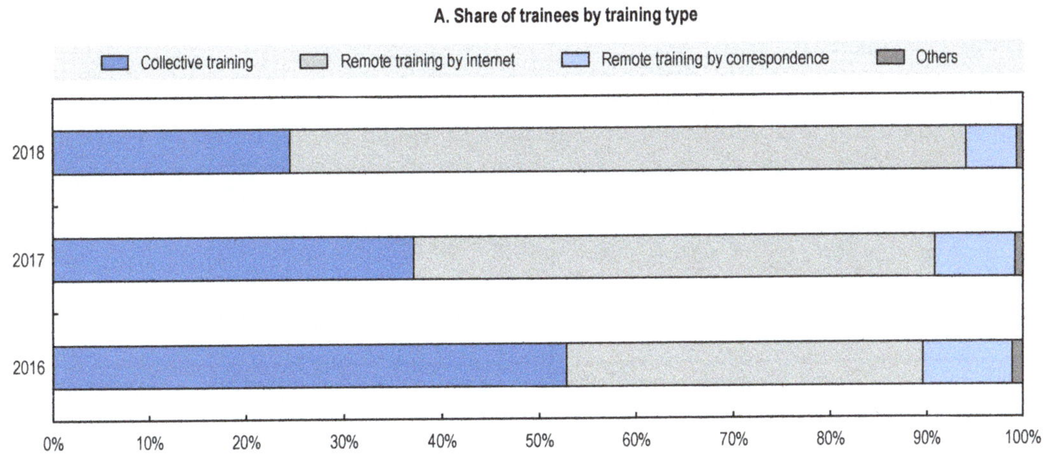

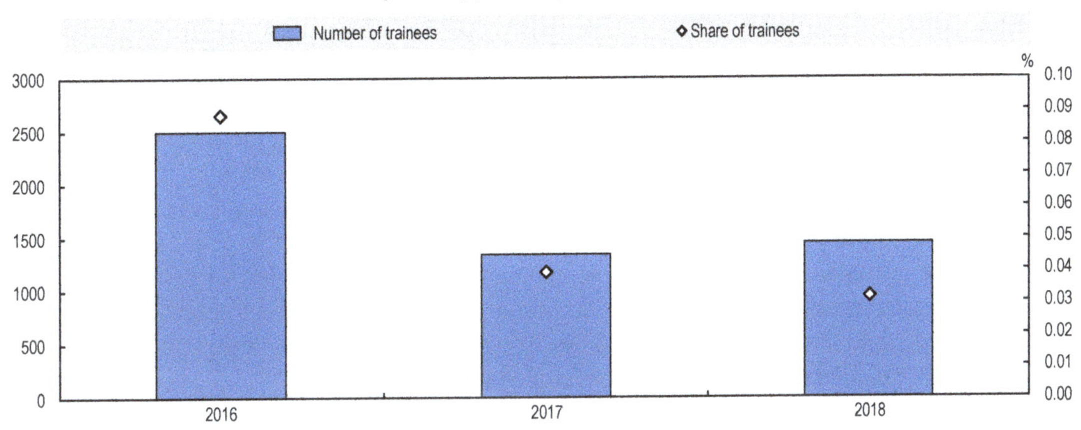

Note: Data include the following projects that subsidise employer-provided training: (1) subsidy for employer-provided training, (2) National HRD consortium, (3) region-industry tailored training, (4) Work and Study dual system.
Source: Administrative data provided by the Ministry of Employment and Labor.

Systematic on-the-job training (S-OJT)

S-OJT was launched in 2018 to foster and facilitate customised on-the-job training for SMEs, which may have difficulty in using external training institutions due to labour shortages and lack of personnel. The HRD Korea selects about 150 companies through the competition process every year. The main supports include: a) training course development by which external experts analyse the tasks that require training and provide a firm-specific on-site training programme; b) capacity building of in-house trainers including trainees coaching techniques; c) supports for administrative procedures and professional consulting related to training by matching professional support agencies; d) subsidies of training costs and training teacher allowances. A total of 122 companies were selected and supported by this programme in 2018. The average annual expenditure was KRW 24 million (about EUR 18 774[23]) per company.

SMEs training support centres

SMEs training support centres were open in 2018 by designating professional agencies as consulting centres to provide professional services to promote SMEs' participation in training. A total of five centres, including two in 2018 and three in 2019, have been selected as SME training support centres through open bidding process. The selected institutions are the Korea Chamber of Commerce and Industry (Busan Institute of Human Resources Development and Gwangju Institute of Human Resources Development), the Korea Productivity Center, the Gyeonggi Employers Federation and the Korea University of Technology and Education.

The main contents of support are: a) providing guidance and consultation on the government-funded programmes; b) searching and supporting of participating companies; c) providing vocational training consulting, including training course design; and d) supporting of administrative procedures related to training. In 2018, 1 559 SMEs benefited from the *SMEs training support centres*. The amount of support for each centre is KRW 600 million (about EUR 480 623) per year.

Annex Table 2.A.2. Number of beneficiaries (firms) in SME support centres (2018)

Total	Training information	Training consulting	S-OJT consulting	Training Implementation
1559	1141	216	135	67

Source: Administrative data provided by the Ministry of Employment and Labor.

Subsidy for paid training leave

The subsidy for paid training leave financially supports employers who grant their workers time off work to train. SMEs eligible for preferential support (see Box 2.3) need to provide training for at least 20 hours and give their employees at least 5 days of paid leave. The subsidy covers the wage of participants, which is subsidised at 150% of the minimum wage. Since 2011, additional support is given to SMEs to partially subsidise the wage of replacement workers. This additional subsidy is granted when three conditions are met. The employers need to: continuously provide training for at least 120 hours; give employees at least 30 days of paid leave; and hire replacement workers. The eligibility criteria for large firms are more stringent than for SMEs, and the subsidy is also less generous (Annex Table 2.A.3).

Annex Table 2.A.3. Subsidies for paid training leave

Eligibility criteria and subsidy

	SMEs (eligible for preferential supports)		Large firms	
	Subsidy	Eligibility criteria	Subsidy	Eligibility criteria
Training cost	Same as subsidy for employer-provided training	At least 20 training hours for 5 days	Same as subsidy for employer-provided training	At least 180 training hours for 60 days. Workers with min. 1 year of tenure.
Worker's wages	Working hours × hourly minimum wage × 150%	At least 20 training hours for 5 days	Working hours × hourly minimum wage × 100%	At least 180 training hours for 60 days. Workers with min. 1 year of tenure.
Replacement worker's wages	Working hours × hourly minimum wage × 100%	At least 120 training hours for 30 days	Not provided	Not eligible

Source: OECD 2018 Policy Questionnaire: Readiness of Adult Learning Systems to Address Changing Skills Needs.

The take-up of paid training leave is on the rise in recent years, and KRW 19.3 billion (about EUR 15.1 million) were provided for 19 676 workers at 5 285 workplaces in 2018. The number of beneficiaries has nearly doubled over the 2015-18 period, and the participation of small firms with less than 50 employees has increased even more significantly from 4 916 in 2015 to 12 419 in 2018 (Annex Figure 2.A.3). However, the take-up of the subsidy for the replacement worker's wages was extremely low at only six participants in 2016.

Annex Figure 2.A.3. Number of beneficiaries of paid training leave, by firm size

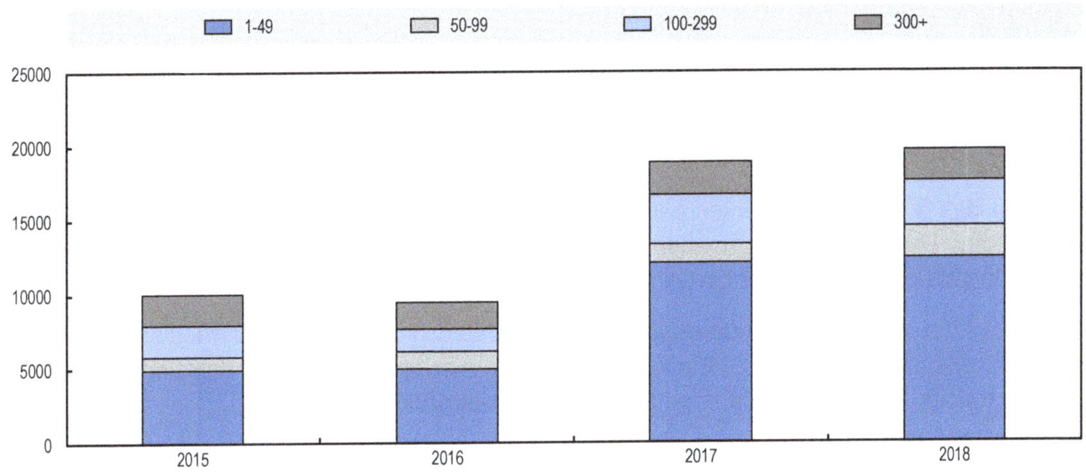

Source: Administrative data provided by the Ministry of Employment and Labor.

Under the Employment Insurance Act, the annual support ceiling for SMEs is 240% of annual levy paid. However, 96.5% of SMEs have an annual ceiling of only KRW 5 million (about EUR 3 911), so they cannot conduct long-term paid leave training for their workers under such a low annual ceiling. To address this challenge, Korea launched a pilot project in August 2018 to encourage the use of long-term (over 30 days) paid leave training for SMEs. Through this project, SMEs can receive additional funding for paid leave training that does not count into the annual ceiling.

National Human Resources Development Consortium

Under the National Human Resources Development Consortium programme (i.e. CHAMP) – launched in 2001 – large firms, employers' associations and universities establish joint training centres, which conduct consortium projects to provide customised training for workers in SMEs. In August 2018, a total of 216 joint training centres had been set up, and participating institutions were evenly distributed between large firms, employers' association and universities (Annex Table 2.A.4).

Annex Table 2.A.4. Joint training centres by operation institution, 2018

Total	Large firms	Public institutions or NGOs	University	Polytech	Employers' associations, etc.
216	45	37	35	26	73

Source: Administrative data provided by the Ministry of Employment and Labor.

On top of the subsidy for employer-provided training, the government further subsidises infrastructure costs for joint training up to KRW 2 billion (about EUR 1.6 million) per year. Training facilities and equipment costs are provided within the limit of KRW 1.5 billion (about EUR 1.2 million) per year and operating cost are provided within the limit of KRW 400 million (about EUR 0.3 million) per year (80% of projected cost respectively). Programme development costs are also covered up to a maximum of KRW 100 million (about EUR 0.1 million) per year (100% of projected cost).[24]

The National HRD Consortium has made a significant contribution to increasing SME participation in vocational training. As of 2018, 124 230 of SMEs and 252 159 workers had benefited from this programme.

The programme accounted for 25% of the total government spending on vocational training for incumbent workers.

Training Centres by the Ministry of SMEs and Start-ups

Since 1982, The Ministry of SMEs and Start-ups (MSS) operates programmes aimed at providing educational opportunities to SME workers to enhance their business and job-related skills.

The MSS provides 600 training courses per year through 5 training centres under the Korea SMEs and Start-ups Agency. The programme provides training for both employees and CEOs/business owners and around 50 thousand people per year participate in this programme.

The training involves a short-term courses (3/4/5 days), divided into beginner, intermediate and advanced levels to encourage participation by SMEs workers. Participation fees are paid by the employees, but 50% to 60% of the training costs are reimbursed through the Employment Insurance.

Training content is defined based on surveys of skill demands by companies. Many efforts are currently being made to reform existing curriculum into new industry and smart factory courses. Therefore, the participation of SMEs interested in building smart factories is expected to increase.

Work-Study Dual system

The Work-Study Dual System introduced in 2013 is a Korean-style apprenticeship, which enables young people to acquire relevant job competences through the structured theoretical education at education/training institutions and practical training in workplaces.

To be eligible for the programme, firms need to have at least 50 full-time employees (at least 20 full-time employees for joint training centres), they have to hire trainees and provide NCS-based off-site and on-site training for 1 year to 4 years.

Eligible firms can receive a subsidy to cover the costs of training and related infrastructure costs, including the costs of developing education and training programmes and the cost of consulting services to develop learning tools.

The Work-Study Dual System is spreading rapidly among companies, with the number of companies selected for the programme jumping from 1 897 in 2014 to 14 110 in 2018. By 2018, a total of 11 217 participating companies had actually developed training programmes tailored to their needs with government subsidies and had actively provided practical training for 76 076 training workers (Annex Table 2.A.5).

Annex Table 2.A.5. Trend of Work-Study Dual System

	2014	2015	2016	2017	2018
Selected firms	1 897	5 212	8 492	11 688	14 110
Training firms	752	2 816	6 207	9 228	11 217
No. of training workers	3 154	14 318	34 378	57 423	76 076

Source: Administrative data provided by the Ministry of Employment and Labor.

Although this programme is opened to companies of all sizes, it is especially contributing to skills development for SMEs. Indeed, some 95.8% of the selected firms are SMEs with less than 300 employee (Annex Table 2.A.6). Most programmes target workers who have already graduated from school (Annex Table 2.A.7).

Annex Table 2.A.6. Selected firms, by firm size (August, 2018)

	Total	Less than 20	20-49	50-99	100-299	300-999	+1000
No. of selected firms	12 977	3 727	4 696	2 347	1 658	443	106
Percentage of total firms	100.0	28.7	36.2	18.1	12.8	3.4	0.8

Source: Administrative data provided by the Ministry of Employment and Labor.

Annex Table 2.A.7. Selected firms, by characteristics of training workers (August, 2018)

	Total	Employees (already graduated from school)		Students		
		Training by Individual firm	Joint Training Centre	High School	Junior college	University
No. of selected firms	20 413	2 763	10 428	5 642	512	1 068
Percentage of total firms	100.0	13.5	51.1	27.7	2.5	5.2

Note: The total includes 7 436 firms that participated in more than one category.
Source: Administrative data provided by the Ministry of Employment and Labor.

Through these programmes, SMEs can secure the necessary skilled talent, foster employees attachment and increase corporate productivity. On their side, trainees can learn the job competencies and skills required by firms while working, and can settle into their jobs early without spending time acquiring unnecessary credentials and qualifications.

According to employers surveys, the job performance of the trainees who completed this programme – defined as a share of the job performance of skilled workers in the firm – has improved from 48.5% (before training) to 81.2% (after training) (Park et al., 2018[37]).

The employment retention rate after training is also relatively good, compared to the Employment Success Package Programmes (ESPP), a comprehensive employment support programmes for the unemployed. The percentage of participants retaining jobs for more than one year after completing the Work-Study Dual system, for example, was 62.6% in 2017, well above that of the ESPP (48.4%).

SME Learning Organization Project

Introduced in 2006, this programme supports SMEs' learning activities and helps them build infrastructures related to training. When an SME sets up a body for organised training bridging work and learning, it may receive subsidies to cover the expense of running the body (e.g. learning group activities, sharing model practice, outside expert consulting, building spaces for learning). The average annual support is KRW 24 million (about EUR 18 774) per company and 91 companies were selected through the public offering process in 2018. In particular, more than 70% of the selected firms are small companies with less than 100 employees (Annex Table 2.A.8). This programme enables SMEs to accumulate and share work-related knowledge and knowhow within the firm systematically.

Annex Table 2.A.8. Learning organisations, by firm size, 2018

	Total	1-99	100-199	200+
Number of firms	91	65	19	7

Source: Administrative data provided by the Ministry of Employment and Labor.

Awareness campaigns and training programmes for CEOs

Korea has put in place various policies to raise awareness among CEOs on the benefit of training:

- September is designated as the month of vocational skill development and various events, such as the National Human Resource Development Conference and the 'Vocational Skills Month' are held every year.
- HRD Korea has a training programme for SME CEOs and HRD managers through their headquarters and branch offices. The objective of this training is to encourage SME CEOs and managers to recognise the importance of vocational skills development and enhance their human resource development capabilities. This programme is free of charge, and training lasts 2 hours for CEOs and 4 hours for managers. In 2018, KRW 410 million (about EUR 320 718) was provided. Some 4 532 people benefited from the programme.

Best-HRD certification awards

The Ministry of Employment and Labor encourages companies to invest in human resource development by awarding Best-HRD Certification to companies that excel in human resource development and management. The selection criteria are geared towards competency-based HRM (hiring, promotion, wages, etc.) and the highest weight is given to the CEO's willingness to invest in human resource development. Companies that have received the Best-HRD certification are given preferential treatment in selecting various SME support projects (such as the SME Learning Organization Project). Since 2006, a total of 1 533 companies have applied for this programme and 676 companies have been certified, including 552 SMEs. Other similar programmes exist in Korea. For example, the Ministry of SMEs and Start-ups operates the "Human resources cultivating SMEs designation programme" to promote human resources investments in SMEs, and provide financial and administrative incentives to them.

Notes

[1] The Korean Workplace Panel Survey (WPS) and the European Continuing Vocational Training Survey (CVTS) are not fully comparable for several reasons: 1) Unlike the WPS, the CVTS excludes firms with less than 10 employees; 2) The CVTS includes legally mandated training – while in WPS most questions exclude legally mandated training; 3) CVTS includes training provided to persons employed who either have a working contract or who benefit directly from their work for the enterprise such as unpaid family workers and casual workers – while in the WPS, most questions refer to regular workers (excluding executives).

[2] This includes both mandatory and other types of training.

[3] i.e. the total training hours of the trained employees divided by the total number of employee in the year preceding the survey.

[4] This refers to the gap in participation between micro and large firms.

[5] Except for Austria, Greece, Japan, Lithuania, Spain and Turkey – where the gap is null or negative.

[6] Informal learning can also help address this challenge.

[7] Source: OECD 2018 Policy Questionnaire: Readiness of Adult Learning Systems to Address Changing Skills Needs.

[8] The replacement workers are chosen among unemployed people with a minimum of 26 weeks of unemployment. The wage follows the collective agreement in the company and the employment period should go from a minimum of 10 hours to a maximum of 26 weeks. At the beginning of 2014, the number of unemployed in job rotation was around 7 000.

[9] The financial resources spent on the programme was only 3 645 million KRW (approximately EUR 2.8 million) in 2018.

[10] For example, industrial policies can encourage SMEs to adopt cutting-edge technologies that could increase workers' productivity, performance, and wages; adjustments in the Employment Protection Legislation (EPL) can decrease labour market duality between regular and non-regular workers; wage setting mechanisms can be designed to reward performance rather than seniority.

[11] The average includes firms with 100 or more employees.

[12] E.g. training that meets certain quality criteria; or that refers to National Competency Standards.

[13] For example, elaborations of the HCCP Survey (2017) show that 66.8% medium-sized firms (100-199 employees) have an annual HRD (training) plan in place, a rate that increases progressively with firm size up to 96.7% for very large firms (with 2 000 employees or more). Similarly, 51.5% of medium-sized firms 'slightly' or 'fully' agree that HRD experts are insufficient, against 23.3% in very large firms.

[14] 11 989 out of 224 302.

[15] Top management leadership in human resources is measured though various factors: (a) ability to treat excellent and talented employees considerately and specially, (b) having a clear vision about HRD, and (c) emphasising the importance of competent people.

[16] Elaborations of the Workplace Panel Survey (2015) show that in Korea, 3.2% of SMEs (with less than 250 employees) report that the most important reason for not implementing or supporting the training is lack of understanding from management.

[17] Partly related to the poor offer and quality of entrepreneurship education available, only 24.1% of women and 38.7% of men in Korea (aged 18-64) say that they have the knowledge and skills to start a business – one of the lowest values in the OECD (OECD/EU, 2017[38]).

[18] Considered the high share of SMEs in the Korean economy (see Chapter 1), these results could point to the fact that many adults (including many older people who go on "honorary retirement" relatively early in their careers) start a new business out of necessity even if they do not feel that they have the skills to do so.

[19] Before the implementation of the policy, the minimum wage in Korea was already relatively high at 53% of median wages in 2017, above the OECD average of 51%.

[20] Source: OECD Labour Database.

[21] This subsidy is the primary channel for incumbent workers to develop and improve their job skills in Korea. On top of financing vocational training for incumbent workers, the Employment Insurance also finances employment security programme to retain or create jobs, as well as unemployment benefits.

[22] Employer-provide training includes five programmes that provide training subsidies to employers: (1) subsidy for employer-provided training, (2) National HRD consortium, (3) region-industry tailored training, (4) Work and Study dual system (5) Stepping stone to employment programme. The budgets and the number of beneficiaries of these programmes are managed and open in one category: employer-provided training.

[23] All currency conversions are based on the exchange of 31 December 2018: EUR 1 = KRW 1 278 38.

[24] While there is no limit to the support period, the maximum amount varies depending on the operation period. Also, the duty fulfilment period of consortium businesses is 6 years after receiving support for training facilities and equipment. If the business is suspended or cancelled before this period ends, they must pay back the subsidies received.

3 Encouraging workers in SMEs to train

Adult learning is important to help workers in SMEs to be ready for the structural changes that lie ahead. However, in Korea, workers in SMEs lag considerably behind workers in larger companies when it comes to access to training. On top of receiving less training from their employers, workers in SMEs also face additional barriers, including lack of time, limited information on training options, and lack of financial resources. This chapter highlights the specific training obstacles that SME workers face.

In Brief

Adult learning is key for SME workers

On top of receiving less training from their employers, SME workers also face additional obstacles to training compared to workers in large firms, such as lack of time, limited information on training options, and lack of financial resources. This chapter analyses the barriers to training that SME workers face. The key findings of the chapter can be summarised as follows:

- Lack of time is the number one training barrier for SME workers. Among SME workers who wanted to participate (more) in training but did not, 63% cited lack of time (for work or family responsibilities) as a key barrier – by far the highest share in the OECD area. Education and training leave, distance learning, modular learning, and recognition of prior learning, are all policy tools that can help (SME) workers to overcome time-related barriers to training. Korea already have these policies in place, but take-up by (SME) workers is rather limited.
- Low-wages put SME workers at a significant disadvantage when it comes to attending training. Some 15% of SME workers who wanted to participate in (more) training did not, because training was too expensive for them, compared to only 6% of workers in larger firms. Korea already provides various financial incentives for SME workers to reduce training costs. One key challenge is that SME workers – compared to workers in large firms – are less likely to benefit from public financial support for training, partly because they are often not eligible (e.g. they are not covered by Employment Insurance).
- Limited information is another key reason for not training, and particularly so for SME workers who cannot rely on the support for their employers for guidance and advice on learning options. Career guidance in Korea is mainly focussed on young students, older people, and the unemployed, while services for incumbent workers are piecemeal and generally less developed. Online career guidance options exist but are scattered across different websites and data sources.

Introduction

Despite the potential benefits of training, Korean SME workers lag considerably behind workers in larger companies when it comes to access to adult learning. Not only SME workers receive less training by their employers (see Chapter 2), they also face additional barriers to training participation. While these barriers are shared by all workers, they can be particularly burdensome for SME workers. The next sections discuss the most important barriers that prevent many SME workers from training, including lack of time, little financial resources, and limited information on training options. This chapter is structured as follows. Section 3.1 highlights how lack of time represent a key barrier to training for many SME workers. Section 3.2 looks at the financial barriers to training they are facing. Section 3.3 analyses lack of information on the available learning options as an additional barrier to training.

3.1. Lack of time

In Korea, one of the key reasons why SMEs workers do not participate in formal or non-formal training is because they lack time – be it for work or family/childcare responsibilities. Stakeholders interviewed in the context of this project reported that lack of time is probably the number one training barrier for SME workers. Existing evidence also corroborates these arguments. Indeed, elaborations of PIAAC data show that in Korea, among SME workers who wanted to participate (more) in training but did not, 52% cited being too busy at work as a key barrier to training – well above the OECD average of 32% and above any other OECD country. Another 11% cited lack of time because of childcare or family responsibilities as a key barrier to training (more) – against an OECD average of 13% (Figure 3.1).

Figure 3.1. Lack of time as a key barrier for training among SME workers

Percentage of SME workers who wanted to participate (more) in training, but did not because of lack of time

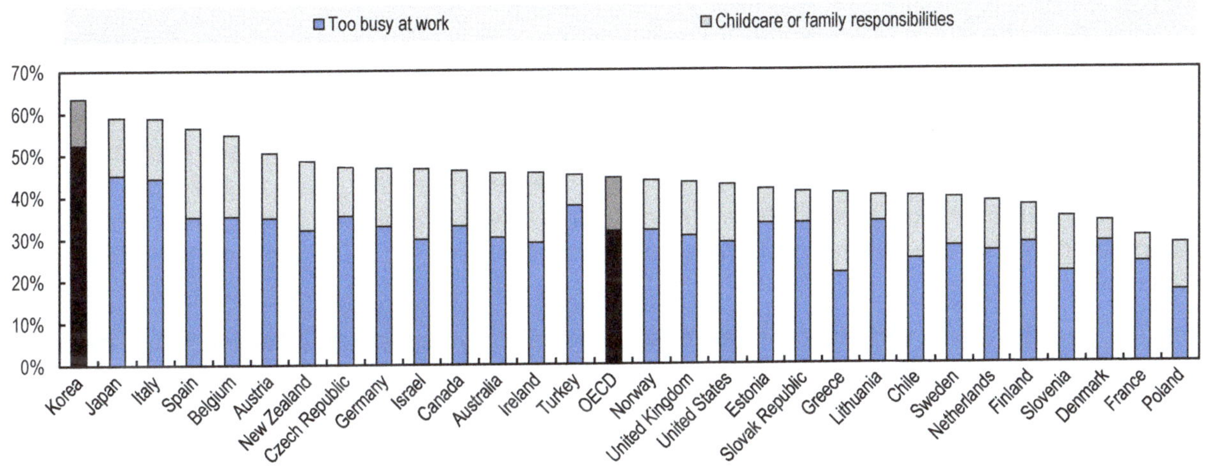

Note: Data refers only to workers in SMEs (250 employees or less).
Source: OECD Secretariat calculations based on the Survey of Adult Skills, PIAAC (2012, 2015).

Lack of time to train reflects a combination of factors. To some extent, it reflects the fact that SMEs often lack staff and experience great difficulties in freeing up time for their employees to undertake training (see Chapter 2). It also reflects traditionally long working hours in SMEs and existing regulation on working time (see Chapter 2). On top of policy measures that tackle SMEs' personnel shortages and balance working hours, there are other policy measures that can help SME workers to combine more effectively their work and family responsibilities with education and training. These include education and training leave, flexible learning provision (e.g. distance learning), as well as modular learning and recognition of prior learning. These policies are discussed in the following sections.

3.1.1. Education and training leave

Education and training leave, i.e. a regulatory instrument which sets out the conditions under which employees may be granted time away from work for learning purposes, is a key policy to mitigate the time-related barriers to employees' training.

Like in many other OECD countries, in Korea workers are allowed to take education and training leave, upon the employer's approval. Korea provides financial compensation for employers that grant paid education and training leave to their workers and meet certain eligibility requirements. In line with best practices found in some OECD countries, subsidies cover not only direct training costs, but also indirect costs (i.e. workers and replacements' wages). Moreover, SMEs benefit from more flexible eligibility criteria and more generous subsidies compared to large firms (see Chapter 2).[1]

Empirical evidence suggests that the education and training leave can improve SME workers' productivity and help firms cover training costs. For example, Lee (2010[1]) finds that SME workers in Korea show higher job satisfaction, organisational commitment, skill level, job performance and cooperation skills after completing paid training leave programmes.

Despite the generous subsidies provided to SMEs, and the positive results associated with their use, education and training leave remains rather under-used in Korea. In 2017, only around 18 800 workers used the leave,[2] accounting for roughly 6% of the employed population.

Low take-up of education and training leave is a challenge that other OECD countries are also facing. In Japan, only 10% of the employers have introduced the education and training leave system.[3] In European Union countries, the take-up of training leave is as high as 2% and as low 0.01% of total employment in Spain (OECD, 2019[2]; CEDEFOP, 2012[3]; Stone, 2010[4]).

There are several reasons as to why the education and training leave is rarely used by Korean (SME) workers. First of all, sometimes workers are simply not aware of its existence. Those who know about the scheme may feel reluctant to request it – conscious that their employers would struggle to secure a replacement worker and that their leave could put excessive burdens on colleagues. Another related challenge is the duration of the leave: in order for SMEs to receive the public subsidy, training should last at least 5 days (20 hours) but often SMEs are unable to free up workers' time for such long periods of time. Low up-take may also reflect the fact that SMEs can reject the request, e.g. if training is not directly relevant to the firm.

One policy option worth considering is to make approval of education and training leave requests compulsory for employers, either by law or through collective agreements. In this way, SME workers would not have to rely upon the goodwill of their employer to use the scheme. Some OECD countries have already started to bound firms to grant education and training leave to their employees (Italy; United Kingdom; Portugal; France) (see Box 3.1).

In Korea, there have already been attempts to make the paid educational and training leave a legal right for workers. In 2007, the Korean National Assembly submitted a 'Draft of the Lifelong Education Act' mandating that employers should allow their workers to take up to 10 days of paid education leave per year. Employers opposed this proposal for fear of increased labour costs, and the draft was never adopted (Oh, Park and Jo, 2016[5]). Since then, discussions on the rights to learn for workers have been continuously conducted. For example, the revision of the Equal Employment Opportunity and Work-Family Balance Assistance Act (on August 2019) institutionalised the right to claim the reduction of working hours on the ground of learning. This is a step in the right direction and Korea may further consider making paid education and training leave a legal right for workers, or at least start re-opening the debate while seeking buy-in from social partners.

To increase the take-up of education and training leave, Korea should:

- *Raise awareness on the existence of education and training leave options among SMEs and SME workers.*
- *Make paid educational and training leave a legal right for workers* or at least re-open the debate on this issue while seeking buy-in from the social partners. This measure should be combined with job rotation schemes to help SMEs to find replacement workers (see Chapter 2).

Box 3.1. Statutory rights to education and training leave across OECD countries

- In the **United Kingdom**, workers (in firms with more than 250 employees)[4] have a statutory right to request education and training leave (i.e. *Right to Request Time to Train*), if training improves the employee's effectiveness in the employer's business, and the performance of the employer's business. Employers are required to give due consideration to such requests and to respond in writing within certain time limits (28 days), and can refuse requests only for a number of recognised business reasons (gov.UK, n.a.[6]).[5]
- In **Italy**, according to a recent collective agreement, since January 2017 all firms in the metalwork industry have to provide 24 hours of training to each worker, every three years. In the absence of training, the worker has the right to participate to external training activities, for which two-thirds of the cost should be borne by the firm up to a maximum of EUR 300 (OECD, 2019[7]).
- In 2009, **Portugal** introduced legislation requiring employers to provide a minimum amount of professional training to their employees annually. Every employee is entitled to a yearly minimum of 35 hours of education and training, which may be postponed for up to two years. Cumulatively, employers are required to give training to a minimum of 10% of their workforce annually. The cost of training is mostly borne by employers (OECD, 2018[8]).
- In **France**, the Individual Training Account for job transitions *(CPF de transition)* allows workers to take time to participate to training with a view to find a new job. Training does not need to be linked to the workers' current job. Workers need to request the *CPF de transition* to the firm, and the employer has 30 days to give a reply. The leave can be delayed for a maximum of 9 months. The delay should be claimed only under certain circumstances, e.g. if the workers' absence undermines the firm's ability to maintain business activities, or in case the number of workers requesting leave at the same time is above a critical threshold set by law: 2% of workers for larger firms (100 workers or more) and 1 worker at a time in smaller firms (100 firms or less). The level of wages paid during the leave depends on various factors, including previous wages, and in some cases (if the wage base is twice the minimum wage or more) the length of the training leave (French Ministry of Labour, 2019[9]). It is worth mentioning that even though employers cannot deny the request for training leave, many requests are rejected by the institutions financing the training, due to limited resources. In 2016, the acceptance rate was 58.5%.

3.1.2. Distance learning

Distance learning is another policy tool to tackle time-related barriers to training and as such it offers growing opportunities for SME workers to close the training gap with workers in large firms. By allowing workers to train at any time and in any place, distance learning could help SME workers to fit training into their busy schedules,[6] while making it possible to take better account of SMEs organisational problems and barriers for training (see Chapter 2) (OECD, 2019[2]; OECD, 2018[10]).

In Korea, the distance learning system is already quite developed. Today a variety of distance education courses are offered by the Korea National Open University (KNOU), cyber universities, traditional universities[7] (Zawacki-Richter and Qayyum, 2019[11]) as well as private training providers. These training programmes target both youth and adult learners. For example, around 70% of the KNOU's students are workers (Yang and Yorozu, 2015[12]).

Distance learning is widely used in Korea (OECD, 2019[13]). According to PIAAC data, 37% of SME workers in Korea state that one of their (non-formal) education and training activities in the past 12 months was organised as distance learning, the highest value in the OECD after Lithuania and Poland, and well above the OECD average of 19% (Figure 3.2).

Figure 3.2. Distance learning, by firm size

Percentage of workers who state that one of their (non-formal) education and training activities in the past 12 months was organised as distance learning

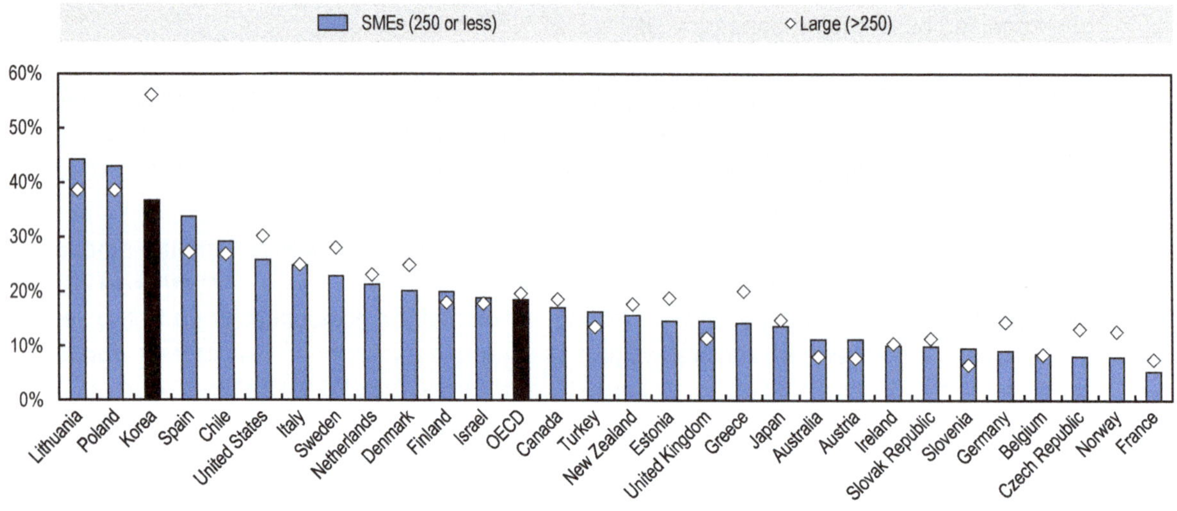

Source: OECD Secretariat calculations based on the Survey of Adult Skills, PIAAC (2012, 2015).

The wide use of distance learning in Korea reflects the plethora of e-learning options available, as well as other factors such as high internet penetration,[8] and a modular learning system that allows individuals to obtain full degrees through online courses. [9]

Despite this positive picture, there is still room for SMEs to catch up with distance learning practices already adopted in larger companies. Indeed, PIAAC data shows that while in OECD countries there is a small variation between larger and smaller firms in the extent to which workers use distance learning, in Korea this gap is very large (19 percentage points) (Figure 3.2).

Other Korean national surveys confirm that e-learning remains much less used in SMEs than in larger firms. For example, elaborations from the Human Capital Corporate Panel Survey show that, in 2016, only around 20% of workers in SMEs participated to e-learning, three times less than workers in firms with 1 000 or more employees (Figure 3.3). It is likely that e-learning is even less widespread in smaller firms (with less than 100 employees), who are not covered by this survey.

Figure 3.3. Types of training programme attended by workers, Korea

Percentage of workers who participated in training by method, by firm size, 2016

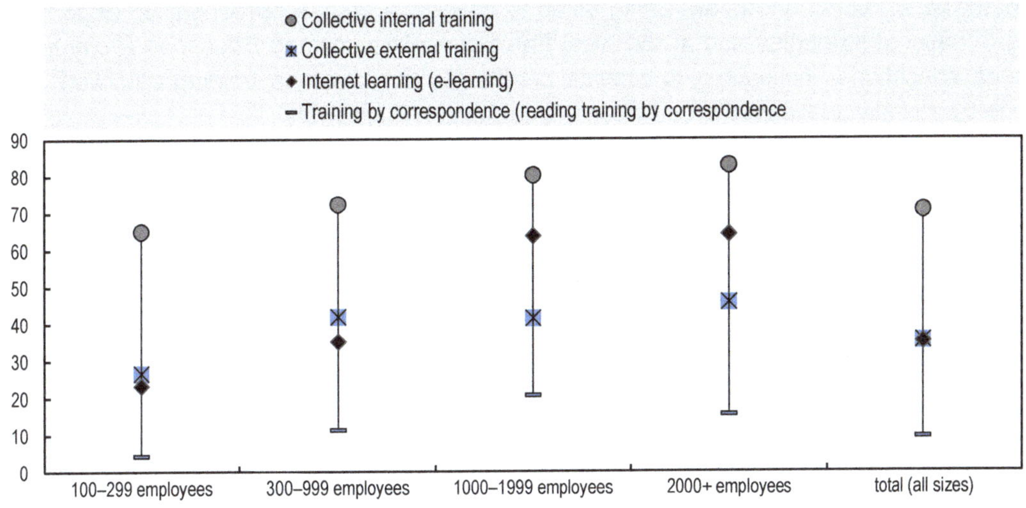

Note: Multiple answers possible.
Source: KRIVET elaborations of the Human Capital Corporate Panel Survey (7th wave, 2017).

While Korea has already paved the way for the development and expansion of e-learning, some key challenges lie ahead. One issue is that workers with low digital skills – such as older workers, or the low-skilled – often struggle to use distance learning options. These workers are often over-represented in smaller firms (see Chapter 1 and 4) so improving their basic digital skills will be key to favour a greater use of distance learning in SMEs.

Another issue is that SME workers can struggle to navigate the plethora of distance learning options available. They often cannot rely on the support of their employer for advice and guidance, and have to look for this type of courses independently. Several online platforms allow individuals to access high-quality e-learning options, but without assistance, SME workers can easily get lost between platforms that are exclusively dedicated to distance learning (K-MOOC; Smart Tech Education Platform), and websites that provide information on both traditional training and e-learning (HRD-net, Neulbaeum) (see Section 3.3).

Further expand access to distance learning to SME workers. This should be done by encouraging SMEs to provide further e-learning opportunities to workers and improving the basic digital skills of vulnerable groups – older workers, or the low-skilled – who are over-represented in SMEs. This would favour a greater use of distance learning among all SME workers, including the most disadvantaged.

3.1.3. Modular learning and recognition of prior learning

Modular approaches are helpful in providing adult learners with greater flexibility on their learning path and can be combined with processes for the recognition of prior learning. They permit learners to combine more easily work with training outside of work – and as such they can help workers tackle time-related barriers to learning. These measures are particularly relevant for SME workers, who often have lower qualifications but may have acquired skills through work experience.

Many universities in Korea today have lifelong learning centres that allow individuals to gain credits little by little until they receive the full qualification. Maister Schools also already apply modular training options.

However, there is still a long way to go to improve modular adult learning across the board and increase its usage. While the Ministry of Education recognises this challenge, there is still not any concrete formal plans to expand the modular learning system further.

On the other hand, recent efforts are being taken to develop a system of recognition of prior learning – including in national strategies and in the legal framework. The *Lifelong Education Promotion Strategy* encourages educational institutions to provide credits for any previous training and work experience undergone by an individual based on a National Qualification Framework.

Recognition of Prior Learning was also made institutionary possible through the revision of the law in 2017. To encourage the use of Recognition of Prior Learning practices, the *fourth National Lifelong Learning Promotion Plan* (2018-2022) launched a trial operation of Match Up, a programme targeted to students, job seekers, and employees that allow them to have their job skills certified from companies in their relevant fields. Match Up aims to operate 50 programmes by 2022 (NILE, 2018[14]).

Despite these positive efforts, the Korean Recognition of Prior Learning System is still in its early stages of development. Korea could learn from the experience of OECD countries, such as France (see Box 3.2), that have a longer history of Recognition of Prior Learning.

Expand modular learning options in formal education and strengthen the Recognition of Prior Learning system. These options permit learners to combine more easily work with training outside of work – and as such they can help SME workers tackle time-related barriers to learning.

Box 3.2. The Recognition of Prior Learning System in France

In 2001, France has started developing a tool for recognition of prior learning (*Validation des Acquis de l'Expérience*, VAE). VAE allows individuals to obtain qualifications that are registered in the National directory of professional certificates (RNCP), by showing they have acquired the necessary skills through work experience.

The VAE can lead to a full or partial recognition. In the latter case, additional training or work experience is needed to obtain the full qualification. Individuals can receive help in preparing their file and in preparing for the jury evaluation. The VAE procedure can be done within the framework of existing training policies, such as the Individual Learning Account (CPF). Additionally, employees can request specific VAE leave (*congé de VAE*).

In 2015 about 42 000 individuals participated in a VAE process to acquire a public qualification, of which almost 60% obtained a full qualification.[10] Among certifying ministries, the Ministry of Education had the highest number of VAE applicants (53% of all applicants), followed by the Ministry of Health and Social Affairs (20%).

Source: OECD (2017[15]), Getting Skills Right: France, OECD Publishing, Paris, https://doi.org/10.1787/9789264284456-en.

3.2. Lack of financial resources

Like in other OECD countries, many workers in Korea decide not to train because they cannot afford it. The direct costs of learning, such as tuition fees and learning materials, may be unaffordable for workers. Attending training may also imply additional indirect costs, including costs for transportation, accommodation, or expenses for the care of children or any other dependants. On top of direct and indirect training costs, workers may also face opportunity costs (e.g. foregone wages during learning periods), which can further discourage training participation.

This situation is exacerbated in SMEs. Analysis of PIAAC data shows that in Korea cost was a barrier to participation for 15% of SME workers (more), compared to only 6% of workers in larger firms (Figure 3.4). These shares are slightly lower than the OECD average, yet Korea lags behind the best performing countries such as Norway, Germany and Finland.

Figure 3.4. Lack of financial resources as a barrier for training, by firm size

Percentage of workers who wanted to participate (more) in training, but did not because too expensive

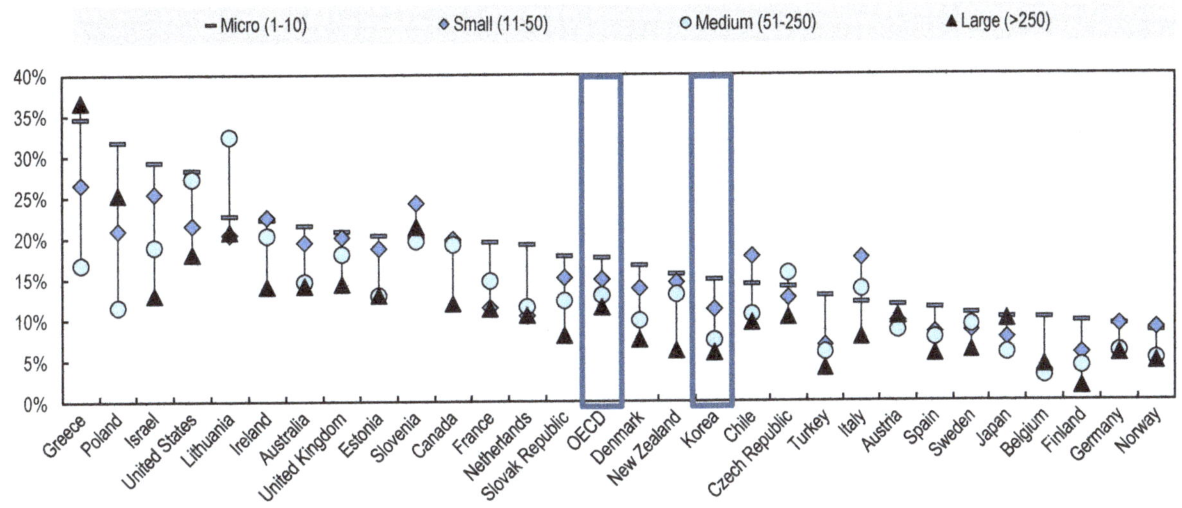

Source: OECD Secretariat calculations based on the Survey of Adult Skills, PIAAC (2012, 2015).

There are several reasons as to why many SME workers perceive training costs as a barrier to learning – much more than workers in large companies. Training costs may be unaffordable for SME workers who on average earn lower wages and have fewer savings. In this context, even moderate course fees and indirect costs to learning can pose a barrier to participation.

Another challenge is that SME workers privately pay for training more often, because they are less often beneficiary of employer-provided training, compared to large firms' workers. Different data sources corroborates these insights. The Korean Labor and Income Panel Survey (19th wave) data shows that in micro-firms, 19% of training workers paid for training themselves, a rate that drops to 8% in small firms and further down to 6% and 1% in medium-sized and large firms respectively.

Similarly, PIAAC data shows that, in Korea, SME workers are less likely to receive financial support for learning activities when compared to Korean workers in larger firms, as well as compared to SME workers in other OECD countries (Figure 3.5). In micro-firms only 56% of training participants have received funding from their employer for (formal or non-formal) learning activities (the 4th lowest value in the OECD), compared to 58% in small firms (OECD average 87%), 70% in medium-sized firms (OECD average 89%), and 75% in large firms (OECD average 91%). Interestingly, in Korea the extent of employer support varies greatly with firm size, a pattern that is not commonly found in the OECD area. The gap between workers in micro- and large firms is 19 percentage points, against an OECD average of 8 percentage points and indeed the highest gap in the OECD after Greece (22 percentage points), at par with Chile and Turkey.

Figure 3.5. Employer-sponsored training, by firm size

Percentage of training participants who have received funding by their employer for (formal or non-formal) learning activities

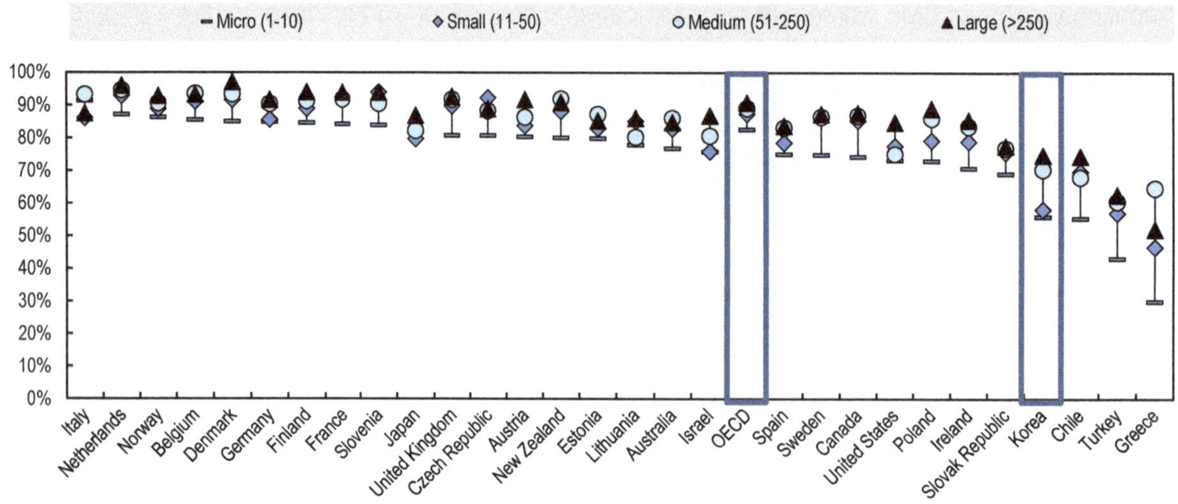

Note: data exclude those who had no employer or prospective employer at that time; and those for whom there were no such costs.
Source: OECD Secretariat calculations based on the Survey of Adult Skills, PIAAC (2012, 2015).

To address these challenges and ensure that lack of money is not a barrier to training for SME workers, Korea has put in place several financial incentives for workers – such as the *My Work Learning Card System for workers* and loans for living costs (see Annex 3.A). These financial incentives often provide preferential treatment for SME workers.

However, not all SME workers are able to use these schemes. One key challenge is that many SME workers are not covered by Employment Insurance and therefore are not eligible to access subsidised training programmes (Yoo, 2011[16]).[11] In 2018, 94.3% of regular workers and 68.5% of non-regular workers in SMEs (less than 300 employees) were covered by Employment Insurance, against respectively 95.9% and 96% in larger firms (300 employees or more) (Figure 3.6).

Other SME workers may be unable to benefit from financial incentives/publicly funded training programmes because they do not meet eligibility criteria, notably on minimum training hours. For example, the *Loan for living costs during vocational training* (see Annex 2.A) gives higher priority to individuals who plan to participate in long training programmes: the longer the training, the higher the scores given to candidates, with full scores given to training that lasts over six months. While it is reasonable to give higher scores to individuals who have no earnings for long periods due to long-term training, this rule obviously penalises many SME workers who are unable to train for such a long time while keeping their job (see Chapter 2).

Another possible explanation is that there are not enough subsidised valuable learning options (Chapter 4). According to stakeholders interviewed in the context of this project, some publicly subsidised training programmes in high demand (e.g. coding) have long waiting lists, and workers have to decide whether to pay out of pocket or wait for a free spot to become available.

Korea has put in place policy measures to address these challenges. For example, in January 2019, the government expanded the coverage of subsidised vocational training to workers who are not enrolled in Employment Insurance, including many workers in SMEs (OECD, 2019[17]). This measure is financed through general account public resources.

Figure 3.6. Workers' coverage of employment insurance

Share of workers covered by employment insurance by firm size and type of employment, 2006-18

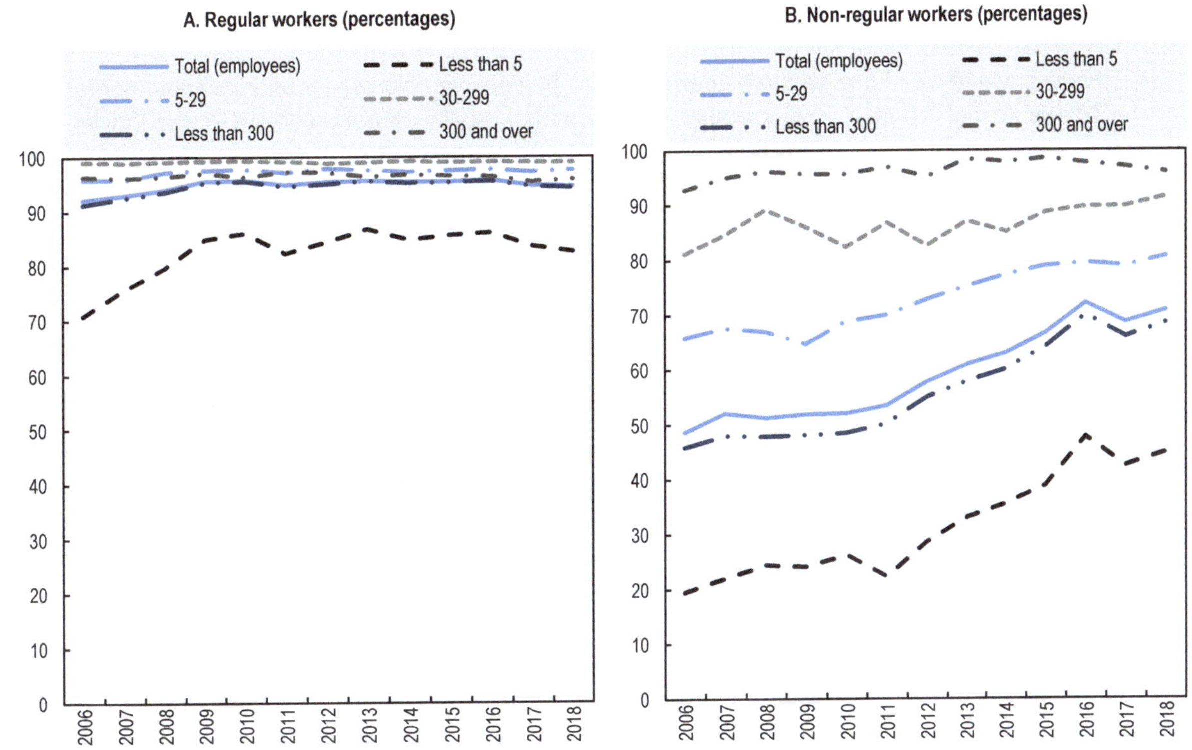

Note: Data on non-regular workers exclude independent contract workers.
Source: Ministry of Employment and Labor (MOEL), Survey on Labor Conditions by employment type, 2006-18.

As another example, in March of 2019, the government announced plans to reform the *My Work Learning Card System*. As of 2020, the existing training account systems for the unemployed and the employed will be integrated into one card system, the *National Learning Card System*. All individuals will be able to enrol in the lifelong learning card and develop their vocational skills regardless of their employment status and whether they have enrolled in the Employment Insurance or not. The card validity period will be increased from 1-3 years (in existing systems) to 5 years, and the amount of support will be increased from KRW 2-3 million per person (approximately EUR 1500-2300) to KRW 3-5 million (approximately EUR 2300-3800). This reform is expected to increase the participation in vocational training among vulnerable people including non-standard workers, who are overrepresented in SMEs, as well as the self-employed.

Similarly to Korea, France has also put in place individual learning accounts (ILAs) targeted to all adults regardless of employment status. These schemes aim to empower individuals to train irrespective of their employment status and attachment. However, a recent OECD study on ILAs shows that careful design is key to obtain high take-up, increase training participation of vulnerable groups, and minimise deadweight losses (i.e. financing training that would have taken place even in the absence of the subsidy).[12]

Good practices for successful design of ILAs include: i) provide high-quality career guidance to help individuals make informed training decisions; (ii) strengthen quality assurance of training providers; (iii) foster the support of employers and a learning culture; (iv) provide financial support that is generous enough to encourage training participation; and (v) keep governance and processes simple (e.g. through well-designed and well-functioning web apps) (OECD, 2019[18]).

To ensure that lack of money is not a key barrier to training for SME workers, Korea should:

- *Continue expanding the coverage of Employment Insurance to all SME workers*. This would allow all SME workers to benefit from the financial incentives to train that are available conditional on EI coverage.
- *Facilitate take-up of the National Learning Card System and closely monitor its implementation.* To ensure high up-take, Korea should: i) provide high-quality career guidance to help individuals make informed training decisions; (ii) strengthen quality assurance of training providers; (iii) foster the support of employers and a learning culture; (iv) provide financial support that is generous enough to encourage training participation; and (v) keep governance and processes simple (e.g. through well-designed and well-functioning web apps). The results of this programme should be also closely monitored.

3.3. Lack of information

One of the reasons why many SME workers do not train is that they lack information. They may be unaware of the benefits of training, may not know what training options are available, or be unsure about what training programmes are of good quality and bring best results. This may be a challenge particularly for SME workers, who cannot rely on the support of their employers for career advice and information on training options.

Partially as a result of this lack of information, Korean SMEs workers seem to have low motivation and willingness to train – in line with patterns observed in other OECD countries. According to PIAAC data, 35% of SME workers in Korea did not participate (further) in training but reported that, over the previous 12 months, there were learning activities that they would have wanted to participate in. Although this is share higher than the OECD average of 25% (Figure 3.7), the majority of SME workers in Korea are still not willing to train (further) – pointing to the need to invest in policies to increase their engagement in learning.[13]

Figure 3.7. Willingness to train by group, by firm size

Percentage of workers who did not participate in (further) training but would have liked to

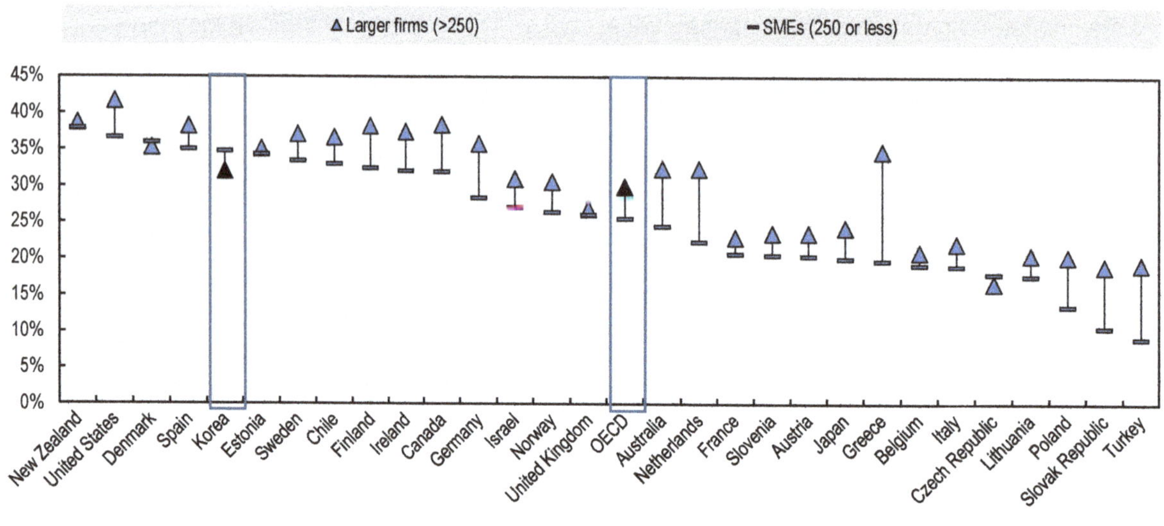

Note: Share of adults who did not participate (further) in training but report that, over the previous 12 months, there were learning activities that they would have wanted to participate in.
Source: OECD Secretariat calculations based on the Survey of Adult Skills, PIAAC (2012, 2015).

Career guidance services could potentially help SME workers to better understand their training needs and navigate the plethora of training opportunities available to them. These services are particularly important for SME workers who often cannot count on the guidance typically provided by HR departments in larger firms, nor can they afford private counselling. Moreover, career guidance is particularly useful for SME workers who tend to change jobs more frequently (see Chapter 1) and may need advice during job transitions.

Career guidance in Korea is mainly focussed on young students, older people, and the unemployed, while services for incumbent workers are piecemeal and generally less developed (Hooley, 2019[19]).

Career guidance for incumbent workers can in theory be provided by public employment services (PES). However, PES career guidance services face several limitations:

- First, there is a shortage of PES counsellors. With a caseload of more than 600 registered jobseekers per staff, PES counsellors are often overloaded and unable to deliver adequate career guidance to workers (Yang, 2015[20]; OECD, 2018[10]).
- The Korean PES administration is seriously under-resourced by international standards: public expenditures on PES administration (e.g. delivering services, dealing with clients) account for 0.04% of GDP, the fourth lowest share in the OECD area and well below the OECD average of 0.13%.
- The bulk of the PES counsellors' work revolves around the unemployed and jobseekers, rather than incumbent workers. Data on PES career guidance services delivered to unemployed/workers is not available, but anecdotal evidence suggests that incumbent workers are given less priority.
- Existing rules oblige the unemployed to consult with PES counsellors for training advice, while these obligations do not apply to workers. As a result, it is likely that workers rely much less on PES counselling services than the unemployed. For example, the unemployed are required to consult with PES counsellors to make use of the Individual Training Account (ITA), while employees can apply for the ITA online without having to consult a PES counsellor first (see Section 3.2).
- PES counsellors are not always well-placed to guide workers in their training decisions. They focus on minimising moral hazard and promoting training provided by the government, but they are not trained to understand the rapid changes that are taking place in the labour market and to advice workers accordingly.

Beyond the PES, other public institutions in Korea provide career guidance to workers. However, these organisations are often targeted at disadvantaged workers. For example, *Job Hope Centres* are mainly targeted at older workers approaching retirement age and willing to prepare for a second career. Similarly, the *Korea Job World* – an institution designed to help people obtain a realistic view about possible professional choices and prospects, and to give career advice based on individual interests and aptitude – is open to all, but is mainly focussed on youth.[14]

Public career guidance aside, companies could also play a key role in providing training counselling services to their employees. They could advise workers on career progression opportunities within the firm, and guide them through available training options that would help them seize such opportunities. However, Korean firms – and SMEs in particular – are rarely involved in career guidance. According to the Workplace Panel Survey data, only 2.1% of small firms (1-49 employees) implemented career counselling[15] as a programme for career development, compared to 19.8% of medium-sized firms (50-249) and 28.1% of large firms (250+) in 2015. Korea could learn from the experience of France, where employers have to set up, every two years, a professional meeting (*entretien professionnel*) to discuss the career progression and training opportunities with their employees (Box 3.4).

Beyond face-to-face career guidance services, online career guidance platforms can also help workers to make informed training decisions. Korea counts numerous online career guidance platforms that provide information on training programmes. These include HRD-net, *Neulbaeum*, regional lifelong learning portals, and Q-Net. Two online career guidance platforms are specifically designed to provide access to, and information on, e-learning programmes: K-MOOC and Smart Training Education Platform (see Box 3.3 for a description of these websites).

Box 3.3. Online platforms on training programmes: Korea

HRD-net

In Korea, the most notable example of online platforms on training programmes is HRD-net, a website launched in 2002 by the MoEL that provides a wealth of information on subsidised training programmes available, including on the duration of the course, training costs, as well as training quality information (OECD, 2019[13]; OECD, 2017[21]). HRD-net is a successful example of an online database on adult learning: it counts over 11 million members (as of May 2018) and around 160 000 visits per day, and it acquired the Web Accessibility Quality Mark in 2018.[16]

Neulbaeum

Neulbaeum, established in 2014, provides online (and offline) lifelong education information, including learning opportunities, learning outcomes and information on training centres. It collects and consolidates data from 17 regional lifelong learning centres on a single platform. 67 institutions and 830 000 courses are registered on the platform in Korea.

Q-Net

Q-net provides general information on the qualification system and how it has changed. It also provides basic information on how to obtain qualifications. Q-net provides a customised service for users by recommending qualifications he/she might be interested in and providing information on benefits people enjoy after obtaining qualifications and careers related to the qualification.

Regional lifelong learning portals

Similar to the "*Neulbaeum*" at the national level, each region operates regional lifelong learning portals, which provide lifelong learning information and courses. For example, Seoul lifelong learning portal provides information on lectures related to employment/qualification, foreign languages, family/health, hobbies/culture, and ICT.

K-MOOC

K-MOOC is a national platform developed in 2015 and operated by the National Institute for Lifelong Education (NILE), where universities can offer their distance learning courses (Bandalaria, 2018[22]). It has 357 000 registered users, and offers 776 000 courses. In the future, there are plans to introduce paid services, favor exchange with other international MOOC courses, and completion of the courses are to be consolidated into the Academic Credit Bank System. There is also a willingness to expand the training offer further: one of the goals of the 'fourth National Lifelong Learning Promotion Plan (2018-22)' is to develop 30 new courses each year after 2019 (NILE, 2018[14]).

Smart Training Education Platform (STEP)

Smart Training Education Platform (STEP) is a platform launched in October 2019 by the Ministry of Employment and Labour (MoEL) which provides comprehensive information on e-learning programmes and supports the infrastructure to facilitate the operation of training programmes that integrated on/offline courses. Starting from 2020, more than 200 training contents will be newly added every year.

Although they play an important role in disseminating information on adult learning and facilitating access to training, these platforms face several challenges. For example, *Neulbaeum* has a user-friendly interface, but its usage is limited. In 2018, the annual number of visitors in Neulbaeum was 175 578 people (MoE/NILE, 2019[23]). K-MOOC provides high-quality distance learning lectures, but completion rate remains low, at 8.8% (Soo-jin, 2017[24]).

Also HRD-net, which is considered a case of best practice and was awarded the Web Accessibility Quality Mark in 2018, faces several limitations. First, HRD-net does not include information on all training programmes available. For example, it includes only programmes provided under the aegis of certain ministries (mainly MoEL) and excludes training programmes provided by local governments. Secondly, HRD-net can be difficult to navigate for workers and could be made more user-friendly.[17]

Another key challenge is that workers may struggle to navigate the numerous competing online career guidance platforms available. There is a plethora of Skills Assessment and Anticipation (SAA) information – conducted by different institutions, but this information is scattered across different sources (see Chapter 5). This fragmentation is symptomatic of a coordination failure in adult learning, and is partly due to the fact that career guidance is under the supervision of different ministries, including the Ministry of Education and the Ministry of Employment and Labor, while regional authorities also have a role to play (Chapter 5).

Going forward, Korea should adopt a one-stop shop solution that brings these platforms together. This would avoid duplication, minimise overlaps, and help users navigate training options in an easy way. A one-stop shop solution would also help the government develop an administrative information system on adult learning, which could track individuals' history of participation in different training programmes.[18] Korea could learn from the experience of OECD countries that have already taken steps in this direction (see Box 3.5).

The Korean government is already taking action to improve career guidance. For example, as of 2019, the MoEL is developing the next generation Work-net and HRD-net to be more user-friendly, to enhance their linkages with other databases (e.g. Employment Insurance Database), and to offer more comprehensive information on training programmes (including training programmes of ministries other than MoEL).

Going forward, further efforts will be needed in Korea to provide better career guidance to workers. Strengthening career guidance will become all the more important in the future, as Korea is progressively trying to shift the responsibility to train away from firms and towards workers, notably through the implementation of the *National Learning Card System*, a training subsidy that is given to all workers regardless of employment status (see Annex 3.A and section 3.2). The international experience shows that to be successful, schemes of this type need to be combined with efforts to support workers in their training decisions through quality career guidance (OECD, 2019[25]; OECD, 2019[18]).

Improving career guidance to (SME) workers will require efforts to:

- *Expand public career guidance services beyond traditional target groups* (jobseekers; the unemployed) and towards incumbent workers. This includes better preparing the PES to provide career guidance to workers, as well as putting in place public career guidance services dedicated to all workers.
- *Encourage company career guidance provision*, particularly in smaller firms. Firms could advise workers on career progression opportunities within the firm, and guide them through available training options that would help them seize such opportunities. Public authorities together with employer representative bodies should collaborate in providing information to SMEs and their workers on the availability of career guidance services.
- *Create a one-stop-shop online career guidance platform*. Existing Skills Assessment and Anticipation (SAA) information should be put together in one place. This would avoid duplication, minimise overlaps, and help users navigate learning options in an easy way.

Box 3.4. Career guidance for workers in selected OECD countries

Public career guidance

- In **France**, the Advice for Professional Development (*Conseil en Évolution Professionnelle*, CEP) was launched in 2014, offering free and personalised career advice to assist individuals in their professional development. Individuals who decide to pursue a career change are offered support to develop their career. More specifically, individuals can benefit from a one-to-one meeting to analyse their professional situation; they can get advice to define their career objectives and they can receive support on implementing their career plans. The CEP is available for all employed and unemployed individuals. In principle, workers can access the CEP outside of working hours, although collective agreements can allow the CEP to take place during working hours. All employees can participate at their own initiative in CEP without having to inform their employer. Employers need to inform their employees of the existence of the CEP, for instance in the context of the professional interview (*entretien professionnel*) (The Adecco Group, 2019[26]; OECD, 2017[27]).[19]
- In **Luxembourg**, the House of Guidance (*Maison de l'Orientation*) opened in 2012 following the collective effort of five departments across the Ministries of Education, Labour and Higher Education. The house provides a one-stop shop for education and labour market orientation. Previously targeted at a younger age group, there has been a greater focus on adult learners since 2017.

Private / company career guidance

- In **France**, employers have to set up a professional meeting (*entretien professionnel*) every two years, in which they discuss career progression opportunities with their employees and the training that can advance these opportunities (OECD, 2017[27]). Every six years, the meeting needs to include a review of the professional pathway of the employee, to show whether the employee has benefitted from the professional meetings in the last six years. When the six-year review shows that an employer did not organise the required bi-annual meetings, or when no sufficient career progression options were provided to the employee, medium-sized and large firms can be sanctioned. Work councils (*Comité d'entreprise*), individual employees and labour inspectors all play a role in detecting infringements. Sufficient career progression options are defined as having benefited from at least two out of three career progression actions: i) participation in at least one training course, ii) acquisition of at least one professional certificate, either through training or through Recognition of Prior Learning (called VAE), and iii) salary or professional progression. Sanctions take the form of additional contributions to the employee's Individual Learning Account (CPF) that need to be paid by the employer to the relevant training fund. However, smaller firms are less likely to provide professional interviews than larger companies: 25% of workers in micro-firms (less than 10 employees), less than 50% of workers in small firms (10-49 employees), and 75% of workers in large firms (250 or more employees) benefit from professional interviews in France.

Box 3.5. One-stop-shop online career guidance platform: good practices from OECD countries

Australia

The Australian myskills website (www.myskills.gov.au) allows users to consult available vocational training courses and providers within the proximity of a certain location. For each course the average course fee is provided, as well as information on whether or not subsidies or VET student loans are available. Details are also provided on the average duration of the course, students' satisfaction and the availability of online learning options. In addition, for each course the percentage of graduates in employment or further training is provided, as well as the percentage of graduates who improved their employment status and the median salary of graduates.

Canada

The Canadian Job Bank website (http://www.jobbank.gc.ca/home) allows users to search for occupations in specific regions or nation-wide. Key facts and figures about the occupations are provided in the following areas: wages, outlook, jobs, requirements and skills. For example, the detailed wage information shows median, high and low wages for the occupation in the selected region, province and Canada. The "jobs" part of the occupational profile allows users to consult available vacancies for the selected occupation and region. The job requirements section describes the education and training pathways. Finally, the website provides information on the skills and knowledge usually required in the occupation, and the degree to which nine essential skills (e.g. reading, digital technology) are used.

Denmark

The Danish website UddannelsesGuiden (www.ug.dk) brings together information on general education, higher education and adult/continuing education. It further includes information on the structure of the Danish labour market, the role of industries and businesses and descriptions of the most common occupations and jobs in the Danish labour market. Users can access further information and guidance via chat, phone or email.

New Zealand

The Ministry of Business, Innovation and Employment in New Zealand provides detailed information about labour supply and demand on its Occupation Outlook website (https://occupationoutlook.mbie.govt.nz/) (and mobile app). The list of occupations provides an attractive and easy-to-understand synthesis of the labour market and training information, showing an indication of wages in the occupation, training fees and job prospects. The website outlines how to enter each occupation, how many individuals are studying in related fields, how many are employed, and what the average incomes are. It also shows the prospects of getting a job in that occupation after completing the required qualification. In terms of income and employment prospects, information is provided about average wages, but also about past, current and prospective employment levels in the occupation. The outcomes of graduates for the qualification associated with the occupation are also provided, showing the share of graduates that are in employment, in further study, receiving benefits or are oversees (three years after completion).

Norway

The Norwegian Utdanning website (www.utdanning.no) provides information about occupations in the country. For each occupation, information is available on tasks, typical workplaces and soft skills (or personal characteristics) requirements. Interviews with workers in the occupation are presented to give a better understanding of what the job is like. The website also provides information about the qualification(s) associated with the occupation, data on the occupations in which individuals with the associated qualification are employed, and data on the educational profile of workers in the occupation. Additionally, the website shows information about average wages in the occupation, by gender and working time (fulltime or part-time). A useful feature of the website is that the number of firms that employ workers in a specific occupation and related occupations is shown (as well as the number of workers), and users can easily access information about the employers by region.

Scotland (United Kingdom)

The Scottish My World of Work website (http://www.myworldofwork.co.uk/) brings together information on careers, education and training programmes and job vacancies. For example, the website describes the types of tasks usually done in each occupation, the working conditions, entry requirements and skill requirements. The website has information to help individuals assess their own skills.

Sweden

The Yrkeskompassen website (https://arbetsformedlingen.se/) in Sweden allows users to browse occupations and learn about their labour market needs. For each occupation the degree of competition in the labour market is provided within one year and within the next five years. Occupations that are defined as having low competition have higher labour demand than labour supply, which means that it is easy for people with the right skills to find employment in that occupation. In addition, the website provides comprehensive descriptions of occupations, including the associated education and training options, as well as links to available vacancies on the PES website.

Source: OECD (forthcoming[28]), Skills for Jobs in South Africa: Labour market imbalances by occupations, industries and skills, OECD Publishing, Paris.

References

Bandalaria, M. (2018), “Open and Distance eLearning in Asia: Country Initiatives and Institutional Cooperation for the Transformation of Higher Education in the Region”, *Journal of Learning for Development*, https://oerknowledgecloud.org/sites/oerknowledgecloud.org/files/301-1520-4-PB.pdf. [22]

CEDEFOP (2012), *Payback clauses in Europe: supporting company investment in training*, CEDEFOP, European Centre for the Development of Vocational Training, http://dx.doi.org/10.2801/75534. [3]

Department for Business Innovation & Skills (2011), *Consultation on the Future of the Right to Right to Request Time to Train Regulations*, Department for Business Innovation & Skills, https://assets.publishing.service.gov.uk/government/uploads/system/uploads/attachment_data/file/207563/11-1052-consultation-right-to-request-time-to-train-regulations-response.pdf. [31]

French Ministry of Labour (2019), *Projet de transition professionnelle*. [9]

gov.UK (n.a.), *Training and study at work: your rights*, gov.uk, https://www.gov.uk/training-study-work-your-rights/employers-decision-and-responsibilities. [6]

Hooley, T. (2019), *International approaches to quality in career guidance*, Skills Norway, Oslo, https://www.kompetansenorge.no/globalassets/karriere/international-approaches-to-quality-in-career-guidance.pdf. [19]

Institute for Employment Studies (2017), *Appraisal of the Right to Request Time to Train Regulations*, UK Department for Education, https://assets.publishing.service.gov.uk/government/uploads/system/uploads/attachment_data/file/653435/Appraisal_of_the_Right_to_Request_Time_to_Train_Regulations.pdf. [32]

Jeong, S., G. McLean and S. Park (2018), “Understanding informal learning in small- and medium-sized enterprises in South Korea”, *Journal of Workplace Learning*, Vol. Vol. 30 No. 2, 2018/Emerald Publishing Limited, http://dx.doi.org/10.1108/JWL-03-2017-0028. [30]

KEIS (2017), *Performance evaluation of In-service training*. [29]

Lee, Y. (2010), “Analyzing the Supervisors’ Perception of the Paid Training Leave System on the Performance of Employees in Small and Middle-Sized Corporations”, *Journal of Agricultural Education and Human Resource Development*. [1]

Limited, E. (ed.) (2016), “Paid educational leave and self-directed learning: Implications for legislation on the learning leave scheme in South Korea”, *European Journal of Training and Development*, Vol. Vol. 40 No. 3, 2016, http://dx.doi.org/10.1108/EJTD-07-2015-0055. [5]

MoE/NILE (2019), *White paper on Lifelong Education*, Ministry of Education and National Institution for Lifelong Education. [23]

NILE (2018), *2018 Lifelong Learning in Korea*, National Institute for Lifelong Education, http://pascalobservatory.org/pascalnow/pascal-activities/news/lifelong-learning-korea-june-2018-nile. [14]

OECD (2019), *Adult Learning in Italy: What Role for Training Funds ?*, Getting Skills Right, OECD Publishing, Paris, https://dx.doi.org/10.1787/9789264311978-en. [7]

OECD (2019), *Getting Skills Right: Future-Ready Adult Learning Systems*, OECD Publishing, Paris, https://doi.org/10.1787/9789264311756-en. [25]

OECD (2019), *Individual Learning Accounts: Panacea or Pandora's Box?*, OECD Publishing, Paris, http://www.oecd.org/publications/individual-learning-schemes-203b21a8-en.htm. [18]

OECD (2019), *Investing in Youth: Korea*, OECD Publishing, Paris, https://doi.org/10.1787/4bf4a6d2-en. [13]

OECD (2019), *OECD SME and Entrepreneurship Outlook 2019*, OECD Publishing, Paris, https://dx.doi.org/10.1787/34907e9c-en. [2]

OECD (2019), *The future of work: How does Korea compare? OECD Employment Outlook 2019*, OECD, Paris, https://www.oecd.org/korea/Employment-Outlook-Korea-EN.pdf. [17]

OECD (2018), *Skills for Jobs*, OECD Publishing, Paris, https://www.oecdskillsforjobsdatabase.org/data/Skills%20SfJ_PDF%20for%20WEBSITE%20final.pdf. [8]

OECD (2018), *Towards Better Social and Employment Security in Korea*, Connecting People with Jobs, OECD Publishing, Paris, https://dx.doi.org/10.1787/9789264288256-en. [33]

OECD (2018), *Working Better with Age: Korea*, Ageing and Employment Policies, OECD Publishing, Paris, https://dx.doi.org/10.1787/9789264208261-en. [10]

OECD (2017), *Getting Skills Right: France*, OECD Publishing, Paris, https://doi.org/10.1787/9789264284456-en. [27]

OECD (2017), *OECD Skills Strategy Diagnostic Report: Korea 2015*, OECD Skills Studies, OECD Publishing, Paris, https://dx.doi.org/10.1787/9789264300286-en. [21]

OECD (2013), *Korea: Improving the Re-employment Prospects of Displaced Workers*, Back to Work, OECD Publishing, Paris, https://dx.doi.org/10.1787/9789264189225-en. [34]

OECD (forthcoming), *Skills for Jobs in South Africa: Labour market imbalances by occupations, industries and skills*, OECD Publishing, Paris. [28]

OECD/EU (2017), *The Missing Entrepreneurs 2017: Policies for Inclusive Entrepreneurship*, OECD Publishing, Paris, https://dx.doi.org/10.1787/9789264283602-en. [15]

Soo-jin, K. (2017), *Edudonga*, http://edu.donga.com/?p=article&ps=view&at_no=20171002092340248506. [24]

Stone, I. (2010), "Encouraging small firms to invest in training:", *UK Commission for Employment and Skills* Issue No. 5, https://core.ac.uk/download/pdf/4151307.pdf. [4]

The Adecco Group (2019), *S'orienter aujourd'hui*, The Adecco Group. [26]

Yang, J. and R. Yorozu (2015), *Building a Learning Society in Japan, the Republic of Korea and Singapore*, UNESCO Institute for Lifelong Learning, https://files.eric.ed.gov/fulltext/ED564132.pdf. [12]

Yang, S. (2015), *The Public Employment Service in the Republic of Korea*, International Labour Organization. [20]

Yoo, K. (2011), *The Introduction and Development of Employment Insurance (EI) in Korea*, Korea Labor Institute, http://dl.kli.re.kr/dl_image/IMG/02/000000008089/SERVICE/000000008089_01.PDF. [16]

Zawacki-Richter, O. and A. Qayyum (2019), *Open and distance education in Asia, Africa and the Middle-East: National perspectives in a digital age*, SpringerBriefs in Education. [11]

Annex 3.A. Financial incentives for workers

My Work Learning Card System for workers

From 2007 to 2019, the Korean government implemented a training account system named 'My Work Learning Card System for workers'. Financial support was provided to vulnerable workers in the form of a voucher, including: SME workers, non-regular workers, soon-to-be retirees, workers in unpaid leave, workers aged 45 years or older in large firms, workers with an average monthly wage of less than KRW 2.5 million in large firms, and those who have not received employer-provided training for three years. The support subsidises 60% to 100% of training costs, depending on the training courses and characteristics of participants, within the limit of KRW 2 million (about EUR 1 564) per year (KRW 3 million – about EUR 2 347 – for 5 years) (Annex Table 3.A.1). Participants in the programme increased rapidly from 7 638 in 2007 to 311 401 in 2018. SME workers accounted for 62.8% of the total beneficiaries in 2016 (KEIS, 2017[29]).

Annex Table 3.A.1. Scale of subsidies in My Work Learning Card System

Training Course	Training cost	
	Workers eligible to My work learning card system	Workers with preferential treatment
Collective training (all courses except food service)	80%	100%
Foreign language course and food service	60%	60%
Internet course	100%	100%

Note: Workers with preferential treatment refer to non-regular workers, soon-to-be retirees in SMEs and workers in unpaid leave.
Source: HRD-net, Guide on the government-supported training programmes.

My Work Learning Card System has contributed to increasing opportunities for SME workers to participate in the training of their own choice. Indeed, workers in SMEs have used My Work Learning Card System much more often than workers in large firms. For example, during the period 2006 to 2015, 32% of the total trainees in smaller firms (1-4 employees) received only employee-directed training against 7% of trainees in large firms (Annex Figure 3.A.1). This may be because all workers in SMEs can apply for this programme while only some qualified workers in large firms can.

Annex Figure 3.A.1. Share of employer- and/or employee-led training by firm size (2006-15)

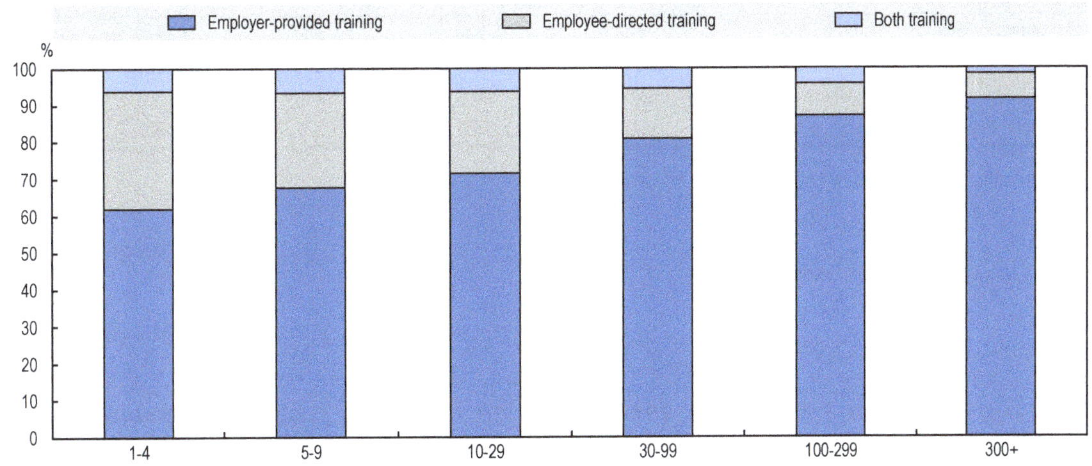

Note: Employee-directed training refers to the training by My Work Learning Card system for workers. 'Both training' means the case where employees received both employer-provided training and employee-directed training.
Source: KEIS (2017[29]), "Performance evaluation of In-service training".

Although My Work Learning Card System was an innovative programme to increase training participation for SME workers, the training account system was divided into a system for the unemployed[20] and one for the employed. This made it difficult for vulnerable workers to select suitable training courses, especially if they changed employment status.

To address this challenge, in 2020 the Korean government has reformed My Work Learning Card System and merged the two systems into one: the National Learning Card System. Under the new system, all individuals can be issued a National Learning Card and develop their vocational skills irrespective of their employment status and whether they are enrolled in the Employment Insurance or not. The card validation period is increased from 1-3 years to 5 years and the amount of support is increased from KRW 2-3 million (about EUR 1 564-2 347) to KRW 3-5 million (about EUR 2 347-3 911).

Loans for living costs during vocational training

This loan programme is available to vulnerable people, such as the unemployed and non-regular workers, to cover their living costs while on training. The loan limit is KRW 2 million (about EUR 1 564) per month and the annual interest rate is 1%. The loan amount is capped at a total of KRW 10 million – about EUR 7 822). Exceptionally, the total ceiling of the loan is up to KRW 20 million (about EUR 15 645) for people who work in the Special Employment Support sectors (see Chapter 5)or live in the employment crisis areas designated by the Ministry of Employment and Labor. A trainee can defer the loan up to three years and then pay back the money in instalments over a maximum of five years.

The number of loans increased in the period 2014-17, but decreased significantly in 2018. Most of the beneficiaries are the unemployed and the up-take of non-regular workers was only 3.4% of all beneficiaries in 2017 (Annex Table 3.A.2).

Annex Table 3.A.2. Trend in Loans for living costs during vocational training

		2014	2015	2016	2017	2018
Number of trainees	Total	9 892	9 830	9 090	10 476	7 309
	Unemployed	9 612	9 341	8 677	10 125	N.A
	Non-regular workers	280	489	413	351	N.A
Amount of Support Fund (KRW, MN)		23 992	27 754	27 326	40 982	41 133

Source: Administrative data provided by the Ministry of Employment and Labor.

Notes

1 In SMEs (with less than 150 full-time employees), part of training costs and workers' wages are subsidised when employers grant paid leave for at least 20 training hours for 5 continuous days. Since 2011, there is an additional financial support covering the wage of the replacement worker, when SMEs grant paid leave for at least 120 training hours for 30 continuous days and hire a replacement worker. Conversely, for larger firms (more than 150 employees), training must last at least 180 training hours for 60 continuous days and must be provided to workers with at least 1 year tenure. Moreover, the level of the wage subsidy is lower and does not cover replacement workers' wages.

2 Source: OECD 2018 Policy Questionnaire: Readiness of Adult Learning Systems to Address Changing Skills Needs.

3 Source: OECD 2018 Policy Questionnaire: Readiness of Adult Learning Systems to Address Changing Skills Needs.

4 In recent years there have been several discussions in the United Kingdom on whether to extend the right to employees of SMEs (with fewer than 250 employees). A consultation process was launched in 2010 among businesses of different sizes. The consultation results showed that smaller businesses felt an extension would affect them negatively and disproportionately, largely because of short-term administrative impact of missing staff and the cost of temporarily replacing them: 70% of small employers did not want the extension of the right to SMEs. The government decided to take no immediate action and to collect more evidence before making any changes to the right (Institute for Employment Studies, 2017[32]; Department for Business Innovation & Skills, 2011[31]).

5 These reasons include: training does not benefit firms' business; firms would run up extra costs for the business and would not be able to meet customer demands; impossibility to re-organise the work among other members of staff; impossibility to recruit extra staff; damage to quality and business performance; not enough work for the employee to do at the times they intend to work; conflicts with planned structural changes.

6 Of course, there is only so much that can be achieved through distance learning, as not all training programmes can be delivered on-line. Technical training that require a more practical component may be difficult to be delivered online. For instance, Korean Polytechnics do not offer any distance learning programmes reflecting the practical nature of the training programmes they deliver.

7 20% of university lectures can be taught online.

[8] As of December 2018, in Korea there were 41.1 fixed broadband subscriptions per 100 inhabitants, the 6th highest rate in the OECD. Source: OECD Broadband statistics http://www.oecd.org/sti/broadband/broadband-statistics.

[9] Through Academic Credit Bank System. The "Academic Credit Bank System" allows recognising various experiences and learning outside a formal education setting and converting them as credits. Those who have accumulated certain amounts of credits through the Academic Credit Bank System can be granted with a bachelor's degree, or an associate degree. As of 2018, 435 education institutions have participated in the Academic Credit Bank System, through which 51 611 people were able to get a degree.

[10] Participation in VAE for non-public qualifications is not registered.

[11] As discussed in Chapter 5, workers who are not covered by Employment Insurance are not eligible to receive financial incentives for training, or reimbursements for training costs. While EI in principle covers all employees on a mandatory basis, certain groups of workers are legally excluded. These include: a) employees who work less than 60 hours per month or 15 hours per week; b) businesses with less than five employees in the agricultural, forestry and hunting industries; c) most foreign workers; and d) workers aged 65 and over. Moreover, even employees not explicitly excluded are often not insured, and non-compliance is particularly acute among workers in smallest firms, low-wage, and non-regular workers. Many smaller firms – which operate with very small profit margins – may find it unaffordable to pay for insurance premiums. Low-wage and non-regular workers may also try to avoid paying insurance premiums to increase net wages (OECD, 2013[34]; OECD, 2018[33]).

[12] The most known example of this scheme is the Compte personnel de formation (CPF) in France. However, only around 6% of individuals have used the CPF in one year, mainly among the unemployed or the high-skilled. Studies have pointed to the importance of raising awareness about this scheme and providing high-quality career guidance to help individuals make informed training decisions (The Adecco Group, 2019[26]).

[13] Interestingly, SME workers in Korea are also more motivated and willing to train compared to workers in larger firms, whereas the opposite is true in the vast majority of OECD countries. There may be several reasons as to why SME workers are more willing to train than workers in larger companies. First of all, in Korean SMEs, learning is totally up to individual willingness, while large companies typically make interventions if an employee experiences skill gaps relative to his/her job (Jeong, McLean and Park, 2018[30]). Further, and perhaps more importantly, SME workers' motivation to train may reflect their willingness to find a better quality job in a larger firm or in the public sector (Jeong, McLean and Park, 2018[30]). This is not surprising in a context of labour market duality where SMEs typically offer low-quality, low-pay, and less-protected jobs while larger firms offer employment stability and high wages (see Chapter 1). Different wage-setting practices adopted across firms of different sizes may also explain these patterns. Larger firms often adopt seniority wages – a wage system that rewards seniority rather than performance (see Chapter 1) – while SMEs often do not implement any pre-defined wage tables. In the view of several observers interviewed in the context of this review, seniority wages generate very predictable career pathways and could potentially reduce workers' motivation to train and upskill in large companies.

[14] The Korea Job World is an interactive vocational experience centre providing career guidance to the public in general, and young people in particular. It consists of an 80 000 square metre, six-story building, offering visitors a unique opportunity to explore and experience various occupations and career opportunities in an interactive way. It is designed to help people obtain a realistic view about possible professional choices and prospects, and to give career advice based on individual interests and aptitude.

[15] In the WPS, career counselling is defined as an activity that helps workers identify career plans and provides appropriate advice.

[16] Web Accessibility Quality Mark is a certification system designated by the Ministry of Science, ICT and Future Planning that recognises the level of web accessibility of excellent sites that comply with the Korean Web Content Accessibility Guidelines so that the disabled and the elderly can use the website with ease.

[17] This is particularly true for disadvantaged workers – over-represented in SMEs, such as the low-skilled and older workers – who often lack the basic ICT skills needed to use online services.

[18] At the time of writing, HRD-net does not collect information on the life history of trainees and is not able to follow workers through different training programmes, jobs and employment statuses – which limits its ability to provide tailored advice to individuals.

[19] Between 2015 and July 2018, around 5.8 million individuals used the CEP. However, in 2019 only less than 7% of active people (either employed or unemployed) knew about the CEP and how it works. Although the CEP is supposed to benefit all individuals, the vast majority of users are the unemployed, and the Public Employment Service seems to be the actor more often engaged in the delivery of the CEP. The use of the CEP among workers is much less substantial.

[20] My Work Learning Card System for job seekers is a voucher system that provides job seekers a certain amount of money (KRW 2-3 million (about EUR 1 564-2 347) per year depending on the level of household income), which allows them to choose training programmes and institutions within the given financial limit.

4 Ensuring that training is of high quality and aligned with skill needs

In order for training to be effective and attain the desired objectives it needs to be of high quality and aligned with skills needs. This chapter analyses the extent to which training programmes provided by or available to SMEs are useful, of high quality, and aligned with labour market needs. The chapter also provides examples of national policies implemented in Korea to promote training quality and presents international good practice examples from OECD countries.

In Brief

High training quality is key

High training quality is key to ensure that SMEs and SME workers can make the most of adult learning programmes. This chapter analyses whether training is useful, of high quality, and aligned with labour market needs. The key findings of this chapter can be summarised as follows:

- The usefulness of training could be improved in Korea. Only a third of SME workers find their formal or non-formal job-related training activity very useful for their job – well below the OECD average of 53% and lower than any OECD country except for Japan.
- Training is associated with positive wage returns for SME workers in Korea, suggesting potential gains in productivity. SME workers' participation in formal and non-formal training is associated with higher wages (8% and 10% more respectively). For workers in larger firms, wage returns are virtually inexistent, probably reflecting seniority-wage practices rather than low-quality training.
- More could be done to build the capacity of SMEs to provide training that addresses their skill gaps. The key challenge is that Korean SMEs often lack the capacity to assess their skill needs beyond the short-term. In Korea, 28.3% of small firms, 24.6% of medium-sized firms, and 17% of large firms do not at all review the skills and competences required by employees based on the business environment and company strategy.
- Korea has a plethora of Skills Assessment and Anticipation (SAA) information, which is used by policy makers to design adult learning strategies, develop training programmes, and determine whether subsidies should be allocated to adult learning programmes/providers or not. However, SAA information could be better leveraged to help SME workers make informed career decisions. Indeed, SAA information is often scattered, delinked, and dispersed across different online platforms, making it difficult to use.
- The recent development of National Competency Standards is an important step forward to make skills development more aligned with labour market needs. However, there are implementation challenges, including the mismatch between NCSs and industry needs; the rapid obsolescence of the NCSs framework; as well as the lack of expertise of teachers and lecturers in adopting NCSs.
- Digital skills are crucial in the context of the 4th industrial revolution. Yet, some 72% of workers in micro-firms have low problem-solving skills in technology-rich environments, a rate that declines evenly to 50% in large firms. Despite this challenge, IT-related training is the least frequently provided training in SMEs. What is more, publicly financed training programmes related to the 4th industrial revolution are scant. Industry 4.0 training programmes are typically more expensive than more traditional courses, and public subsidies are often insufficient to cover such costs.
- Adult learning teachers should be better prepared to teach the skills needed for a changing world of work. Adult learning teachers do not participate enough to refresher training, partly reflecting the fact that continuous training is not mandatory to continue teaching.

Introduction

In order for training to be effective it needs to be of high quality and aligned with skills needs. Indeed, increasing participation is unlikely to have the desired impact on skills if training is of low quality. This chapter analyses the extent to which training programmes provided by SMEs and/or attended by SME workers are useful, of high quality, and aligned with needs.

This chapter is structured as follows. Section 4.1 presents subjective and objective indicators of training quality, drawing from international data sources and placing Korea in the international context. Section 4.2 discusses how to build the capacity of SMEs to train for a changing world of work. Section 4.3 presents how skills assessment and anticipation (SAA) information is collected and used to align training with labour market needs. Section 4.4 discusses existing adult learning monitoring and quality assurance mechanisms. Section 4.5 discusses how training programmes are kept up to date, particularly in the context of the 4th industrial revolution.

4.1. Is training of good quality?

Measuring training quality is not an easy task, as quality is multi-dimensional in nature and is often subjective. This section discusses two specific aspects of training quality, drawing upon internationally comparable data: 1) usefulness of training; and 2) wage returns to training. While these dimensions reflect important aspects of the quality of adult learning programmes, they do not provide a full picture. Additional information is needed to draw a more complete picture of adult learning quality in Korea in comparison to other OECD countries.

4.1.1. Usefulness of training

One way to measure training quality is to assess whether workers perceive training as being useful for their job. The self-reported usefulness of training reflects a personal judgement of the training content, and as such, it reveals one subjective aspect of training quality.

In Korea, SME workers seem to be much less satisfied with training than their peers in other OECD countries (OECD, 2019[1]), according to data from the Survey of Adult Skills (PIAAC). Only a third of SME workers found their formal or non-formal job-related training activity very useful for their job – well below the OECD average of 53% and lower than any OECD country except for Japan (Figure 4.1).

However, SME workers in Korea seem to be slightly more satisfied with training compared to workers in larger companies. The gap between workers in larger companies and SME workers in Korea is 5 percentage points – well above the OECD average (0.6 percentage points) and above some OECD countries where the gap is negative (Denmark, Greece, Ireland, Turkey) or less marked (Figure 4.1).

It is noteworthy that there might be a link between quantity and perceived quality of training. For example, the fact that in Korea SME workers are more satisfied with training than workers in larger companies, can be due to the fact that they train considerably less than workers in larger companies (see Chapter 2), and as a result that they value more the few training programmes they pursue.

Figure 4.1. Workers' self-reported usefulness of training, Korea and OECD countries

Percentage of workers in job-related (formal or non-formal) training who said that at least one training activity was "very useful" for their job, by firm size

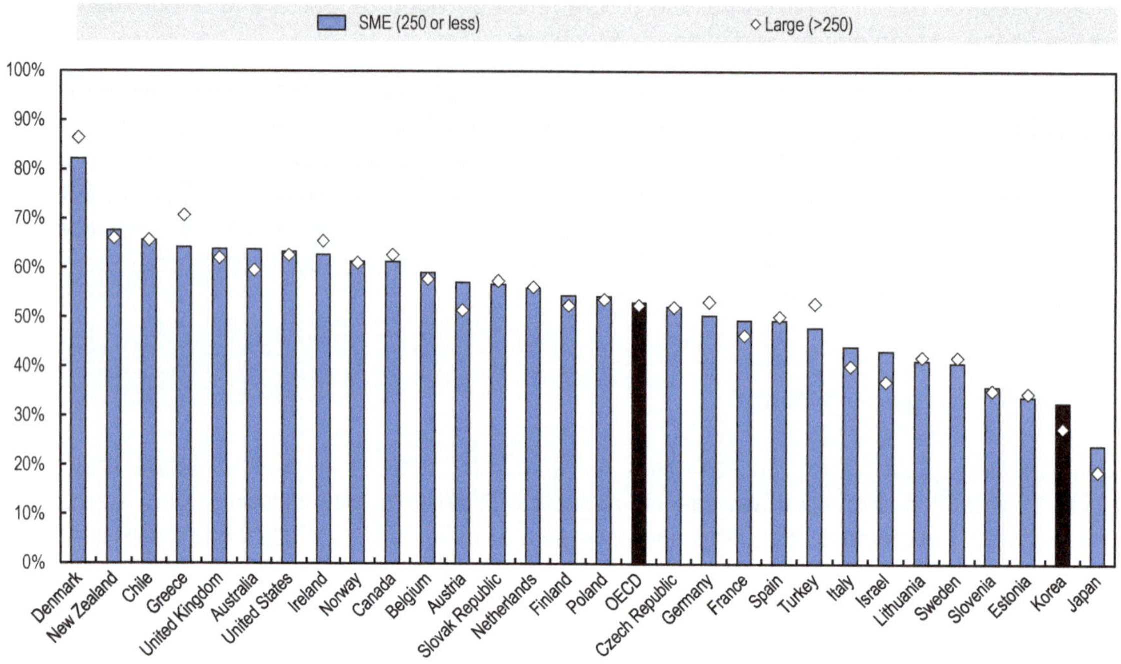

Source: OECD elaborations of the Survey of Adult Skills (PIAAC) 2012: 2015.

4.1.2. Wage returns to training

Wage returns assess the extent to which workers' training participation leads to higher wages. To the extent that wages increases are aligned with increases in the participant's productivity, they can be interpreted as a proxy for training quality.

Using the framework developed by Fialho, Quintini and Vandeweyer (2019[2]), and exploiting PIAAC data, it is possible to estimate the wage returns to training in Korea and other OECD countries. The analysis distinguishes between returns to formal, non-formal and informal training, controlling for a range of individual, job and firm characteristics. The analysis presented in this chapter also disentangles results between SME workers and workers in larger firms.

As shown in Figure 4.2, in Korean SMEs, workers' participation to formal and non-formal training is associated with higher wages, while informal training (i.e. learning by doing the job, learning from others, or learning new things at work at least once a week) negatively correlates to wages. More specifically, formal training participants earn approximately 8% more than non-participants with similar characteristics and in similar jobs and firms, the second highest wage return in the OECD after Chile. Non-formal training participants earn 10% more, just above the OECD average of 9.6%. Conversely, workers exposed to informal learning at least once a week earn approximately 1.7% less than workers not exposed to it. However, the results are statistically significant only for non-formal training.

Interestingly, a completely different picture emerges when looking at workers in larger firms, where wage returns are virtually inexistent regardless of the type of training considered (Figure 4.2). These results could be explained by the fact that larger firms in Korea often adopt seniority-wages, where pay increases are related to workers' seniority rather than productivity and performance (see Chapter 3). It is important to note that for Korea, the results for workers in large firms are not statistically significant regardless of the type of training considered.

Figure 4.2. Returns to training for SMEs, by country

OLS coefficients, from country-specific regressions

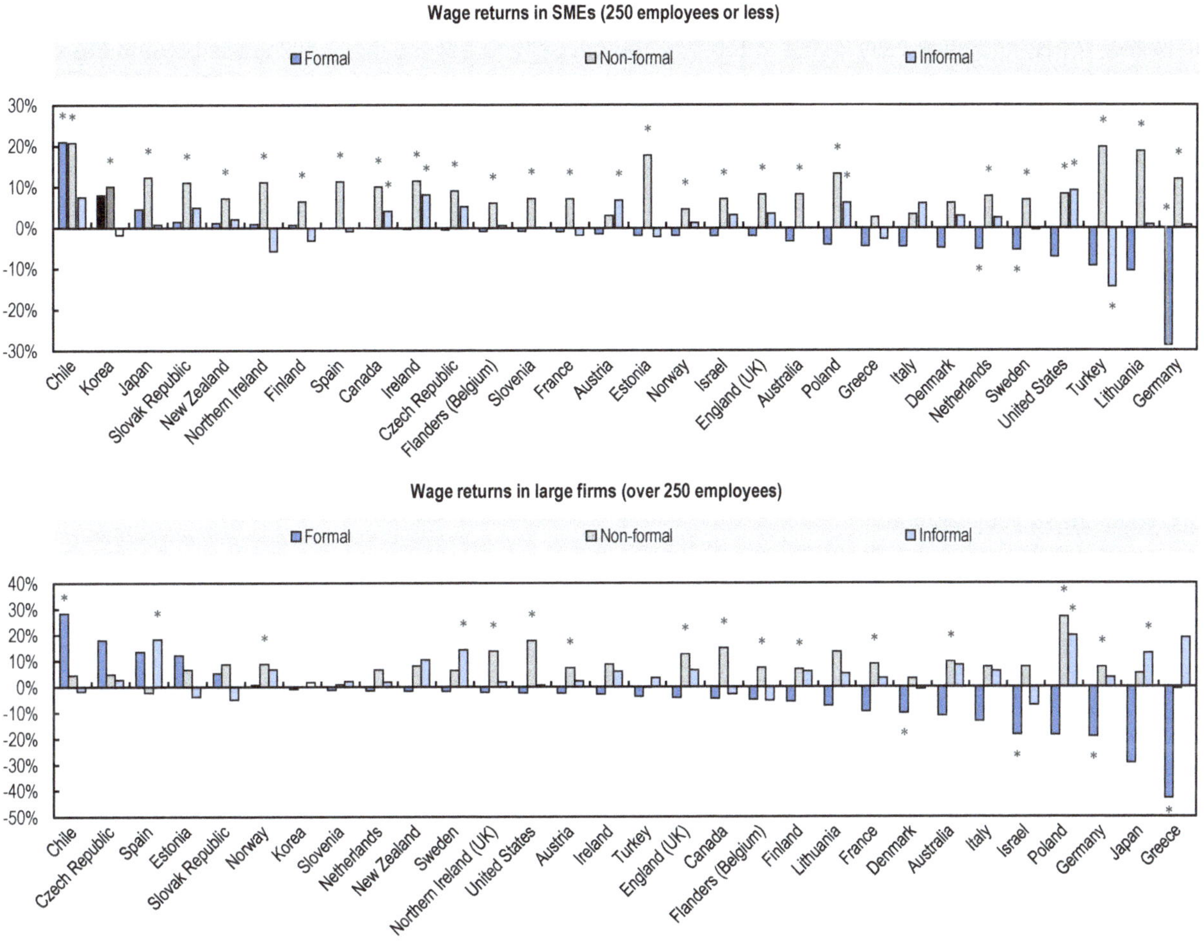

Note: Job-related formal and non-formal training are computed based on workers who report that the latest training activity was job-related. The model includes controls for individual, job and firm characteristics. A Heckman Correction term are included in the model. Values marked by * are statistically significant at the 10%, 5% or 1% level.
Source: OECD Secretariat calculations based on the Survey of Adult Skills, PIAAC (2012, 2015), based on Fialho, Quintini and Vandeweyer (2019[2]), *Returns to different forms of job related training: Factoring in informal learning*, OECD Social, Employment and Migration Working Papers, https://dx.doi.org/10.1787/b21807e9-en.

It is noteworthy that wage returns might reflect factors unrelated to training quality, and therefore results should be taken with caution. For example, wage returns may reflect the degree of flexibility in the wage-setting process. Most importantly, low wage returns may reflect the appropriation by firms of the returns to training.[1] Or, workers may be sent on a training course by their employers to prepare them for a promotion, in which case the wage increase would take place irrespective of productivity gains. Finally, wage returns could also reflect the types of training programmes typically pursued by workers. Indeed, some courses (e.g. health and safety training) are by definition not intended to have any impact on wages. For these courses, low wage returns are unlikely to reflect low training quality.

4.2. Building the capacity of SMEs to train for a changing world of work

SMEs – and firms more generally – have an interest in keeping the skills of their employees up to date, so that they can introduce new technologies and work-organisation methods and stay competitive.

To achieve this objective, SMEs need to understand what skills they need for the development of their businesses. Although SMEs can partly rely on SAA information to understand the training needs of their sector (see Section 4.3), companies also need to improve the assessment of their own skill needs.

In Korea, firms, and especially SMEs, often lack the capacity to assess their skill needs beyond the short-term. They may not have the technical capacity, the financial resources, or the time to undertake such assessments. As a result, many firms (especially smaller firms) do not conduct skills assessment and anticipation analysis on a regular basis.

In Korea, 28.3% of small firms, 24.6% of medium-sized firms, and 17% of large firms do not at all review the skills and competences required by employees based on the business environment and company strategy – according to Workplace Panel Survey (WPS) 2015 data. Only between 14% and 23% of firms, depending on firm size, review the required skills and competences of their employees on a regular basis (Figure 4.3). The remainder of firms carry out such analysis only on an irregularly.

Figure 4.3. Firms reviewing workers' skills and competences, by firm size

Percentage of firms that reviewed employee's required skills and competences based on the business environment and company strategy last year

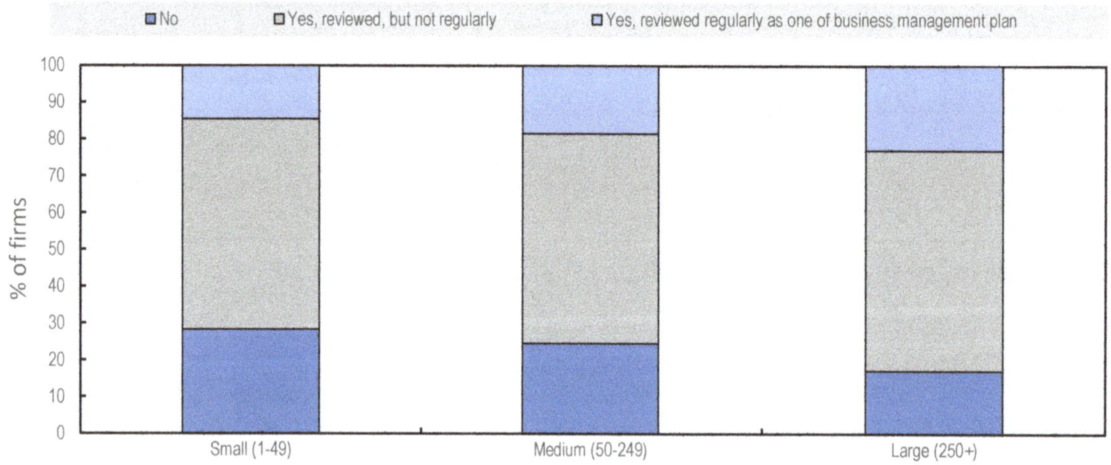

Note: A 'job analysis' is a process for collecting and analysing information on the nature of the work that is entailed in performing a job function and the personal aptitude of the worker that is required.
Source: OECD elaborations of the Workplace Panel Survey (6th wave, 2015).

On top of improving the assessment of their skills needs, firms also need to be able to provide relevant training that addresses skill gaps and prepares employees for the future. However, employers do not always provide training on the skills they need the most.

One key challenge is that Korean SMEs often provide only or mainly mandatory training. Industrial safety and health training is the training programme most frequently provided by SMEs (as well as larger firms), as shown in Figure 4.4. And as discussed in Chapter 3, some 53.7% of small firms and 44.2% of medium-sized firms provide *only* mandatory training to their workers. While knowledge on health and safety is certainly important to reduce work accidents, it does not help in addressing skill gaps or preparing the workforce for emerging skill needs.[2]

Figure 4.4. Content of training provided by firms, by firm size

Percentage of firms providing training, by training content

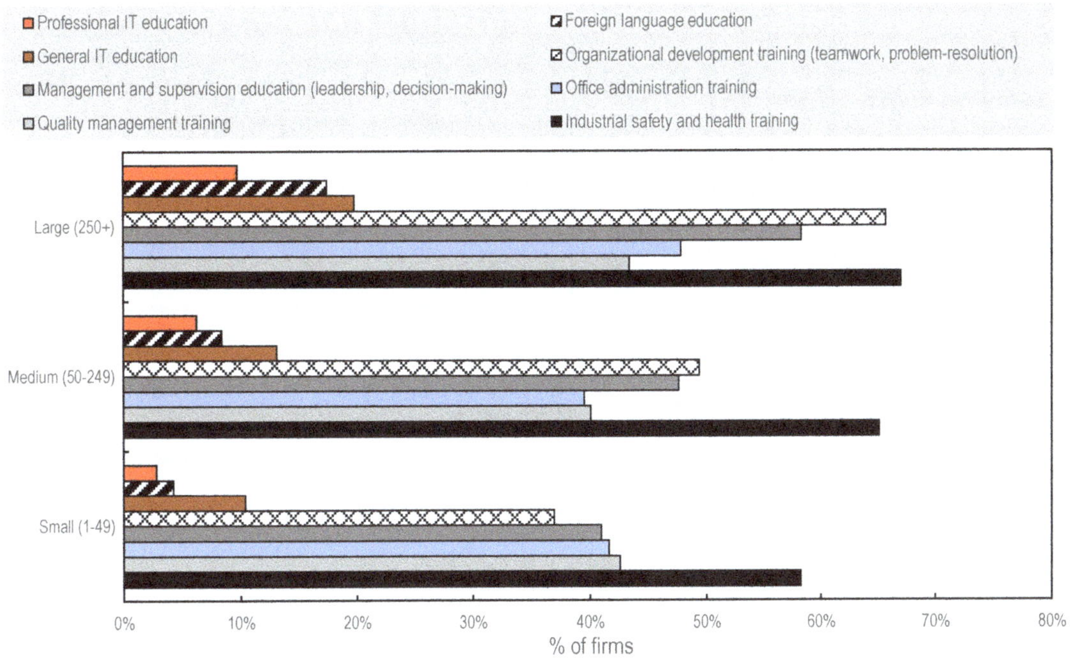

Note: Data refers to all major training programmes implemented at workplace in the past year. Multiple answers are possible.
Source: OECD elaborations of the Workplace Panel Survey (6th wave, 2015).

Another challenge is that training (beyond mandatory) is not always of the highest quality, particularly in SMEs. Looking at national employers and employees' surveys, it seems evident that SMEs (and their workers) are not as positive as large firms (and their workers) about the quality, usefulness, and results of company's official training.[3] This is not so surprising, considered that SMEs rarely have the facilities, infrastructures, as well as the financial and human capital resources to provide high-quality training (see Chapter 3).

For example, according to the Human Capital Corporate Panel Survey (HCCP) (2017) data, only 32.7% of workers in SMEs "fully" or "slightly" agree that their company provides adequate training, 44.4% agree that their company's training is relevant for the job, and 38.6% that their company's training is readily applicable to the job (Figure 4.5). These rates are systematically higher in larger firms.[4]

Figure 4.5. Workers' perception of training, Korea, 2017

Percentage of workers who agree with the following statements regarding the company's official training, by firm size

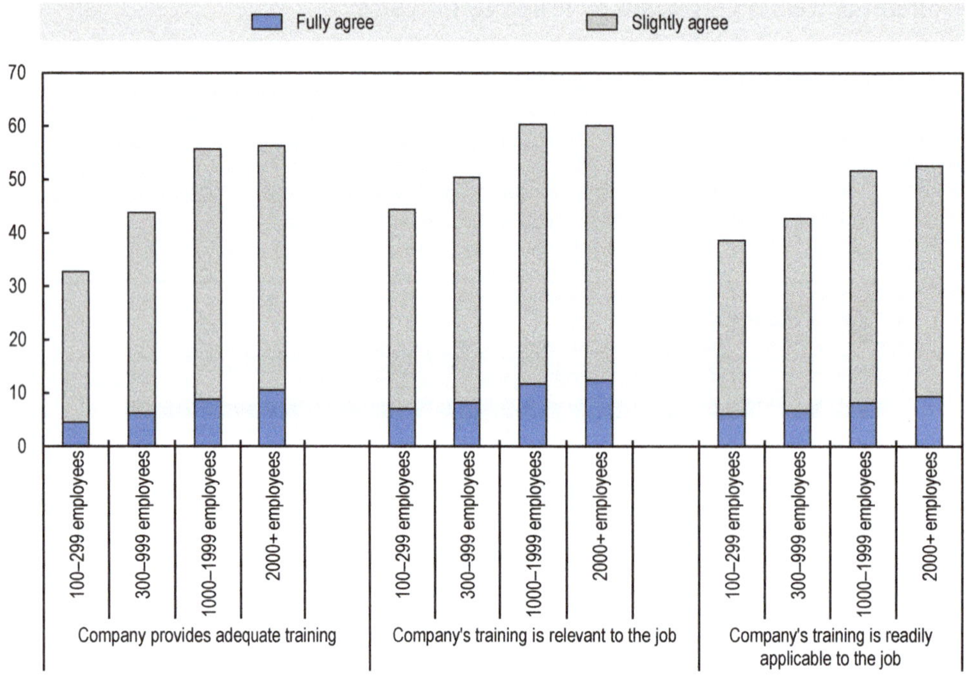

Note: Data refers to company's official training (outside the team or department). Data refer to workers who "fully" or "slightly" agree with the following statements.
Source: KRIVET elaborations of the Human Capital Corporate Panel Survey (7th wave, 2017).

Similarly, SMEs themselves seem to be less satisfied about the impact that their training has on their workers. According to the HCCP data, only 35% of medium-sized firms in 2017 reported that training "highly" or "somewhat" improved the job capability of employees. A minority of medium-sized firms reported that training improved labour productivity (32%), company image (29%), morale of employees (34%), and retention of employees (26%) (Figure 4.6). These rates are systematically lower than rates observed in larger companies.

Figure 4.6. Firms' perceptions of training, Korea

Percentage of firms reporting that training "somewhat" or "highly" improved the following items, by firm size

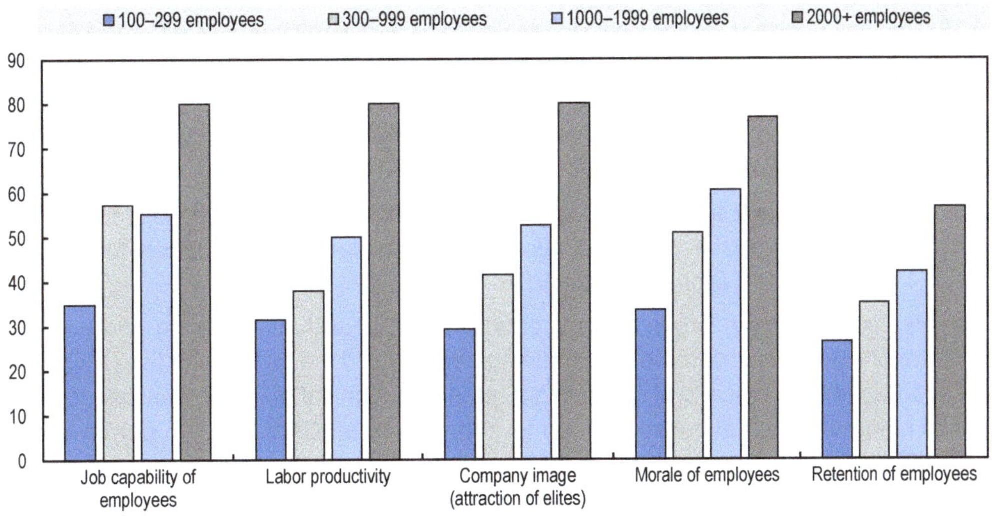

Source: KRIVET elaborations of the Human Capital Corporate Panel (7th wave, 2017).

Firms should also monitor the quality of the training offered to their workers. This monitoring can allow firms to identify the impacts of training on staff's performance, and adjust future training choices accordingly. Yet, many Korean companies still do not monitor whether their training has reached the desired objectives and brings effective outcomes (EPF, 2017[3]). This is particularly true among SMEs. According to WPS data, some 66% of small firms, 55% of medium-sized firms and 29% of large firms did not implement any evaluation of training in the year preceding the survey (Figure 4.7). Unlike what happens in Korean SMEs, most large companies seem to conduct, at least, a trainee satisfaction survey.

Figure 4.7. Firms' evaluation of training programmes, by firm size

Percentage of firms that implemented an evaluation of the training last year

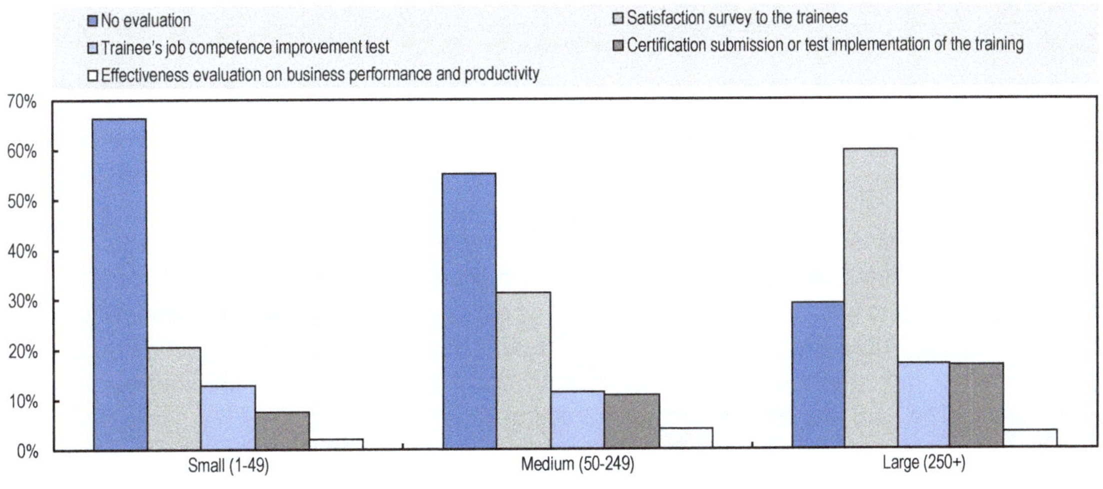

Note: Data exclude the legally mandatory training. Multiple answers possible.
Source: OECD elaborations of the Workplace Panel Survey (6th wave, 2015).

Korea has already implemented several projects to support SMEs to better understand their training needs and offer training accordingly, in line with good practices in OECD countries. These projects include the *SME training (support) centres*, the *S-OJT* project, and the '*Subsidies for Learning Organisations*' (see Chapter 3 for a full description of these programmes):

- *SME Training (Support) Centres* aim to tackle the lack of HRD capabilities of SMEs, by supporting business guidance, company diagnosis, as well as training programme design in SMEs. In 2019, operation institutions include Chambers of Commerce and Industry, employers association, Korea Tech and other institutions. The amount of support for each centre is KRW 600 million (approximately EUR 460 000).
- *S-OJT project*. This is a subsidy that covers the cost of training, job analysis/module development, training delivery, and assessment of results. The average annual support for each company is KRW 24 million in 2019 (approximately EUR 18 500).
- *Subsidies for Learning Organisations* provides SMEs with financial support to hire external consultants to analyse the company's training needs, build the capacity of the CEO and managers, and accompany the process of becoming a learning organisation.[5] The subsidy covers 70% of the cost of hiring an external consultant, up to a maximum of KRW 3 million per firm (approximately EUR 2 265).

These programmes provide targeted coaching to companies to identify their skill needs, and offer financial incentives alongside advice and guidance, in line with international best practices (OECD, 2019[4]). However, take-up remains low. For example, the S-OJT programme is still at its early stage of development and today remains quite small scale, with only 122 selected companies in 2018. Similarly, in 2018, only 91 SMEs were supported from the *Subsidies for Learning Organisations* programme. To increase take up, Korea could task Regional and Industry Skills Councils with administering the programmes or informing firms about the existence of these programmes. Box 4.1 provides good practice international examples that Korea could learn from.

Korea should encourage SMEs to conduct an analysis of their training needs on a regular basis. For this to happen, Korea should increase the take-up of programmes that aim to help SMEs to better understand their training needs and offer training accordingly. Korea could task Regional and Industry Skills Councils with administering these programmes or informing firms about the existence of these programmes.

Box 4.1. Build capacity of employers to train for a changing world of work: the experience of Finland and Germany

Finland

Finland has a financial incentive that goes hand-in-hand with building the capacity of companies to identify their training needs and deliver training. The Joint Purchase Training (*Yhteishankintakoulutus*) supports employers who want to retrain existing staff or set-up training programmes for newly recruited staff. Offered by the Public Employment Services (PES), it supports employers to define their training needs, select the appropriate candidates for training and find an education provider to deliver the tailored training. The PES also part-finances the training.

Germany

In Germany, the initiative 'Securing the skilled labour base: vocational training and education (CVET) and gender equality (Fachkräfte sichern: weiterbilden und Gleichstellung fördern)' supports social partners in increasing adult learning participation and gender equality at work. This initiative funds 93 projects. For example, one project aims to create staff development structures in utility companies in the three German cities of Coburg, Kronach and Lichtenfels. Companies receive coaching and training for key staff on analysing their skill and training need, practical ways of introducing staff development structures and working with partners.

Source: OECD (2019[4]), *Getting Skills Right: Creating responsive adult learning systems*, OECD, Paris, http://www.oecd.org/employment/emp/adult-learning-systems-2019.pdf.

4.3. Assessing and anticipating changing skills needs

Skills assessment and anticipation (SAA) exercises are tools used to collect information on current and future skills needs. SAA exercises collect information on where (i.e. in what economic sectors, occupations, or geographic areas) and when (i.e. now, in the future) the demand and supply of skills are misaligned (OECD, 2016[5]). In adult learning, this information can be used to guide policy makers, training providers, firms, and adults on what training programmes to provide and/or choose. This section looks at 1) the collection of skills assessment and anticipation (SAA) information; 2) the use of SAA in adult learning policy; and 3) how SAA can be used to help (SME) workers make informed training decisions.

4.3.1. Collecting skills assessment and anticipation analysis

In Korea, there is a plethora of SAA exercises to monitor current and future labour force supply and demand. These exercises pursue different objectives, are conducted by different (mainly institutional) organisations, present information at different levels of granularity/aggregation, use different time horizons (current, future), and adopt different dissemination practices to make the results publicly available. The most important SAA exercises include:

- *Occupational Labour Force Survey at Establishments.* The survey is conducted every six months by the MoEL. The purpose of the survey is to collect information on current labour demand and shortages. Indicators collected include the current number of employees, number of new hires, number of vacancies, scheduled number of employees to be hired, reasons for not hiring. Indicators are disaggregated by occupation, industry, firm size, region, and skill level.[6] The results of the survey are available on a dedicated website and are published in a report twice a year (see Chapter 1).
- *Medium- to Long-Term Labor Demand and Supply Forecast.* This forecast exercise is conducted every year by the Korea Employment Information Service (KEIS). It identifies and anticipates long-term skills supply and demand at the macro level, covering a time-span of ten years. Results are disaggregated at the industry, occupation, and skills level. The results of the forecast are available on a dedicated website, they are published in an annual report, and micro-data are also accessible.
- *Regional and Industry Skills Councils Surveys.* Since 2013, Skills Councils conduct an annual survey on training and skills demands for each region and sector of the economy, on around 2 500 companies. The results of the analysis are published in an annual report and is available on a dedicated website, and micro-data are also available.
- *Labor Supply and Demand Forecast Caused by the Fourth Industrial Revolution.* Conducted every year by the MoEL, the exercise aims to forecast industry-specific growth, looking at the number of employees by industry and occupations on a time-horizon of about 15 years. The results of the survey are available on a dedicated website, and they are also published in an annual report.

Table 4.1 provides a summary of these and other SAA exercises available in Korea.[7] On top of these institutional assessments, training providers sometimes also independently conduct skills needs surveys to better understand the training needs of firms and develop an adequate training offer. For example, in order to develop training programmes aimed at improving the job competencies of workers,[8] several Korean Polytechnic Universities conduct a demand survey among enterprises at the end of each year.

Table 4.1. Selected examples of SAA exercises in Korea

Name of SAA exercise	Organisation	Disaggregation	Time Span	Frequency	Dissemination
Occupational Labour Force Survey at Establishments	MOEL	Occupation/Industry/Firm size/regional/skills	Current	Every six months	Report; website
Medium- to Long-Term Labor Demand and Supply Forecast	KEIS	Occupation/Industry/skills	Future (10 years)	Every year	Report; website; free micro-data
Survey on Regional Workforce and Vocational Training Need (Regional Skills Councils survey)	MOEL	Regional/skills/NQSs	Current	Every year	Report; website
Industry Skills Councils Survey	MOEL	Occupation/Industry/Qualifications/NQSs	Current	Every year	Report; website; free micro-data
Labor Supply and Demand Forecast Caused by the Fourth Industrial Revolution	MOEL	Occupation/Industry/Skills	Future (15 years)	Every year	Report; website
Survey on Establishment of Small and Medium Enterprises	Ministry of SMEs and Startups	Occupation/ Industry/Firm size/Regional	Current	Every year	Report; website; free micro-data
National Skills Outlook	KRIVET	Occupation/Industry/Firm size/skills/NQSs	Future	Every year	Report; website
Survey on Vocational Training in Enterprises	MOEL	Industry/Firm size/Skills	Current	Every year	Report; website; free micro-data
Survey on industrial skills supply and demand	Ministry of Trade, Industry and Energy	Occupation/Industry/Firm size/ Regional	Current	Every year	Report; website; free micro-data
Survey report on SME technology and technical skills	Korea Small Business Institute	Occupation/Industry/Firm size/Skills	Current	Every year	Report; website; free micro-data
Korea Labour and Income Panel Study	KLI	Skills	Current	Every year	Report; website; free micro-data
Human Capital Corporate Panel	KRIVET	Skills	Current	Every year	Report; website; free micro-data

Source: OECD Questionnaire "Readiness of Adult Learning Systems to Address Changing Skills Needs"; OECD Questionnaire "Anticipating and Responding to Changing Skills Needs"; additional information provided by the MoEL.

4.3.2. Making use of SAA information

The collection of skill assessment and anticipation (SAA) information is not a self-serving tool. Its key purpose is to inform policy-makers, firms, training providers, and individuals, so that they can provide/access appropriate adult learning programmes that address current and emerging skill gaps.

Like in other OECD countries, SAA information in Korea is used in a number of policy fields, including adult learning (OECD, 2016[5]). One of its main uses is to develop adult learning programmes that respond to the needs of firms. To give one example, the results of *Surveys on Regional Workforce and Vocational Training Need* and the *Industry Skills Councils Surveys* are used to develop region/industry-customised training programmes (HRD Korea, 2017[6]). This information is also used by the MoEL to shape public adult learning programmes (e.g. Work-Study Dual System) and by the Public Employment Services to identify their training offer.

SAA information is also used to determine whether financial subsidies should be allocated to adult learning programmes/providers or not. For example, in the National HRD Consortium Programme (see Chapter 3), demand surveys are conducted via e-mail, and several stakeholders – e.g. firms, employers' organisations, and other government-recommended associations – are consulted to evaluate whether training corresponds with their needs. Training programmes that are based on demand surveys are more likely to receive government funding, and surveys that are poorly conducted can lead to disqualification.

On top of guiding training providers, SAA information is also used by policy makers to design national strategies/policies on adult learning. To give one example, the results of the 5th *Science and Technology Foresight* analysis fed into the '4th Master Plan for Science and Technology' (2018-2022) (Ministry of Science and ICT, 2017[7]). Similarly, the "The Innovation Plan for Vocational Competency Development in response to labour market changes" developed by the MoEL in 2019 reflects the results of "*Labor Supply and Demand Forecast Caused by the Fourth Industrial Revolution*".

4.3.3. Helping workers make informed training choices

SAA information should also be leveraged to help workers make informed career decisions – e.g. through career guidance that makes full use of SAA information. Training choices have important implications for workers' lives. They can influence their income, well-being, job-security, and career progression opportunities. However, it can be difficult for workers to understand which occupations and skills are most in demand in the labour market. It is also a challenge for them to identify whether their skills are up to date and are still relevant for their jobs/occupations. Hence, tailored information on training must be available to all workers. As discussed in Chapter 3, in Korea SAA information is often scattered, delinked, and dispersed across different online platforms. Many users may find it difficult to navigate the existing SAA exercises and may struggle to find the information they are looking for. As suggested in Chapter 3, going forward Korea should create a one-stop-shop solution to career guidance, in line with practices already adopted in other OECD countries.

4.4. Monitoring and ensuring high-quality adult learning programmes

The Korean adult learning system is characterised by a large number of training programmes, delivered by a multitude of training providers, including government bodies, public and private training providers, and firms' in-house training.[9] In such a large and scattered market, ensuring that training meets basic quality standards is key to ensure that workers and firms have access to good quality options.

In Korea, two national bodies are responsible for assessing and monitoring the quality of the adult learning system: the Korean Skills Quality Authority (overseeing public and private training provision) and HRD Korea (overseeing firms' in-house training) (see Annex 4.A).

The Korean Skills Quality Authority (KSQA), established in April 2015 under the responsibility of the MoEL, is the national body dedicated to quality assurance in the adult learning sector (excluding firms' in-house training). The KSQA is in charge of providing accreditation to training providers, assessing their effectiveness and quality, and detecting fraudulent practices (see Annex 4.A for a description).

The KSQA provides accreditation to training providers that meet certain minimum quality standards. After a thorough assessment of training outcomes (such as completion rates, satisfaction surveys), and of the adequacy of on-site operations and facilities (such as trainers, facilities and equipment) the KSQA provides a score (up to 100 points) that reflects overall performance (Table 4.2). If the training provider receives a score inferior to 60, the request for accreditation is rejected.

Table 4.2. Assessment items used for accreditation

Assessment areas	Assessment items	Points
Training outcomes (60 points)	Completion rate	20
	Satisfaction survey	20
	Ration of NCS-based courses	5
	Trainee assessment results	10
	Training courses opening rate	5
On-site operations and facilities (40 points)	Organisation operations	6
	Training course management	8
	Facilities and equipment	10
	Trainers	10
	Trainee management	6

Source: KSQA (2019[8]), KSQA Introduction, PPT.

The KSQA-accreditation is valid for a period of 1, 3 or 5 years, depending on overall performance. In 2018, 26% of training providers were not given/renewed accreditation because they did not meet minimum quality criteria. 1-year accreditation was granted to 62.5% of the training providers assessed, 3-year accreditation was given to 10%, and 5-year accreditation was given to only 0.8% (Table 4.3).

Table 4.3. KSQA-accreditation results, 2018

Number and % of training providers

Category	Total	5 years	3 years	1 year	Rejected
Total	4 597(100%)	38(0.8%)	462 (10%)	2 874 (62.5%)	1 223 (26.6%)
Renewal	3 156 (100%)	38(1.3%)	462 (14.6%)	1 893 (59.9%)	763 (24.2%)
Initial	1 441 (100%)			981 (68.1%)	460 (31.9%)

Source: KSQA (2019[8]), KSQA Introduction, PPT.

But the work of the KSQA goes beyond accreditation. As described in detail in Annex 4.A, accredited training providers are monitored on a regular basis by KSQA, the performance of their training offer is assessed regularly, and they are audited to ensure that they do not engage in fraudulent practices.

KSQA's assessments and evaluations are used in several important ways to improve the quality of the Korean adult learning system. For example, they are used to:

- *Establish the level of government financial support.* Korea adopts a performance-based funding system, whereby the outcomes of KSQA accreditation processes and audits are directly reflected in government funding decisions as well as the extent of administrative support provided by the government. For example, training providers that do not manage to receive KSQA accreditation are not entitled to receive any government financial support. [10]
- *Provide excellence labels for best performing training providers.* Training providers with good performance assessment results can participate to a call for best practice tender and be designated as 'organisation of excellence'.
- *Inform individuals/firms about the quality of each training provider/training course.* The results of KSQA assessments and evaluations are available on HRD-net (see Chapter 3). By allowing individuals and employers to have access to relevant and up-to-date information on the quality of different training providers, the KSQA helps users to make informed choices about which training to invest in. Indirectly, this also creates a virtuous circle of competition among training providers that drives quality up.

HRD Korea's branch offices are responsible for conducting regular evaluations of firms' in-house training (e.g. training provided by the firm). Employers can apply for approval of a training course up until 5 days before the start of the training, and Korea's branch offices decide whether to approve or reject the applications.

Basic requirements for approval include adequate training space and minimum training hours. For example, the training course is disqualified if it does not provide a dedicated learning space. Minimum training hours for employer-provided training should be at least 16 hours for 2 days (for SMEs, at least 8 hours for one day). Training content should also comply with minimum standards. For example, the training should be job-relevant and appropriate teaching staff should be provided. Training courses for hobbies, entertainment, sports, and classes to prepare for foreign language tests are rejected, and so are mandatory training courses (e.g. occupational health and safety, sexual harassment prevention, personal information protection).

During the training period, HRD Korea monitors training delivery to identify fraudulent or poor training practices. To do that, HRD Korea uses data collected from HRD-Net and other relevant databases, and carries out on-site visits. When on-site visits are not possible (e.g. because training takes place during the week-end or at night time), phone calls are conducted to check trainees' attendance. Moreover, after the end of the firms' in-house training, participants are asked to complete a survey designed to assess satisfaction with the operation and management of the training programmes, the on-the-job application of what was learned during the training, and skills improvement levels.

HRD Korea regional offices/branches are responsible for providing advice and guidance to companies that offer in-house training for the first time, e.g. on how to prevent fraud and low-quality training. Moreover, regional offices/branches collect information on training programmes and providers operating at the regional level, and report it to the headquarters every two months. The Training Quality Improvement Centre in the headquarters assembles this information in a comprehensive report that allows regions to benchmark themselves with one another.

HRD Korea headquarters also conduct a performance evaluation of their regional offices/branches. The evaluation assesses their performance based on a number of criteria, such as training completion rates; to what extent SMEs provide in-house training; whether regional offices/branches provide support for firms' in-house training (e.g. competency-building training for in-house training staff; consultation prior to training); and whether regional offices/branches monitor training to prevent fraud.

As of today, for each training provider/training course, HRD-net includes information on quality. Quality indicators include completion rates, satisfaction of participants, and acquisition of units of competences based on the National Competency Standards (NCSs).[11] As shown in Figure 4.8, completion rates of training programmes for employees have decreased in Korea over the past years, and particularly so among workers in SMEs. In 2010, 89% of workers in SMEs completed their training, a rate that decreased to 83% in 2018. Completion rates for workers in large firms have dropped by only 2 percentage points in the same period. On the other hand, satisfaction scores have increased for all training participants, including SME workers.

Figure 4.8. Completion rates and satisfaction scores of training programmes for employees, by firm size and year

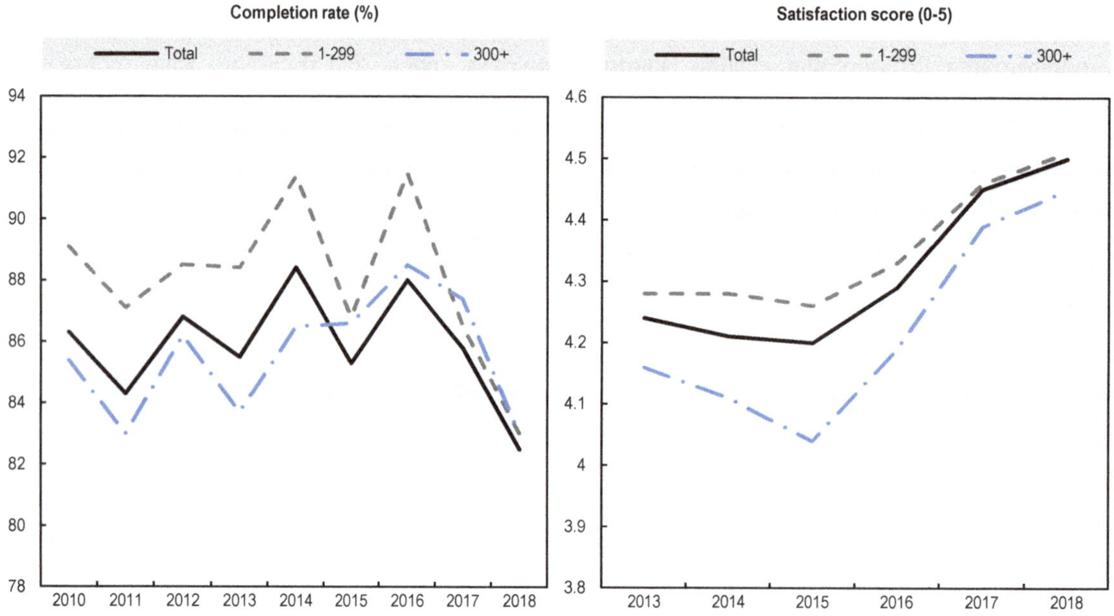

Note: Data refers to training programmes for employees only. It refers to all employer-provided training – including training that is monitored by the KSQA and HRD Korea. Training programmes for employees include subsidy for employer-provided training; paid leave training; my work learning card system for workers; National HRD Consortium; Work and Study Dual System; Subsidy for organised study at SMEs. Completion rates refer to the percentage of training participants that completed the training programme. Satisfaction scores go from 0 (least satisfied) to 5 (most satisfied).

Source: Korea Employment Information Service (KEIS) elaborations of the HRD-Net database.

According to stakeholders interviewed in the context of this project, the indicators used to measure the quality of training for incumbent workers (e.g. completion rates; satisfaction rates) could be expanded and improved. Collecting adequate indicators on the quality of training providers/programmes is challenging, especially when it comes to training for incumbent workers (see Chapter 3).[12] Perhaps Korea could learn from countries that collect more detailed indicators on training quality. In Singapore, for example, *SkillsFuture SG* has developed a Training Quality and Outcomes Measurement (TRAQOM) Survey Initiative that gather feedbacks from all training participants on quality and outcomes – at the end of the training as well as six months afterwards. The indicators include detailed satisfaction scores for quality (trainer and course content, learning, customer service), and outcomes (ability to apply learning; better job performance; expanded job scope).[13]

4.5. Keeping training content up-to-date

To keep abreast of changing skill needs in the labour market, adult learning systems need to dynamically respond to changes. Korea must put in place structures and mechanisms that allow for the continuous review of the training offer, the content of training and the delivery methods. This section discusses 1) the use of National Competency Standards in adult learning; 2) how to ensure that adult learning teachers are well-prepared; 3) the ability of the adult learning system to provide the skills for the 4th industrial revolution.

4.5.1. Using National Competency Standards in adult learning

Since 2013, Korea has been working on the development of a National Competency Standards (NCS) framework – in a joint initiative between the Ministry of Employment and Labour (MoEL) and the Ministry of Education (MoE). The framework defines a set of competencies (e.g. knowledge, skills, and attitudes) required to effectively perform a job or task in each industry (OECD, 2019[9]). A total of 1 001 NCSs have been developed by 2019.

With a strong push from the government, diverse groups of stakeholders – e.g. Industry Skills Councils, sectoral associations, corporates, and academia – participated in designing the NCS for all types of occupations.

The development of the NCSs is an important step forward to make skills development more aligned with labour market needs. For example, NCSs could be used to minimise the discrepancies between what training providers offer (and therefore what workers learn) and what industries need. Also, NCSs could prove an effective tool for recognising and validating the skills that workers have acquired throughout their careers, posing the basis for the development of a strong system of Recognition of Prior Learning (RPL) (see Chapter 3).[14] Further, NCSs could be used to conduct more accurate and granular skills assessment and anticipation (SAA) analysis – encouraging different actors to adopt the same definitions of skills. When used in recruitment practices, NCSs could encourage firms to focus on candidates' practical skills and performance rather than their qualifications – a practice which could potentially help mitigate skills mismatches, and reduce biases in hiring. Finally, NCSs could support Korean transition away from seniority-wages and towards more job-oriented wage-setting practices, for example by linking jobs to a set of competencies in a clearer and more transparent way – which could have indirect consequences on workers' motivation to train.

The government is already operationalising and promoting the effective use of the NCS in adult learning. For example, certain adult learning programmes (e.g. the Work and Study Dual System) are already developing around NCSs units. Public training institutions, such as Korean Polytechnics, are gradually developing/adjusting their curricula to integrate NCSs. Also private training providers are increasingly incentivised to use NCS-based modules. For example, the use of NCSs is one of the key criteria used by the KSQA to provide accreditation to, and assess the performance of, training providers (see Annex 4.A).[15] All in all, among the 948 NCSs developed by 2018, 934 (98.5%) have been applied in vocational training and qualifications.

Despite NCSs' potential benefits, and their ongoing implementation in adult learning, several stakeholders claim that the Korean adult learning system is not yet ready to make full use of NCSs. First, there seems to be a mismatch between NCSs and industry needs. Stakeholders consulted for the initial development of the NCS were not representative of all sectors in the economy, and industry involvement was relatively passive, with a weak mutual feedback system in place (Choi, 2015[10]).

Another key challenge is to update the NCSs framework to keep up with technology advances, especially in some sectors where new technologies are being introduced rapidly. With the rapid introduction of new technologies and in the context of rapidly changing labour markets, the NCSs gets outdated relatively quickly.[16] In addition, as argued by several training providers, NCSs do not capture the skills taught in new, more innovative, training programmes – e.g. training that develops the skills needed for the 4th industrial revolution (see Section 4.5).

Another issue is training duration. Each NCS competency unit requires a different number of training hours[17], and most require between 30 and 50 hours of training. However, adult learning courses typically last much less long than this, especially when offered by SMEs. For example, according to WPS data, for the vast majority of firms (59% of SMEs and 49% of larger firms), the average annual training time per person is 16 hours or less (Table 4.4). Elaborations of the HCCP data (2017) confirms that most training lasts between 1 and 3 days (Figure 4.9). To address this issue, Korea gives the training institution the flexibility to increase the training hours by up to 50% or reduce it to at least one hour for each unit.

Table 4.4. Annual training time per person (hours)

Percentage of firms, by firm size

	SME (less than 250)		Large firm (250+)	
	%	Cumulative %	%	Cumulative %
8 hours or less	20	20	12.6	12.6
9-16 hours	39.1	59.1	36.6	49.2
17-24	19.9	79	22.5	71.7
25-32	9.9	88.9	9.7	81.4
33-40	0.7	89.5	2.5	83.9
More than 40	10.5	100	16.1	100

Note: Annual training time per person is defined as the total training hours of the trained employees divided by the total number of employee. It excludes mandatory training.
Source: OECD elaborations of the Workplace Panel Survey (6th wave, 2015).

Figure 4.9. Duration of training, Korea, 2017

Percentage of workers who participated to company official's training in a year, by the number of days and firm size

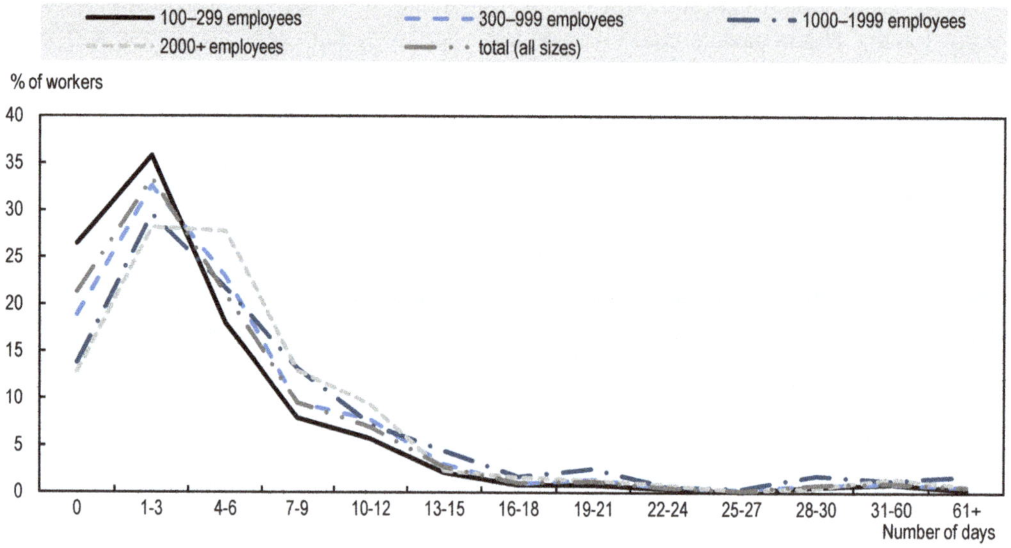

Note: Data exclude internet learning, and learning by correspondence.
Source: KRIVET elaborations of the Human Capital Corporate Panel Survey (7th wave, 2017).

Another challenge is that training providers are facing several obstacles to implement NCSs. The lack of expertise of teachers and lecturers in adopting NCSs, the increased workload related to learner evaluation, and demotivation due to frequent performance assessments – seem to be some of the strongest obstacles faced by training providers (Choi, 2015[10]).

Successful implementation of NCSs will also depend on the involvement of firms and workers, which will need to use the NCS in developing lifelong career paths and managing hiring and promotion. However, today workers/labour unions are not particularly interested in the NCS, given the firmly ingrained seniority-based wage system. Employer associations and firms are also not particularly interested in the NCSs unless they are given a strong incentive to recruit, train and assess workers based on these standards (OECD, 2015[11]).

The government is already implementing positive steps to favour a better implementation of the NCSs. For example, competency-based hiring and blind recruitment have been introduced into public sector firms since July 2017. Further, consulting on NCS-based hiring and personnel management has been provided to SMEs, with a total of 1 044 benefitting from the programme in 2018. In addition, in April 2019, the MoEL announced an innovation plan for NCS quality management, which will assess the status of the NCS and propose future directions for improvement.

In a view to enhance the adoption of NCSs by firms and training providers, Korea should:

- *Improve the process of developing/updating NCSs*, ensuring that users' views are fully reflected in the process. In particular, it will be crucial to expand the roles of industry and labour representatives in updating current NCSs and developing new ones. This will ensure that NCSs are aligned with industry needs.
- *Monitor the implementation of NCSs through dedicated assessments.* These surveys should assess whether NCSs are being used by firms and training providers, and what challenges they are facing. The results should be used to review NCS-related processes accordingly.
- *Applying NCSs to training institutes in a more flexible way.* For example, minimum NCS adoption standards for training should be eased. Training providers should be given greater autonomy in the provision of short-term (less than 40 hours) NCS-based training.

4.5.2. Preparing adult learning teachers

Ensuring that adult learning teachers are well prepared is key for training quality and for keeping training content up-to-date. Teachers need to participate in adult learning in order to keep pace with new emerging skills needs and the introduction of new technologies.

In Korea, training options for adult learning teachers exist but are not mandatory, and several observers argue that there is a need to develop adult learning teachers' skills even after they have acquired the certificate to become a lifelong learning educator (NILE, 2015[12]; Yang and Yorozu, 2015[13]). A recent survey on the perception of refresher training shows that 58.1% of teachers and instructors agree or completely agree that they need refresher training (KoreaTech HRDI, 2019[14]).

According to PIAAC data, Korean teachers (including adult learning teachers) participate in training much less than teachers in other OECD countries. In Korea 67.5% of teachers participate in formal and non-formal job-related training in a given year, well below the majority of OECD countries and below the OECD average of 72.1% (Figure 4.10).

Figure 4.10. Teachers' participation to training

Percentage of teachers participating to formal and non-formal job-related training in the previous 12 months

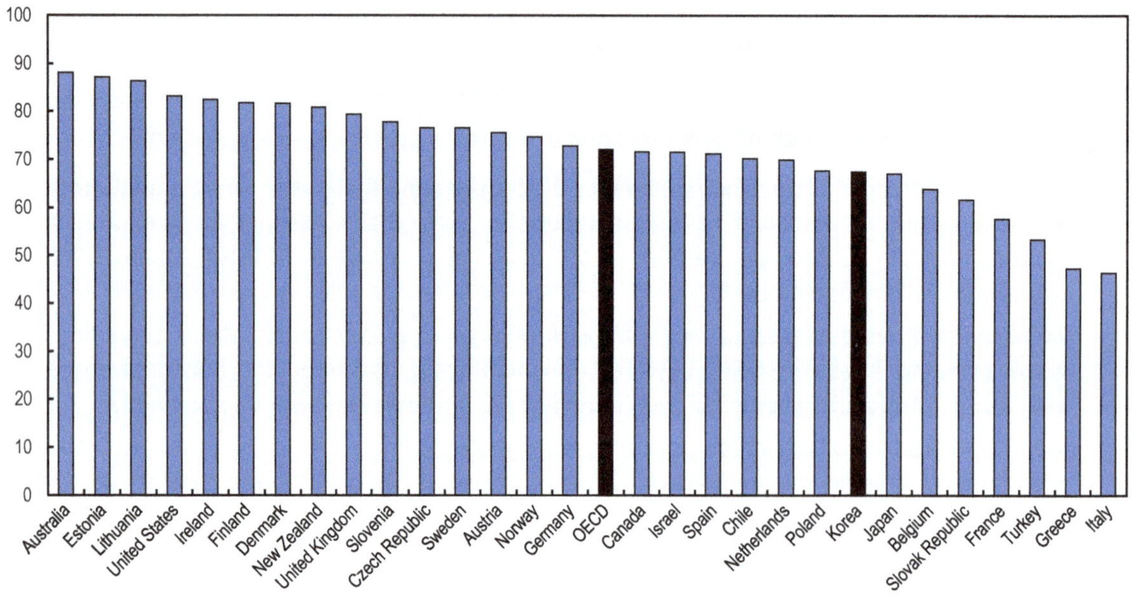

Note: Share of teachers answering "Yes" to the question "Do you feel you need further training in order to cope well with your present duties?". Teachers are adults self-reporting working in the following two-digit occupations as classified by the International Standard Classification of Occupations (ISCO-08): Teaching Professionals (ISCO 23).
Source: OECD Secretariat calculations based on the Survey of Adult Skills (PIAAC) (2012; 2015).

Another issue is that adult learning teachers generally face poor working conditions in Korea – with low and stagnating wages, and poor career advancement opportunities. This may make the profession little attractive and may also reduce teachers' willingness to retrain and advance in their careers.

Korea could learn from the experience of neighbouring countries that have been taking positive steps in adult learning teachers' continuous skills development. For example, in Singapore, SkillsFuture SG has put in place an Adult Education Network, i.e. a professional membership scheme that enhances professionalisation and continual skills development of adult educators. It offers a series of continuing professional development programmes and access to rich resources. To provide incentives to high-quality teaching, SkillsFuture SG also identifies adult educators recognised for pedagogical and professional excellence (SkillsFuture SG, 2019[15]).

Korea is already taking steps in the right direction. In January 2019, a bill on provision of regular refresher training for vocational teachers and instructors was brought to motion. The revision entails that vocational teachers shall regularly (every three years) attend vocational skill development projects such as refresher training provided by the MoEL. A plan announced in April 2019 aim to expand participation to refresher training from 13 000 in 2019 to 35 000 by 2020 (KoreaTech HRDI, 2019[14]).

To ensure the high quality of adult learning teachers, Korea should:

- *Make refresher training mandatory for adult learning teachers,* as is currently being discussed by the government.
- *Enhance working conditions and wages of adult learning teachers* as a way to make the profession more attractive and increase teachers' willingness to train and upskill.

4.5.3. Providing the skills for the 4th industrial revolution

Digital devices and software are introduced and updated with increasing frequency. In Korea like in other OECD countries, adult learning systems need to provide training that develops and maintains (especially SME) workers' ICT skills, help them work with new technologies, and prepare them for the needs of the 4th industrial revolution[18] (OECD, forthcoming[16]).

There is a high and growing demand for digital skills among Korean firms. For example, a survey of 800 firms (including SMEs) conducted in 2014 by the Federation of Korean Industries (FKI), shows that for 77.5% of respondents, IT skills are the most needed skills in the world of work (FKI, 2014[17]).

Supply and participation to 4th Industrial Revolution training has increased in the past years, especially among SME workers. According to Seol (2019[18]), the number of SME workers that participated to 4th Industrial Revolution training (e.g. 3D print, big data, AI, smart manufacturing) went from over 70 000 in the first half of 2013 to over 136 000 in the second half of 2017.

Despite positive improvements observed in the past years, more could be done. The first challenge in Korea will be to equip SME workers with at least basic ICT skills and close the gap with large companies. As discussed in Chapter 1, some 72% of workers in micro-firms have low problem-solving skills in technology-rich environments, a rate that declines evenly to 50% in large firms – according to PIAAC data.

Another challenge is to encourage SMEs to provide digital skills training. Today, IT-related training remains the least frequently provided training in SMEs – according to WPS data (see Figure 4.4). In a given year, professional IT education is provided only by 3% of small firms, 6% of medium-sized firms, and 10% of large firms. Similarly, general IT education is provided only by 10% of small firms, 13% of medium-sized firms, and 20% of large firms.

Another challenge is that publicly financed training programmes related to the 4th industrial revolution exist but are scant, according to several stakeholders. The demand is too high compared to the offer, and as a result there are long waiting lists to access such programmes.

Another issue is training cost. Industry 4.0 training programmes, particularly specialist training courses, are typically more expensive than more traditional courses, and public subsidies are often insufficient to cover such costs. This is partly due to the fact that training cost are linked to (and increase with) training duration, and 4th industrial revolution training programmes typically have a longer duration. For example, according to Seol (2019[18]), in the period 2013-17, the average hours of 4th-industrial-revolution-related training is 43 hours compared to less than 30 hours for other types of training. Another issue is the hourly training cost – which tends to be higher in innovative sectors where teachers are paid higher wages. For example, the hourly wage of block chain instructors is KRW 200 000-400 000, which is well above what government subsidies typically cover. New machinery and equipment facilities can be costly as well.

The Korean government already recognises the need to equip workers with the skills needed for the 4th industrial revolution. Various ministries have developed adult learning strategies that aim to achieve this objective, e.g. the MoEL with the '3rd basic plan for vocational skills development', and the Ministry of Sciences and ICT with the '4th Master plan for Science and Technology (2018-2022)' (Ministry of Science and ICT, 2017[7]; MoEL, 2018[19]). Social partners are also taking steps. The Economic, Social and Labor Council (ESLC) finalised a tripartite framework agreement in February 2018 on the 4th Industrial Revolution, and adult learning is part of the framework.

On top of these strategic efforts, concrete policy measures have also been put in place. For example:

- Local lifelong learning systems are offering basic digital literacy training for vulnerable adults, such as the middle-aged and women after career breaks.

- MoEL has allocated, since September 2019, KRW 5 billion (about EUR 4 million) to provide financial incentives to firms providing new technology training – which cover three times of current NCS unit costs.
- In 2017, the Ministry of SMEs and Startups together with The Ministry of Trade, Industry and Energy, have established the *SMEs Programme for Smart Manufacturing*. This project aims to provide financial support to help cover large scale infrastructure investments often needed for SMEs to fully engage in the digital transformation. The programme finances up to 50% of the costs of digital technology adoption (OECD, 2019[20]). The goal is to have more than 30 000 smart factories operating with the latest digital and analytical technologies by 2025. As a complement to this measure, the government will provide support to help train 100 000 skilled workers to operate fully automated manufacturing sites through various educational programmes. Some initial impact evaluation analysis shows productivity improvement signals in firms using smart factory programmes (MSS, 2019[21]).

Korea needs to put in place a broad set of measures that aims to tackle the challenges highlighted above. These include policies to:

- *Continue providing free or subsidised basic ICT training programmes*, particularly to at-risk population groups. Basic ICT courses could be targeted to SME workers, or to vulnerable groups who are over-represented in SMEs (e.g. older workers; low-qualified).
- *Continue channelling financial incentives to innovative training options*. For example, Korea should continue providing more generous financial incentives for training programmes in emerging industries/sectors.
- *Expand the training offer of Industry 4.0 training programmes* by, for example, making these programmes more widely available and reducing waiting lists.
- *Develop new National Competency Standards (NCSs) to cover emerging sectors*. Ensure that all relevant stakeholders are involved in the process in a timely manner. The process for adding new NCSs could be made shorter so NCSs are more responsive to changing needs.

References

Choi, D. (2015), *A study on Establishment of Quality Management System for National Competency Standards(NCS)-based VET Curriculum*, Korea Research Institute for Vocational Education and Training, Seoul, http://www.krivet.re.kr/eng/eu/ec/euABAVw.jsp?pgn=1&gk=&gv=&gn=M05-M052010314. [10]

EPF (2017), *The Role of the Private Sector in VET*, EPF Working Paper, https://www.bibb.de/dokumente/pdf/epf_the_role_of_the_private_sector_in_vet_official.pdf. [3]

Fialho, P., G. Quintini and M. Vandeweyer (2019), "Returns to different forms of job related training: Factoring in informal learning", *OECD Social, Employment and Migration Working Papers*, No. 231, OECD Publishing, Paris, https://dx.doi.org/10.1787/b21807e9-en. [2]

FKI (2014), *Perceptions of employment of college graduates Workers Survey*, The Federation of Korean Industries, http://www.fki.or.kr/FkiAct/Promotion/Report/View.aspx?content_id=f6b08182-ac93-4da3-960b-f86ec5cf0f94&cPage=1&search_type=3&search_keyword=%b0%ed%bf%eb. [17]

HRD Korea (2017), *35 Years of HRD Korea: Together with the Korean People toward the World*, HRD Korea, http://www.hrdkorea.or.kr/design/image/eng/HRD_35years_Eng.pdf. [6]

KoreaTech HRDI (2019), *Facilitation of refresher training for vocational teachers and instructors*, KoreaTech Human Resources Develoment Institute. [14]

KSQA (2019), *KSQA Introduction*. [8]

Ministry of Science and ICT (2017), *The 5th Science and Technology Foresight (2016-2040): Discovering Future Technologies to Solve Major Issues of Future Society*, Korean Ministry of Science and ICT. [7]

MoEL (2018), *The Employment Insurance White Paper*, Korean Ministry of Employment and Labor. [19]

MoEL (2016), *A Proposal for the Reform of the Vocational Competency Development Training System in preparation for the 4th Industrial Revolution*. [23]

MSS (2019), *Results of Performance Analysis of Smart Factory Support Project*. [21]

NILE (2015), *Lifelong Learning Educator in Korea*, National Institute for Lifelong Education, http://cradall.org/sites/default/files/2015_Lifelong_Learning_in_Korea_Vol.2_0.pdf. [12]

OECD (2019), *Adult Learning in Italy: What Role for Training Funds ?*, Getting Skills Right, OECD Publishing, Paris, https://dx.doi.org/10.1787/9789264311978-en. [4]

OECD (2019), *Digital Innovation: Seizing Policy Opportunities*, OECD Publishing, Paris, https://doi.org/10.1787/a298dc87-en. [20]

OECD (2019), *Individual Learning Accounts: Panacea or Pandora's Box?*, OECD Publishing, Paris, https://doi.org/10.1787/203b21a8-en. [1]

OECD (2019), *Investing in Youth: Korea*, OECD Publishing, Paris, https://doi.org/10.1787/4bf4a6d2-en. [9]

OECD (2019), *OECD Skills Outlook 2019: Thriving in a digital world*, OECD Publishing, Paris, https://doi.org/10.1787/df80bc12-en. [22]

OECD (2016), *Getting Skills Right: Assessing and Anticipating Changing Skill Needs*, Getting Skills Right, OECD Publishing, Paris, https://dx.doi.org/10.1787/9789264252073-en. [5]

OECD (2015), *OECD Skills Strategy Diagnostic Report: Korea*, OECD Publishing, Paris, https://doi.org/10.1787/9789264300286-en. [11]

OECD (forthcoming), *OECD Economic Survey: Korea 2020*, OECD Publishing, Paris. [16]

Seol, G. (2019), *The Fourth Industrial Revolution and Workers in SMEs: Korean case*, Korea Research Institute for Vocational Education and Training (KRIVET). [18]

SkillsFuture SG (2019), *TVET 2019: Open the future.* [15]

Yang, J. and R. Yorozu (2015), *Building a Learning Society in Japan, the Republic of Korea and Singapore*, UNESCO Institute for Lifelong Learning, https://files.eric.ed.gov/fulltext/ED564132.pdf. [13]

Annex 4.A. The Korean Skills Quality Authority

The Korean Skills Quality Authority (KSQA), established in April 2015 under the umbrella of the Ministry of Employment and Labour, is the national body dedicated to quality assurance in the adult learning sector (excluding firms' in-house training). The activities of the KSQA are five-folds: 1) training organisation assessment (accreditation); 2) training evaluation; 3) training performance assessment; 4) trainee evaluation; 5) fraud investigation.

Training organisation assessment (accreditation)

Through the training organisation assessment, KSQA provides accreditation to training providers that meet certain minimum quality standards. KSQA first checks the provider's appropriateness, i.e. it monitors whether the training provider complies with existing regulation and assesses its financial soundness (e.g. whether it respects national and local tax legislations).

Then, KSQA carries out an evaluation[19] that assesses the performance of the training provider based on a number of dimensions and provides a score (up to 100 points) that reflects overall performance. In this evaluation, KSQA assesses training outcomes (60 points) such as courses completion rates, satisfaction surveys, and trainee evaluation results.

KSQA also carries out an on-site assessment (40 points) which evaluates other organisational aspects, such as facility and equipment, trainers, and trainee management. The final score determines whether the training provider is entitled to receive the accreditation, as well as the duration of validity of such accreditation.

If the training provider receives a score inferior to 60, accreditation is rejected. Conversely, training providers that receive at least 60 points receive accreditation. The validity of such accreditation is 1, 3 or 5 years, depending on overall performance. Only accredited training providers are allowed to receive financial support from the government, and preferential support is given to best performers.

Training evaluation

After being accredited, training providers are assessed on a regular basis by KSQA. KSQA adopts a different evaluation procedure for assessing collective training (i.e. class-based; face-to-face training) and distance training.

- **Collective training**: The quality of collective training is assessed using a number of criteria, including compliance with NCSs, training hours, facilities, as well as training assessment strategies. The evaluation is conducted by an evaluation committee composed of thematic experts.[20] Around 30 000 collective training courses are assessed every year. The results of the assessment are displayed in HRD-net; and a report is published on an annual basis and is available to the general public.
- **Distance training**: distance training includes internet-based training, smart training (e.g. delivered through virtual reality), and mail-based training – delivered by private training providers, by the national HRD consortium and by corporate universities. The quality of distance training is assessed based on a variety of criteria, such as skills development/improvement. The results of the evaluation are summarised in a final grade (A, B, C) that reflects the quality of the e-learning training provider. Better grades give training providers access to more generous government subsidies. Around 20 000 distance training courses are assessed every year by the KSQA.

Training performance assessment

The training performance assessment evaluates the performance of central and regional government VET projects, as well as the HRD Consortium, and Work-Learning Dual System. It looks for potential duplication/overlaps among training programmes and reviews the alignment of training courses with skills needs. It also selects training providers suitable to develop talent in the context of the 4th industrial revolution.

Trainee evaluation

Through the trainee evaluation, KSQA evaluates the achievement level of trainees. Among other dimensions, the trainee evaluation assesses whether the participants who completed training courses have acquired the expected skills as measured by the NCSs. The results of the trainee evaluation are used in different ways: they are directly communicated to training providers, in a view to encourage them to improve the quality of their services; they are used to help KSQA decide whether accreditation should be renewed; they are used to determine the level of government financial support.

Annex Table 4.A.1. Trainee evaluation, assessment items

Assessment area	Points	Detailed items	Points
Assessment strategy	25	Assessment strategy is appropriate for its target and the purpose of training	10
		Assessment tools are suitable for measuring trainee's performance	15
Assessment implementation	35	Pre-assessment on trainees is implemented in order to be responsible to the needs of trainees	7
		Assessment activities have been implemented as initially planned	23
		Accurate and accessible information about assessment is provided to trainees	5
Follow-up management	10	Follow-up management is properly conducted depending on trainee's assessment result	10
Sample assessment (assessment on trainees)	30	Trainees achieve unit of NCS	30
Additional points	5	Financial incentives are properly distributed to trainers and assessors, in applicable	3
		The trainees results of NCS based training are systematically managed	2

Source: KSQA (2019[8]), KSQA Introduction, PPT.

Fraud investigation

The KSQA has a *Fraud Investigation Centre* that systematically investigates and prevents fraudulent practices among training providers. The *Fraud Investigation Centre* has different functions: i) it detects suspicious training providers, by analysing big data patterns and conducting audits/investigations; ii) it prevents fraud, by providing prevention training, as well as by disseminating casebooks, flyers and other prevention material to training providers; iii) it provides incentives to training providers to comply with rules, by integrating the results of fraud investigations into certification procedures and training evaluations.

Notes

[1] Thus, indirectly, workers pay for their training, as their wages do not increase in line with the productivity gain by the firm.

[2] A similar challenge is found in OECD European countries, where on average 21% of training hours are spent on compulsory training – according to the Continuing Vocational Training Survey (CVTS).

[3] Including both in-house training and entrusted training.

[4] Differences between Figure 4.1 and Figure 4.5 reflect the fact that the former includes all job-related training, including training initiated voluntarily by the worker, while the latter includes only training initiated by the firm. Differences may also reflect the different definitions of SME workers: in Figure 4.1 a SME worker is defined as an employee working for a firm with 250 employees or less, while in Figure 4.5 a SME worker is defined as an employee working for a firm with 100-299 employees.

[5] Further subsidies are available for setting up learning groups and to fund staff responsible for managing these groups. Funds can be also used to provide training to CEOs and staff responsible for learning activities. The final set of subsidies allows companies to take part in peer-learning activities and share their experience of building a learning organisation.

[6] The skill level classification employed in the Occupational Labour Force Survey at Establishment classifies the skill level by five categories with regards to work experience, educational attainment and certificates: skill level 1 refers to an occupation with no requirement for experience, diploma, and certificate; skill level 2-1 refers to an occupation that requires less than a year of experience or craftsman certificate or educational attainment of high school graduate; skill level 2-2 refers to an occupation that requires one to two years of experience or industrial engineer certificate or educational attainment of two-year college graduate; skill level 3 refers to an occupation that requires two to ten years of experience or engineer certificate or educational attainment of university graduate or master degree; skill level 4 refers to an occupation that requires more than ten years of experience or professional engineer certificate or educational attainment of doctoral degree.

[7] Additional SAA studies are conducted on a more ad-hoc basis. For example, in 2014 the Federation of Korean Industries (FKI) conducted a survey on 800 Employees (including SMEs) to assess the skills required in the Digital Economy.

[8] Called "enhancement training programmes".

[9] Various adult learning programmes are implemented by national, regional, and local governments. In the public sector, 40 Korean Polytechnic University campuses offer courses for adults and 26 universities have instituted adult learning centres. 16 Regional and 17 Industry Skills Councils are have started to deliver their own training programmes, in line with regional and industry needs. The private sector also plays an important role in delivering adult learning programmes. There are around 7 000 private training providers in Korea. Large companies (such as Samsung, LG, and Hyundai) have established their own closed employee training system. On top of traditional courses, distance learning is also expanding: the offer of cyber and open universities can be found alongside thousands of e-learning courses offered by online portals such as K-MOOC and Neulbaeum (see Chapters 2 and 3).

[10] Since 2019, the Korean government has fully abolished government subsidies for non-job-related mandatory training, and has reduced support for job-related mandatory training from 100% to 50% of training costs. This is a step in the right direction: using the public purse to finance compulsory training risks generating large deadweight losses (i.e. financing training that would have taken place even in the absence of the subsidy), on top of representing a missed opportunity to provide workers with the skills needed to adapt to future labour market challenges.

[11] For jobseekers' training, the KSQA uses other indicators to assess training quality, such as employment rates after training.

[12] Training quality is particularly hard to measure when it comes to workers' training, as opposed to training for the unemployed, for which indicators such as employment rates, wages, employment retention period after training, can be used.

[13] Similarly to what happens in Korea, the aggregated results are published online while the detailed results are shared with training providers.

[14] The Learning Experience Recognition System was made institutionary possible through the revision of the law in 2017, but there have been no cases of recognition for work experience.

[15] The ratio of NCS-based courses out of the total number of training programmes provided, is one of the criteria used to receive certification by the KSQA. For continuous assessment of training providers, KSQA requires 40% of curricula compliance with NCS.

[16] NCSs framework is updated every three years.

[17] For example, in the case of big data analysis (NCS), the training time is different for each unit, e.g. visualisation of big data analysis results (40 hours), building data for analysis (20 hours) and data analysis based on machine learning (80 hours).

[18] To reflect the demand for new industries and new technologies, the Korean government launched the training programme for nurturing pioneers for the 4th Industrial Revolution in 2017. This programme defines eight training areas for the 4th Industrial Revolution, which include smart factory and robot, IoT (Internet of Things), big data and AI (Artificial Intelligence), information security, bio-chemical innovation, finance and technology, unmanned aerial vehicle, and AR (Augmented Reality) or VR (Virtual Reality) (MoEL, 2016[23]).

[19] Organisation Competency Assessment.

[20] Experts are called Subject Matter Experts.

5 Improving the financing and governance of the Korean adult learning system

In Korea, like in other OECD countries, the governance and financing of the adult learning system involves many actors. While the Ministry of Employment and Labour is the main body responsible for training policies, other ministries and local governments are also involved in adult learning. Stakeholders such as firms, trade unions, and training providers, also have a key role to play. This chapter examines the financing and governance of the Korean adult learning system, focussing on the programmes available to SMEs and SME workers.

In Brief

Adult learning financing and governance is key for enhancing training opportunities in SMEs

Korea has put in place many adult learning policy measures to enhance training participation in SMEs. These programmes are financed by different actors and fall under the responsibilities of different government bodies and stakeholders. This chapter examines the financing and governance of adult learning in Korea. The key findings of this chapter can be summarised as follows:

- In Korea, training programmes for employees are mainly financed through a levy-grant system paid by employers that feeds into the Employment Insurance Fund. Despite the preferential support given to smaller firms, SMEs still do not use the financial incentive system as much as large firms do. In 2018, some 29.7% of insured SME workers took part in the training financed by the Employment Insurance, compared to 54.8% of workers in large firms.[1]
- Social partners have very limited responsibilities over adult learning financing. This is very different from what can be observed in many OECD countries with a training levy in place, where social partners are often responsible for managing (at least part of) the funding for adult learning.
- While the Ministry of Employment and Labour (MoEL) is the primary actor and funder of adult learning, other ministries and the local government also play a role. In a view to promote a whole-of-government approach in adult learning, in recent years Korea has updated the legal framework to prevent different ministries from implementing similar and overlapping programmes.
- Korea's adult learning system has remained relatively centralised. However, recognising the important role that local actors could play in adult learning, MoEL has steadily increased the funding for local governments to implement adult learning programmes. MoEL is also empowering local quadripartite councils – i.e. an integrated governance body involving labour, management, government and civic groups, which deals with local employment, human resource development, and industrial relations in many regions.
- In recent years, the government has been taking steps to better involve social partners in adult learning. One important initiative was the establishment of regional skills councils (RSCs) and industry skills councils (ISCs). However, much remains to be done to ensure that these bodies can successfully fulfil their roles. Some of the challenges revolve around the lack of experience of the personnel; the weak cooperation between RSCs and ISCs; the imbalance of responsibilities between employers' organisations and trade unions; and the fact that RSCs and ISCs are financially dependent to the government.
- Social dialogue at firm level could also be improved. Labour-Management Councils (LMCs) in Korea could represent a valid tool for workers and firms to jointly identify training needs, regularly discuss the quality of training programmes undertaken, and explore best training options. Despite their potential, the influence of LMCs on adult learning issues remains weak, especially in SMEs.

Introduction

In Korea, like in other OECD countries, the governance and financing of the adult learning system involves many actors. A variety of ministries, local governments, and other stakeholders have some degree of responsibility over adult learning. This chapter provides an overview of the Korean adult learning system, focussing on financing and governance. The chapter is structured as follows. Section 5.1 provides a snapshot of how the adult learning system is financed. Section 5.2 describes how the governance of the adult learning system is organised.

5.1. Financing adult learning

Adult learning in Korea is financed through two main channels: general accounts and the Employment Insurance Fund. Funding from general accounts are primarily used for training for the unemployed or vulnerable groups. The Employment Insurance Fund is mainly used for training for incumbent workers or the unemployed with an employment insurance record (see Box 5.1 for a description of the Korean Employment Insurance system).

Box 5.1. The Employment Insurance system in Korea

The Employment Insurance (EI) system of Korea, introduced in 1995, is a compulsory social insurance that aims to prevent joblessness, promote employment, and improve workers' vocational skills. Korea's EI system finances unemployment benefits, vocational training for incumbent workers and the employment security to retain or create jobs.

All employers and employees are obliged to pay an insurance premium into the EI fund and are entitled to receive training subsidies or unemployment benefits. EI premium rates include a rate for employment security and vocational skills development programmes, and a rate for unemployment benefits (Table 5.1).

Table 5.1. Employment Insurance premium rates paid by employers and employees

Percentage of the total taxable wage bill

	Total	Employer	Employee
Unemployment Benefits	1.30	0.65	0.65
Employment security and vocational skill development programmes	Between 0.25 and 0.85 (depending on firm size)	Between 0.25 and 0.85 (depending on firm size)	None

Source: MOEL (2018[1]), Employment Insurance White Paper.

The EI system has gradually expanded its coverage. As a result, the number of people insured went from just over 4 million at its inception, to 13.4 million in 2018. However, coverage is still far from universal. According to the Economically Active Population Survey (Supplementary Results by Employment type), in 2018 the ratio of the number of insured persons to the number of salaried workers was around 71.6% (87% for regular workers and 43.6% for non-regular workers, respectively).

Low coverage means that many workers are not entitled to benefit from training programmes financed through EI. To tackle this issue, in January 2019 the Korean government expanded the coverage of EI-funded training programmes to workers who are not enrolled in EI – using general account budgets. The government also plans to introduce an unemployment assistance scheme in 2020 to reduce "blind spots" in social protection.

Over the last decade, as shown in Figure 5.1, total expenditure on training has gradually increased reaching KRW 2.58 trillion (about EUR 2 billion) in 2018. Vocational training programmes in Korea rely mainly on the Employment Insurance Fund paid by employers. Indeed, in 2018, some 81% of the funding came from the Employment Insurance Fund.

Figure 5.1. Trends in government spending in VET, by financing sources

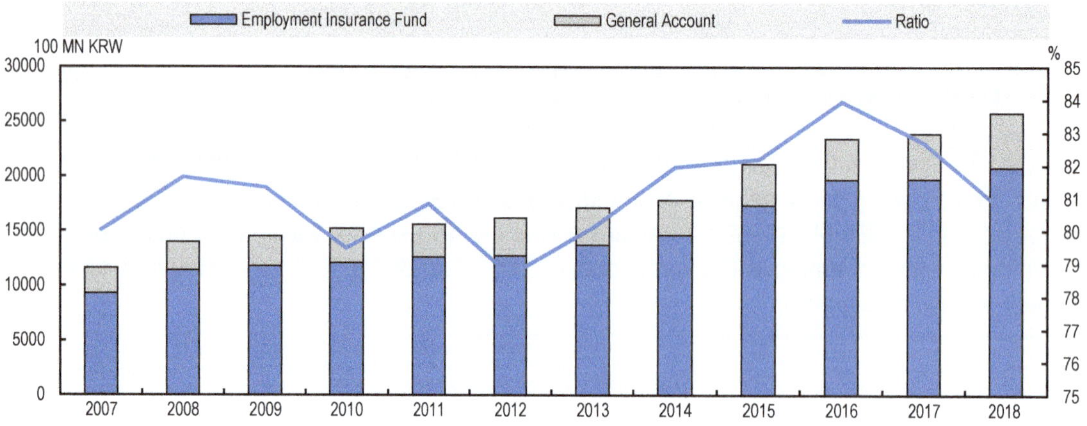

Note: Ratio refers to the percentage of the funding that comes from the Employment Insurance Fund. Data excludes initial vocational education and includes only VET for workers, job-seekers, and disadvantaged groups.
Source: MoEL (2019[2]), Employment and Labor White Paper.

The employment insurance system is funded by a levy-grant scheme. All employers have to contribute to the EI fund, and are entitled to get rebates of training levies to recover the training costs for their workers. The advantage of such a system is that it encourages employers to provide in-company training for their workers, either directly or through outsourced providers. Another advantage is that training programmes are more demand-driven, since they are organised or purchased by the firms themselves in accordance with their needs (Lee, 2016[3]).

The Korean employment insurance system gives more favourable financial incentives to SMEs. Indeed, premium rates vary from 0.25% to 0.85% of the total taxable wage bill depending on firm size, with lowest rates applying to firms with less than 150 workers and highest rates applying to firms with 1 000 or more workers (Table 5.2).

Moreover, rebates are higher for SMEs than for large firms. The level of rebates for SMEs is at 100% of the training costs and up to a total of 240% of training levies paid. Conversely, for large firms it is at 40% of training costs, up to a total of 100% of training levies paid (Table 5.2).

Table 5.2. The Korean levy-grant system under the Employment Insurance

	Contribution and maximum rebates rate		Subsidy rate of training cost (%)
	Insurance premium rate (%)	Maximum rebates rate (%)	
Less than 150 employees	0.25	240	100
SMEs (eligible for preferential supports)	0.45	240	100
Large firms with less than 1 000 employees	0.65	100	60
Large firms with 1 000 or more employees	0.85	100	40

Note: SMEs (eligible for preferential supports) refer to Preferentially Supported Enterprises in the Employment Insurance Act. The number of employees in this category varies by industry, i.e. 500 or less in manufacturing, 300 or less in mining, construction, and telecommunications, 200 or less in wholesale and retail trade, and 100 or less in other industries. See Chapter 3 for further information.
Source: MoEL (2019[4]), Employment Insurance White Paper.

As a result, the training levy recovery rate (which reflects the difference between training levy and rebates) is higher for SMEs than large firms. For example, in 2018, the recovery rate for SMEs with 50 to 99 employees was about 61%, compared to just 8.4% in large firm with 1 000 or more employees (Figure 5.2).

Figure 5.2. Average training levy recovery rate, by firm size, 2018

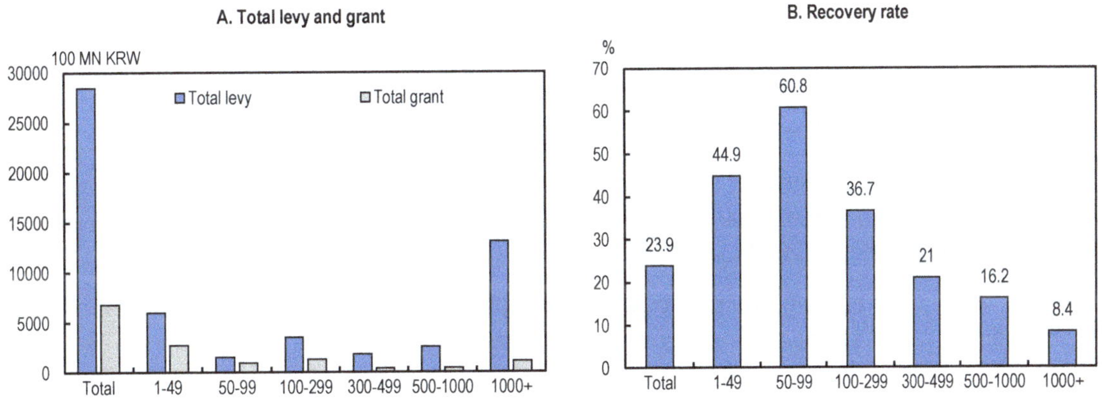

Note: Recovery rate refers to the difference between total training levy paid and rebates received through grant.
Source: MoEL (2019[2]), Employment and Labor White Paper.

Although it has served as an effective incentive for companies to conduct job-related skills training, the levy-grant system is not flawless. Despite preferential treatment given to smaller firms, SMEs still do not use the financial incentives system as much as large firms do. According to Employment Insurance administrative data, in 2018 some 29.7% of total insured SME workers (less than 300 employees) took part in the training financed by the Employment Insurance, compared to 54.8% of workers in large firms (with 300 or more employees). Participation rates are even lower for workers in micro- or small firms (Table 5.3.).

Table 5.3. Training participation rate of EI insured workers by firm size

	2011	2012	2013	2014	2015	2016	2017	2018
Total	31.3	31.0	31.1	29.0	23.4	25.5	28.7	36.6
1-299	21.1	18.8	22.2	21.2	16.8	17.3	21.4	29.7
1-49	17.0	14.2	19.8	19.1	11.8	11.6	14.0	21.2
50-99	24.4	21.4	20.4	19.9	23.2	27.3	33.7	42.1
100-299	35.0	33.9	32.1	29.3	30.9	32.5	41.8	55.0
+300	59.5	62.0	54.3	49.1	41.0	47.5	48.3	54.8
300-499	44.1	40.5	37.4	33.4	33.9	39.2	50.4	62.9
500-999	52.0	49.0	43.0	40.6	38.1	42.1	46.8	58.9
1000+	66.2	71.7	61.9	55.7	43.6	51.3	48.2	51.5

Note: Training participation rate refers to the percentage of workers who take training financed by the Employment Insurance among the total EI-insured workers.
Source: Administrative data provided by the Ministry of Employment and Labor.

This situation shows how, as discussed in Chapter 2, financial incentives alone are insufficient to favour training in SMEs. Besides training costs, SMEs also face other obstacles – such as poaching risks, asymmetry of information on available training options, and administrative burdens to arrange training and recover levies – that needs to be tackled to favour skills investments.

In the Korean levy-grant system, workers' training is largely financed through the premiums that employers pay into the employment insurance fund. Although in theory the Employment Insurance Committee – which is composed of various social partners – provides advice on the direction of vocational skills development programmes, in practice their voices are not always heard.

In the medium- to long-term, there is room for Korea to look at the experience of OECD countries with a training levy in place, where social partners are generally responsible for managing financial resources, at least in some sectors (OECD, 2019[5]).

For example, in Italy, the training levy paid by employers (0.3% of payroll) is directly managed by the *Fondi Interprofessionali*, i.e. associations run by social partners that aim to finance workers' training (see Box 5.2). Similar training funds exist in other OECD countries such as the Netherlands (O&O), and Ireland (Skillnet Ireland). As another example, in Sweden, Job Security Councils – associations run by social partners that are responsible for ensuring smooth transitions from one job to another, through training and other measures – are financed by a levy paid by employers (0.3% of payroll).

Allowing social partners to manage a training budget – e.g. part of the employment insurance fund[2] – could empower employers and workers to work together on adult learning, increase their knowledge and understanding of adult learning challenges, and better align training to the needs of firms and workers. For example, one option could be to allow the Regional and Industry Skills Councils to manage at least part of the training budget (see Section 5.2.3). For this to happen successfully, parallel efforts should be taken to enhance social partners' interest and involvement in adult learning, and strengthen their capability to manage funding in a transparent manner.

Box 5.2. Training funds in Italy

Training Funds (hereafter TFs) are associations run by social partners that finance workers' training, using resources collected through a training levy imposed on employers. The main policy goal of the Training Funds is to provide incentives to firms to invest in the human capital of their workers and promote continuous learning and skills development opportunities.

One distinctive feature of Training Funds is that they are run by social partners. Training Funds' management boards comprise equal numbers of representatives appointed from employers and workers' organisations. All types of training programmes financed need to be agreed by social partners.

While Training Funds work autonomously, they function under the umbrella of government bodies. The Ministry of Labour and Social Affairs authorises the establishment of new Training Funds after verifying compliance with a set of requirements, and can temporarily suspend or terminate them if these requirements are no longer met.

Training Funds are financed through a levy-grant mechanism. Firms can allocate part of the 'mandatory contribution for involuntary unemployment' – 0.3% of workers' payroll, paid to the INPS (*National Institute for Social Security*) – to a Training Fund of their choosing.

If a firm voluntarily joins a Training Fund, the INPS directly transfers the 0.3% to the selected Training Fund. Companies that do not elect to join a Training Fund still need to pay the 0.3%, which integrates government budgets and can be used to serve different purposes.

Since their inception, Training Funds have rapidly increased their importance and outreach. From 2004 to 2017, the number of firms enrolled in a Training Fund has tripled and the number of workers covered by the scheme has doubled. Today Training Funds cover almost 1 million firms and over 10 million workers, capturing almost the totality of potential adherents. Managing EUR 603 million in 2017, Training Funds represent one of the most important sources for financing workers' continuous learning in Italy.

Source: OECD (2019[6]), *Adult Learning in Italy: what role for training funds?*, OECD Publishing, Paris.

5.2. Governance mechanisms in adult learning

In Korea, like in other OECD countries, adult learning is a complex policy area. It covers a variety of programmes with different objectives and target groups. As a result, the responsibility for adult learning often falls under several ministries, different levels of government and social partners. In this context, good coordination mechanisms are essential to ensure that policies do not overlap and complement each other. This section provides an overview of the governance of the Korean adult learning system and describes what Korea is doing to improve co-ordination across different actors involved in adult learning.

5.2.1. Horizontal (inter-ministerial) co-ordination

As in other OECD countries, adult learning in Korea is under the responsibility of several ministries. For example, a total of 11 ministries have implemented 38 projects in the field of adult learning policy in 2019.

The Ministry of Employment and Labour (MoEL), however, is the primary actor and funder of adult learning. Most adult learning policies are delivered by MoEL implementing bodies, such as HRD Korea and public employment services (in charge of training programmes for employees and the unemployed, respectively).

In adult learning, MoEL is responsible for making and revising laws; designating and managing training facilities; certifying training courses; and subsidising training costs. MoEL also is also responsible for operating public training institutions, evaluating training institutions, and fostering the private training market (MoEL, 2010[7]).

Reflecting its key role in adult learning, MoEL's spending on training programmes is high compared to spending observed in other ministries. Indeed, in 2019, 87.6% of government spending on vocational training were under the responsibility of the MoEL (Table 5.4).

Table 5.4. Government spending on training programmes, by ministry

Government spending on training programmes in 2019 (KRW 100 million)

	Ministry of Employment and Labor	Ministry of Education	Ministry of Science and ICT	Ministry of SMEs and Start-ups	Ministry of Gender Equality and Family	Others
Government spending	17 270	1 088	577	391	217	168
Ratio (%)	87.6	5.5	2.9	2.0	1.1	0.9

Note: Data refer to vocational training budget in each ministry among government-funded job-related budget.
Source: Administrative data provided by the Ministry of Employment and Labor.

While the MoEL is the main body responsible for training policies, the Ministry of Education (MoE) takes charge of overall lifelong education policies including some formal types of adult learning and basic skills training. For example, MoE has selected and supported lifelong education universities and colleges to serve the needs of lifelong learners and workers going back to school to obtain university diplomas (MoEL, 2017[8]). MoE is also supporting local learning centres, which run a variety of lifelong learning courses for adults in the community centres or senior citizen centres (OECD, 2020[9]).

The Ministry of SMEs and Start-ups (MSS) also runs adult learning programmes tailored to the needs of SMEs, in the overarching aim to tackle chronic labour shortages in SMEs. For example, MSS promotes industry-academia cooperation in vocational high schools and junior colleges. Other projects aim to raise awareness among SME CEOs and business owners on the importance of training (see Chapter 2).

Other ministries are also involved in adult learning, and often work on specific sectors or target groups. For example, the Ministry of Science and ICT focuses on the development and use of workforce in science and technology.

All in all, these ministries oversee different adult learning policy areas, rely on different legal frameworks, organise their work around different governance bodies, and use different delivery systems. Table 5.5 provides a summary of the key ministries responsible for adult learning in Korea, and the main frameworks under which they operate. In addition, as shown in Table 5.6, each ministry has its own strategy and masterplan for adult learning.

Table 5.5. Key ministries responsible for adult learning in Korea

	Ministry of Employment and Labor	Ministry of Education	Ministry of SMEs and Start-ups
Policy area	Vocational Skills Development	Lifelong learning	Labour shortages and mismatch
Key legislation	Act on the Development of Vocational Skills of Workers	Lifelong Education Act	Special Act on Support for Human Resources of SMEs
Governance	Employment Policy Council	Lifelong Education Promotion Committee	-
Delivery system	HRD Korea and PES	National Institute of Lifelong Learning	Korea SMEs and Start-ups Agency

Source: OECD 2019 Questionnaire: National Skills Strategy for Korea.

Table 5.6. Adult learning strategies in Korea

	Name of the strategy	Year of implementation
Ministry of Employment and Labor	The 3rd Basic Plan of Vocational Education and Training for Innovation and Inclusive Growth	2018-22
	Innovation Plan for Vocational Competency Development in respond to Labour Market Changes (with Job Council)	Adopted in 2019
Ministry of Education	The 4th Basic Plan for Lifelong learning Promotion	2018-22
	Innovation Plan for Lifelong Vocational and Training	Adopted in 2018
Ministry of SMEs and Startups	SME Manpower Support Basic Plan	2016-20
Ministry of Science and ICT	The 3rd Basic Plan for developing Science and Technology Human Resources	Adopted in 2015
	Support Plan for Nurturing Talents in Science, Technology and ICT in respond to the 4th Industrial Revolution	Adopted in 2019

Source: OECD 2019 Questionnaire: National Skills Strategy for Korea.

The Korean central government is aware that a lack of inter-ministerial co-ordination can lead to overlaps and gaps in adult learning provision, and a whole-of-government approach is needed to achieve better results.

To promote better coordination, Korea has updated the legal framework (Framework Act on Employment Policy) to prevent different ministries from implementing similar and overlapping programmes (OECD, 2019[10]). Alongside updates in the legal framework, and to facilitate implementation, MoEL has been developing and distributing the "Guidelines for the Design and Operation of Government-Funded Employment Programs" every year.

Through this initiative, MoEL examines whether any new government-funded employment programme is similar to or overlapping with any existing programme, e.g. whether they share similar objectives, content, and target groups. The examination results are sent to the government offices concerned and the Ministry of Strategy and Finance. Similar or overlapping projects are not reflected (or included) in the government's budget.

5.2.2. Vertical co-ordination between different levels of government

Korea's adult learning system has remained relatively centralised. Central government has been traditionally responsible for most of legislation, policy design as well as implementation and financing. Conversely, local governments have played a relatively minor role in adult learning, with some notable exceptions in some regions where they directly operate training institutions.

The important role played by the central government is also reflected in how adult learning is financed. As of 2019, the local governments' expenditure on employment supports is KRW 1.4 trillion (about EUR 1.1 billion), representing only 6.1% of the central government's budget (KRW 22.9 trillion, about EUR 17.9 billion). In particular, the vocational training budget stood at KRW 67.8 billion (about EUR 53 million), just 3.5% of the central government's budget (KRW 1961 billion, about EUR 1.5 billion) (Table 5.7).

Table 5.7. Expenditure by types of employment supports, 2019

100 Million, KRW (%)

	Total	Direct job creation	Training	PES and administration	Employment incentives	Start-up incentives	Out-of-work income maintenance and support
Central government (A)	229 308 (100.0)	37 713 (16.4)	19 610 (8.6)	9 867 (4.3)	57 883 (25.2)	25 098 (10.9)	79 139 (34.5)
Local governments (B)	14 051 (100.0)	8 231 (58.8)	678 (4.8)	2 080 (14.8)	2 405 (17.1)	657 (4.7)	-
Ratio [(B/A)×100]	6.1	21.8	3.5	21.1	4.2	2.6	-

Source: Administrative data provided by the Ministry of Employment and Labor.

Recognising the important role that the local level could play in adult learning, the government has been taking steps to encourage local actors to be more engaged in adult learning policy. For example, in 2010 the MoEL introduced the *"Local job creation target notice system"*. Under this system, heads of local governments announce to local citizens the goals and plans associated to job creation, which are to be pursued throughout their term in office. These goals and plans include measures to create jobs, reduce supply demand mismatches, and develop vocational skills. Since 2012, all (a total of 243) local governments have joined the system.

Moreover, during the past years, MoEL has gradually increased the funding for the *"Local-customised job creation support programme"*. The project, in operation since 2006, aims to select and support projects to ensure that local governments can take a lead role in designing and implementing their own training and employment projects (OECD, 2014[11]). This programme has provided an opportunity to broaden local vocational education and training market and contributed to the capacity building of local governments (MoEL, 2014[12]).

Finally, in order to increase local policy co-ordination and integration, in the past years the government has reorganised local governance structures that had overlapping functions. For example, existing bodies were consolidated into local quadripartite councils – a governance body involving labour, management, government and civic groups – which today deals with local employment, human resource development, and industrial relations in many regions. Major training projects initiated by the central government can now be coordinated by local quadripartite councils and going forward a variety of local projects could be actively carried out under their leadership.

5.2.3. Co-ordination between the government and the social partners

Traditionally social partners have played a very minor role in adult learning policy in Korea (OECD, 2019[13]). Because vocational education and training historically had a strategic role for the economic growth of Korea, its coordination has been managed by the state, with little involvement by companies and workers (EPF, 2017[14]). However, recent rapid technological innovation and the deterioration of the employment situation have put great pressures on the adult learning system, setting the scene for the reform of its governance. In particular, strengthening partnerships with private sector stakeholders has emerged as an important policy priority.

Empowering Regional and Industry Skills Councils

Among the various initiatives launched over the last few years to better involve social partners in adult learning, one significant step has been to set up Regional Skills Councils (RSCs) and Industry Skills

Councils (ISCs). The objective of these bodies is to make the adult learning system more responsive to business needs and to introduce more flexibility in the delivery and implementation of vocational training programmes. For example, the two councils support drafting HRD plans, administer skills surveys, and deliver training programmes.

Since 2013, a total of 17 RSCs have been set up. RSCs are led by relevant stakeholders in each region, such as industries representing each region, members from the local government, local employment and labour offices, regional small and medium business administrations, and local education offices (Table 5.8). The main tasks of RSCs are to perform surveys of skills demand for employers in their regions, and to designate joint training centres to satisfy the demands identified through the surveys.

Table 5.8. Stakeholders involved in RSCs

	Total	Trade Union	Employers	Business association	Local and central government	Universities, etc.
No. of Organisation	359	19	16	142	64	118
Ratio	100.0	5.3	4.5	39.6	17.8	32.9

Source: MoEL (2019[15]), Innovative Measures for Vocational Competency Development in respond to labour market changes.

Since 2015, a total of 17 ISCs have also been set up. ISCs are led by business associations/organisations and trade unions representing each industry (Table 5.9). ISCs analyse manpower supply and demand by industry and are actively involved in promoting National Competency Standards (NCS) and the Work-Study Dual System.

Table 5.9. Stakeholders involved in ISCs

	Total	Trade Union	Employer	Business association	Professional organisation	University / research institution
No. of Organisation	372	23	145	136	30	38
Ratio	100.0	6.2	39.0	36.5	8.1	10.2

Source: MoEL (2019[15]), Innovative Measures for Vocational Competency Development in respond to labour market changes.

The establishment of RSCs and ISCs signals a partial devolution of the adult learning governance, and it is seen as a policy shift to make adult learning more responsive to local and industrial demands. Going forward, many of the roles that Korean social partners could undertake more thoroughly – e.g. policy design, quality monitoring, adult learning financing – could be successfully undertaken by RSCs and ISCs.

However, Korea's training market is still strongly influenced by the central government, and much remains to be done to ensure that RSCs and ISCs can successfully fulfil their roles and effectively promote social dialogue on adult learning. Some of the key challenges they are facing include:

- RSCs and ISCs are at an earlier stage of development and still require training and development of their personnel (Moon, Ryu and Jeon, 2019[16]).
- Because they are assisted or funded by the MoEL, they have little autonomy and are still perceived by some stakeholders as a central government body rather than a region- and industry-led initiative.
- Cooperation between RSCs and ISCs remains weak and their operations are segmented and at times overlapping.

- RSCs and ISCs still require more active participation from trade unions (OECD, 2015[17]). For example, of the 17 RSCs, 15 are co-chaired by employers' organisations and local government. Trade unions, on the other hand, co-chair only two RSCs. They have only 1-2 member representatives in RSCs. Recognising this challenge, the Korean government has announced a plan to increase the share of trade union Skills Councils representatives from 5-6% (as of the first half of 2019) to 10% (MoEL, 2019[18]).

To ensure that Regional and Industry Skills Councils can successfully fulfil their new roles and effectively promote social dialogue on adult learning, Korea should:

- *Invest in capacity building of Regional and Industry Skills Councils* and provide adequate training to their personnel.
- *Allow Regional and Industry Skills Councils to autonomously manage a training budget*. This would give them greater autonomy and recognition as a social partners' body rather than as a government body.
- *Ensure better cooperation between Regional and Industry Skills Councils*. This would ensure better coordination and fewer overlaps in roles and responsibilities.
- *Balance the power between employers' organisations and trade* unions. Ensure that trade unions are more equally represented in Regional and Industry Skills Councils.

Make quality assurance a joint responsibility with social partners

Due to their proximity to workers and firms, social partners could play an important role in Korea in promoting training quality and ensuring that training is aligned with skills needs. However, social partners in Korea are not much involved in the quality assurance and monitoring of adult learning programmes. For example, unlike what can be observed in many OECD countries, in Korea social partners do not have representation on national agencies responsible for the quality assurance of adult learning (e.g. the KSQA), they do not participate in the accreditation of training providers, and do not actively collect information on training quality. Perhaps Korea could learn from the experience of OECD countries – such as Belgium, Denmark, Germany and Sweden – that have successfully involved social partners in adult learning quality monitoring mechanisms (Box 5.3).

Social partners should have representation on national agencies responsible for the quality assurance of adult learning (e.g. the Korean Skills Quality Authority); they should participate in the accreditation of training providers; and actively collect information on training quality, for example through surveys among workers and firms.

Box 5.3. Making adult learning a joint responsibility: examples from OECD countries

National Agencies for Quality Assurance

In **Sweden**, the Swedish National Agency for Higher Vocational Education (*Myndigheten för yrkeshögskolan*) ensures the quality of higher vocational education programmes. Both trade unions and employers are represented on the agency's advisory council for labour market issues. The role of the advisory council includes the inspections of providers and programmes, including work-based training elements. The inspections entail observational visits, interviews with students, tutors, teachers and head coordinators. Based on the inspection, as well as an assessments of labour market needs, the council advises the Swedish National Agency for Higher Vocational Education about which training programmes should receive state grants and be included in the higher vocational education offer.

Accreditation of training providers

In **Flanders** (Belgium), since September 2019 there are three accreditation streams for adult learning programmes that benefit from government incentives: i) automatic accreditation for certain (often more general or formal) training programmes (e.g. adult education centres and higher education institutions); ii) accreditation through social partners (*Paritaire Comités*) for training organised at the sector level; and iii) accreditation by the Flemish accreditation commission (*Vlaamse erkenningscommissie*) for all other training. The Flemish accreditation commission consists of social partners.

In **Germany**, certification of trainings in the context of active labour market policies is conducted by certifying bodies (*Zertifizierungsstelle*). One of the better-known certifying bodies, CERTQUA, is run by the leading German employer organisations. Certifying bodies, in turn, need to be accredited by the German Federal Public Employment Agency (*Bundesagentur für Arbeit*). An advisory council, composed of trade unions and employer organisations among other stakeholders, supports the agency in this work.

Collection of data on training quality

Social partners in **Denmark** are involved in the 11 continuing training and education committees, which monitor adult vocational training in different sectors of the labour market. One of the key inputs to the monitoring of programmes and providers is information produced through the system *Vis Kvalitet*. This system collects data from each participant about their satisfaction with the training via a questionnaire, as well as data from a sample of companies whose employees have attended training. Results are used by the committees to identify quality issues and develop remedial action.

Source: OECD (2019[13]), Making Adult Learning Work in Social Partnership, OECD Publishing, http://www.oecd.org/employment/emp/adult-learning-work-in-social-partnership-2019.pdf.

Ensure that trade unions are more actively engaged in adult learning

Trade unions could play an important role in understanding (SME) workers' training needs and reflecting these needs into training programmes. They have incentives to protect the interests of existing workers, ensure that all employees have access to training, and that their skills are sufficiently transferable to allow for mobility across companies.

Yet, traditionally labour unions in Korea have not paid much attention to adult learning issues and seemed to have had a rather passive role on training (Oh and Park, 2012[19]). They have given priority to other working condition issues considered as more urgent and important than training (e.g. seniority-wages; job stability; dismissals).

Sometimes, policy priorities supported by trade unions seem to be in stark contrast with policy measures that could create an enabling environment in adult learning. For example, trade unions understandably provide large support to seniority-wages (OECD, 2018[20]), a system that may considerably reduce workers' motivation to train and upskill.

Another related challenge is that trade unions lack technical expertise on training and skills issues, and they have poor understanding of the training needs of the workers they represent. Perhaps Korea could learn from the experience of OECD countries that have taken steps to build the expertise of trade union members on adult learning issues (Box 5.4).

Box 5.4. Building the expertise on adult learning among trade unions: the experience of selected OECD countries

- In the United Kingdom, the great majority of unions now include Union Learning Representatives (ULRs) in their management structures – i.e. trade union members who encourage the take-up of learning in the workplace, help workers identify training needs and arrange learning opportunities within their companies. Since its inception in 2006, Unionlearn has trained more than 40 000 URLs. Today, there are around 450 jobs within Unions that relate to supporting skills, around 15-20% of all union employment.
- In Italy, the national collective agreement of the chemistry industry appointed a "training delegate", i.e. a trade union representative whose main role is to develop a deep understanding of the workers' skills needs within the sector, and help shape training plans accordingly.
- In Belgium, training of workers' representatives at the company level is an important element of adult learning. Several branches have specific agreements between the social partners, whereby employers pay for the training of workers' representatives and allow their participation to training during working hours.
- In Switzerland since 2017, Movendo, the institute for the training of trade unions (*Institut de formation des syndicats*) has developed a network of ambassadors for continuous learning.

There is also no cultural expectation that skills are a legitimate union business. Unsurprisingly in this context, over the past years, trade unions have developed and implemented only few, often short-lived, training initiatives themselves. The only example found in this review is the Labour Management Joint Training Programme developed in 2006 (OECD, 2020[9]). The programme was designed taking into account the training needs of workers, and was built with the direct involvement of the local tripartite committee. Although the programme was initially supported by the government and evaluated as an excellent case of Labor-Management-Civil-Government collaboration, it was terminated in 2010 due to lack of transparency in the way budgets were being managed. Lack of awareness around the initiative was also an issue of concern.

The little influence of trade unions on adult learning issues also partly reflects the fact that trade unions represent only a minority of the workforce in Korea – particularly among SME workers. This lack of representation may undermine trade unions' ability to defend workers' (and particularly SME workers') rights and weaken their influence on important labour market matters, including adult learning.

Indeed, trade union density (i.e. the percentage of employees that are union members) in Korea is at 10%, well below the OECD average of 26.2% and at the bottom of the OECD ranking after Estonia, France, Lithuania and Turkey (Figure 5.3, Panel A). Similarly, collective bargaining coverage (i.e. the percentage of employees with the right to bargain) is very low in Korea by international standards. Indeed, only 11.8% of employees have the right to bargain, below the OECD average of 47.3% and among the lowest levels in the OECD (Figure 5.3, Panel A).

The absence of trade unions is even more apparent in SMEs. Indeed, trade unions have usually remained focused on workers in very large enterprises, overlooking workers employed in SMEs. As shown in Figure 5.3, Panel B, in 2017 trade union density ranged from 0.2% in small firms with less than 30 employees to 57.3% in large firms with more than 300 employees.

Korea is taking steps in the right direction to expand trade union coverage, including to SME workers. Over the past two decades, Korean trade unions have made efforts to organise the SME and non-regular workers as members of the industrial or regional-level unions, which may more easily represent their interests than enterprise-level unions (mainly organised by large firms and regular workers). These efforts may also provide an effective bargaining structure (beyond the boundaries of a single company) for SME workers to advocate their interests, including on adult learning, at the sector or regional-level.

Figure 5.3. Trade unions and bargaining in Korea and OECD countries

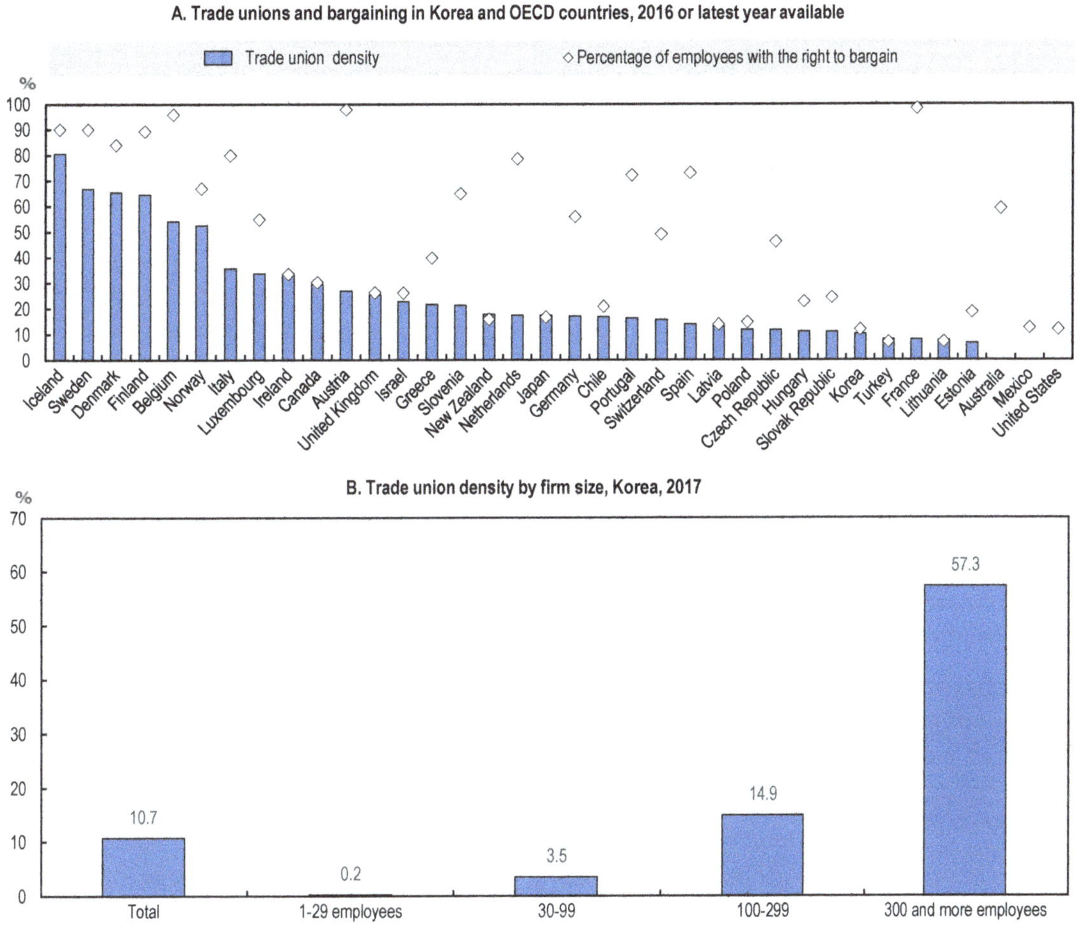

Source: OECD stat for Panel A; and MoEL (2018[21]), "Analysis on trade unions based on data at the local labour office in 2017" for Panel B.

Efforts should be taken to build expertise on adult learning among trade union members. For example, Korean trade unions could appoint dedicated 'training' specialists, whose objectives are to encourage the take-up of learning in the workplace and/or to develop an understanding of the workers' skills needs. Efforts should be undertaken to ensure that trade unions undertake sufficient training themselves, notably on adult learning issues.

5.2.4. Co-ordination between the government and training providers

In addition to social partners, training providers are also important actors in adult learning. The training providers market in Korea is quite fragmented. Private training institutions account for a significant portion of Korea's vocational training market, with 99% of training providers being in the private sector as of 2017 (Table 5.10). However, most institutions rely on government funding and business capacity is relatively small, with only 13% of training provider having 500 or more trainees per year (MoEL, 2017[22]). The competition in the training market has increased after the introduction of My Work Learning Card system in 2008, when individuals were given greater autonomy in making training choices and selecting training providers independently.

Table 5.10. Type of training providers in 2017

Total	Public training institution	Private training institution				
		Subtotal	Provider designated by MOEL	Employers or Employers' organisation	University	Private education institutes
6 884	38	6 846	755	2 937	205	2 949

Source: MoEL (2017[22]), The 3rd Basic Plan of Vocational Education and Training for Innovation and Inclusive Growth.

In this fragmented context, ensuring good coordination between the government and training providers is particularly important. Korea has already established a variety of committees/councils, where training providers and government can meet and discuss training policies. By leveraging these channels, Korea can strengthen its co-ordination between government and training providers to align training programmes to business needs, facilitate the sharing of good practices, and improve training quality.

5.2.5. Promoting social dialogue within firms

Social dialogue at the firm level is also key in adult learning. Indeed, many important training decisions – e.g. whether training should be provided; how much funding should be devoted to training; what types training programmes should be offered to workers – are ultimately taken within firms.

The international experience shows that one way to jointly set priorities for adult learning at company level is to involve staff representatives. Yet, in Korea more could be done in this area. According to several stakeholders, the content of training is often supply- or employer-oriented, and rarely represents the interests and needs of workers (Rok, 2013[23]). Oftentimes, firms unilaterally take training decisions without any inputs from staff.

The little involvement of staff representatives in setting training decision is particularly marked in SMEs, a challenge that Korea shares with other OECD countries (OECD, 2019[13]). Indeed, about half of SMEs in Korea report that workers are not at all involved in training decision: some 44.4% say that workers are informed only once training decisions are taken, and 6% report that workers are not even informed beforehand (against 39% and 5.7% of larger firms respectively) (Figure 5.4) – according to the Workplace Panel Survey (2015).

Figure 5.4. Firms' perception of workers' involvement in decision-making about training, Korea, 2015

Percentage of firms by firm size

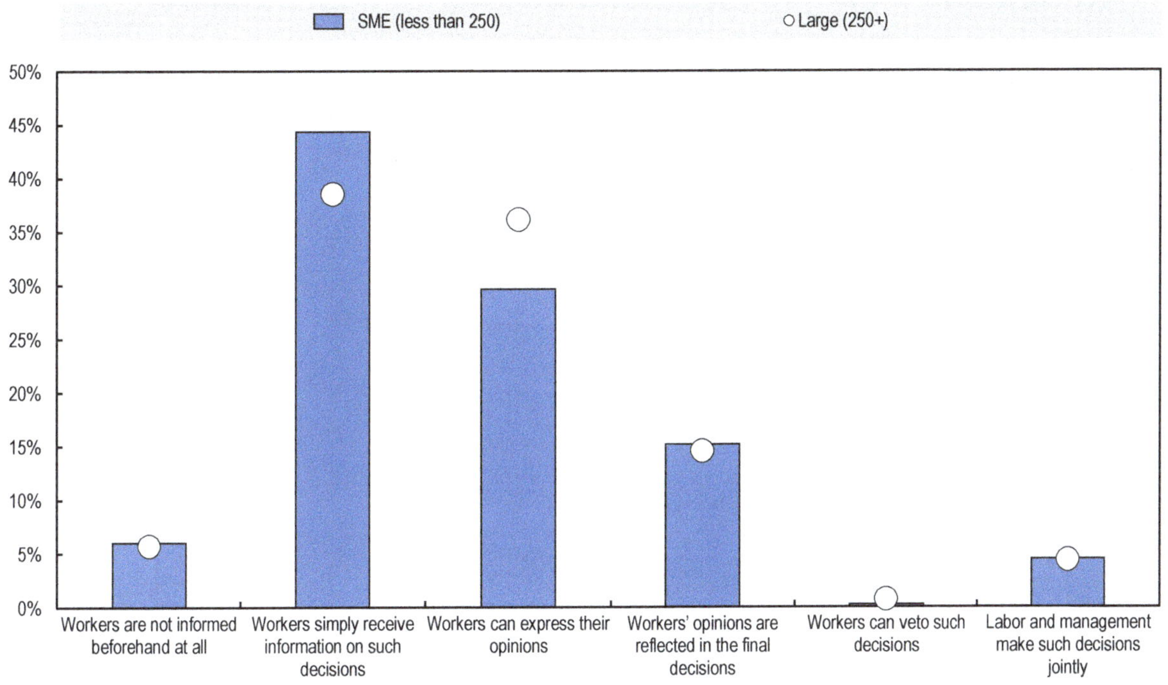

Note: Data refers to workers' involvement either official channels (e.g. unions, labour-management councils) or other unofficial channels.
Source: OECD elaborations of the Workplace Panel Survey (6th wave, 2015).

In this context, Labour-Management Councils (LMCs) could represent a powerful tool to promote better dialogue on training issues between firms and workers. LMCs are consultative bodies formed to help improve the welfare of workers and ensure the sound development of enterprises, through cooperation between workers and employers. They must be composed of company members and employee members in equal numbers, and should hold at least one meeting every three months.

According to the current legal framework, LMCs are able to deliberate on a number of working condition issues, including adult learning. The Act on the Promotion of Workers' Participation and Cooperation specifies that certain matters that are directly related to training (e.g. the establishment of education and training plans) require LMC's approval (ICLG, 2019[24]).

Despite their potential, the influence of LMCs on adult learning issues remains weak, especially in SMEs. First of all, regulation does not bind smallest firms to set up a LMC. The Act on the Promotion of Workers' Participation and Cooperation establishes that only businesses and workplaces with 30 or more regular workers should set up a LMC.

Even when LMCs are in place, they do not seem to put training at the top of their agenda. Although regulation allows LMCs to discuss training issues during their regular meetings, other topics seem to take the bulk of the discussions. Only 20% of SMEs report that training and education is one of the most frequently discussed topics in LMC meetings (Figure 5.5). Conversely, performance-related pay, and safety and health, are reported to be the most frequently discussed topics by over 70% and 50% of SMEs, respectively.

Figure 5.5. Most frequently discussed topics in labour-management council meetings

Percentage of firms by firm size

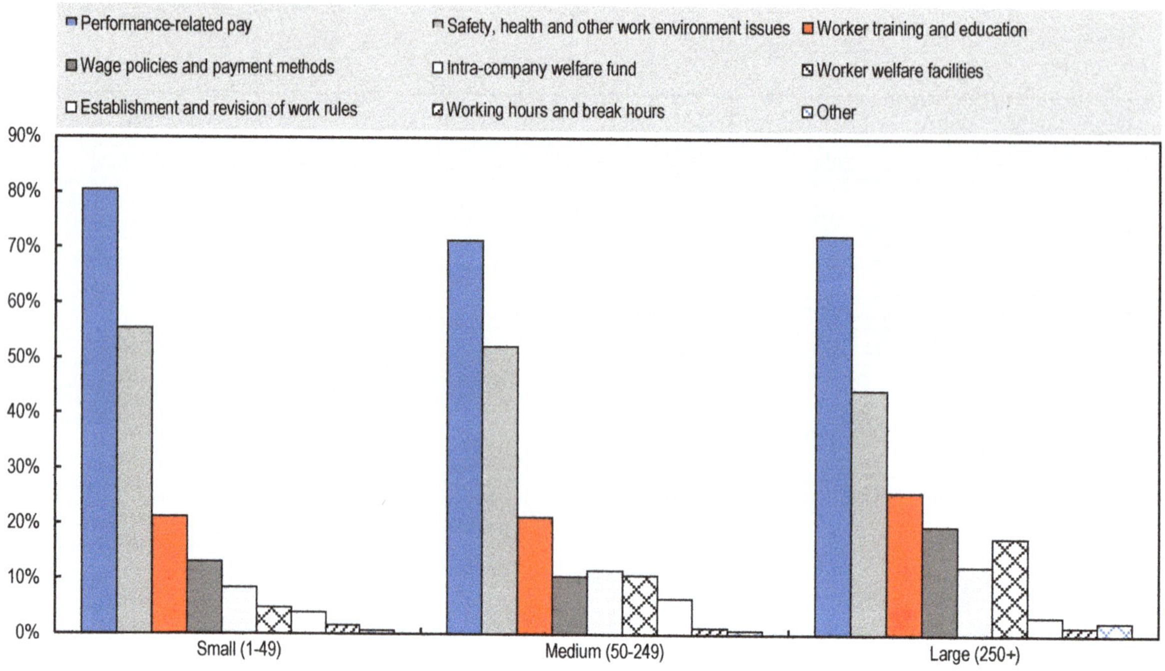

Note: Data refers to the year previous to the survey.
Source: OECD elaborations of the Workplace Panel Survey (6th wave, 2015).

Steps to tackle these ongoing challenges are already underway. In April of 2019, for instance, MoEL announced that preferential financial support will be given to companies that have established training plans that reflect workers' training requests through LMCs. This policy is a clear step in the right direction, and Korea should carry out careful monitoring to assess the impact of the measure on social dialogue within firms.

Strengthen dialogue within firms between employers and workers on adult learning issues. This could be done by continue enhancing the role that Labour-Management Councils play in establishing training priorities within firms. Recent government efforts go in the right direction and should be continued.

References

EPF (2017), *The Role of the Private Sector in VET*, EPF Working Paper, https://www.bibb.de/dokumente/pdf/epf_the_role_of_the_private_sector_in_vet_official.pdf. [14]

ICLG (2019), *Korea: Employment & Labour Law 2019*, Global Legal Group, https://iclg.com/practice-areas/employment-and-labour-laws-and-regulations/korea. [24]

Lee, K. (2016), *Skills Training by Small and Medium-Sized Enterprise: Innovative Cases and the Consortium Approach in the Republic of Korea*. [3]

MoEL (2019), *Employment and Labor White Paper*. [2]

MoEL (2019), *Employment Insurance White Paper*. [4]

MoEL (2019), *Innovative Measures for Vocational Competency Development in respond to Labour Market Changes*. [18]

MoEL (2019), *Innovative Measures for Vocational Competency Development in response to labour market changes*. [15]

MoEL (2018), *Analysis on trade unions based on data at the local labour office in 2017*. [21]

MoEL (2018), *The Employment Insurance White Paper*, Korean Ministry of Employment and Labor. [1]

MoEL (2017), *Survey Report on Labor Conditions by Employment Type*, Korean Ministry of Employment and Labor, http://laborstat.molab.go.kr/newOut/renewal/menu05/menu05_search_popup.jsp. [8]

MoEL (2017), *The 3rd Basic Plan of Vocational Education and Training for Innovation and Inclusive Growth*. [22]

MoEL (2014), *2014 Employment and Labor Policy in Korea*. [12]

MoEL (2010), *Skills Development Policy in Korea*. [7]

Moon, H., D. Ryu and D. Jeon (2019), "The evaluation of learning transfer of industry skills council (ISC) training programs using success case method: Reinforcing role and function of ISC", *European Journal of Training and Development*, Vol. 43/2046-9012, pp. 570-591, https://doi.org/10.1108/EJTD-11-2018-0111. [16]

OECD (2020), *Inclusive Growth in Korea*, OECD Publishing. [25]

OECD (2020), *OECD Skills Strategy Korea, Governance Review*, OECD Publishing, Paris. [9]

OECD (2019), *Adult learning in Italy: what role for training funds?*, OECD Publishing, Paris, https://doi.org/10.1787/9789264311978-en. [6]

OECD (2019), *Getting Skills Right: Future-Ready Adult Learning System*, OECD Publishing, https://doi.org/10.1787/9789264311756-en. [10]

OECD (2019), *Investing in Youth: Korea*, OECD Publishing, Paris, https://doi.org/10.1787/4bf4a6d2-en. [13]

OECD (2019), *OECD Employment Outlook 2019: The Future of Work*, OECD Publishing, Paris, https://dx.doi.org/10.1787/9ee00155-en. [5]

OECD (2018), *Skills for Jobs*, OECD Publishing, Paris, https://www.oecdskillsforjobsdatabase.org/data/Skills%20SfJ_PDF%20for%20WEBSITE%20final.pdf. [20]

OECD (2015), *OECD Skills Strategy Diagnostic Report: Korea*, OECD Publishing, Paris, http://www.oecd.org/skills/nationalskillsstrategies/Diagnostic-report-Korea.pdf. [17]

OECD (2014), *Employment and Skills Strategies in Korea*, OECD Publishing, Paris, https://doi.org/10.1787/9789264216563-en. [11]

Oh, J. and C. Park (2012), *Self-Directed Learning in the Workplace: Implications for the Legislation of Trade Union Education in South Korea*, Adult Education Research Conference, http://newprairiepress.org/aerc/2012/papers/38. [19]

Rok, O. (2013), "Current Status and Direction of Korea's Labor Education Legislation Considered from Lifelong Learning Perspective: Focused on Legislative Review", *Asian Education Research*, Vol. 14/1, pp. 213-241, http://dx.doi.org/10.15753 / aje.2013.14.1.009. [23]

Notes

[1] SME workers are defined as employees working in firms with less than 300 employees.

[2] Collected through the premiums paid by employers relevant to the vocational skills development programmes.

Lightning Source UK Ltd.
Milton Keynes UK
UKHW051135050720
365988UK00002B/6

9 789264 373518